FIGHTER AIRCRAFT

FIGHTER AIRCRAFT

MICHAEL J. TAYLOR

NEW YORK

Photographic acknowledgments

Aeritalia 43 bottom, 116 top, 177; Aermacchi 65, 115, 169 bottom; Aérospatiale 124, 125 top, 126; Agusta 128, 129; Alpha Jet 170 bottom; Atlas Aircraft Corporation of South Africa 114; Beechcraft 163 top; Bell Helicopter Textron 121; Boeing 83, 84, 85 top, 85 bottom, 161 bottom, 182 top; Boeing Vertol 132, 180 bottom; British Aerospace 25, 54, 81 bottom, 93 bottom, 105, 106–7, 108, 147, 158 top, 161 top, 162 centre, 171 top, 183 top; British Aerospace Dynamics 109, 110; Austin J. Brown 33 top; Antonio Camarasa 120; Canadair 104, 146; CASA 157; Cessna Aircraft Company 102, 163 bottom; George Cockle 175 bottom; de Havilland Canada 154, 175 top; Dornier 155 bottom; E.C.P. Armées 59; EMBRAER 153, 164–5; Fairchild Republic Company 44, 98 top, 98 bottom, 103 top; FLYGvapenNYTT 170 centre; FMA 101 bottom; Fokker 30 top, 156 bottom; GAF 152; Gates Learjet 159; GEC-Marconi 131; General Dynamics 29, 31, 86, 87 bottom, 91 top, 91 bottom; Grumman Corporation 67 bottom, 71 top, 71 bottom, 174 top, 183 bottom, 184 top, 184 bottom, 186 bottom; K. Hinata 144, 168 centre, 178 top; Denis Hughes 9 bottom, 12, 13, 32, 33 bottom, 75 top, 76 bottom, 117 top, 117 bottom, 168 top, 173, 178 centre; Hughes Helicopters 122, 139; Israel Aircraft Industries 22, 24, 156 top, 176 top; Israir 23; John Jackson, Louth 14; Geoffrey P. Jones 166 top; Lockheed 187; Lockheed California 72, 149 bottom, 150–1, 186 top; Lockheed Georgia 172 bottom, 172–3; McDonnell Douglas 7, 26, 27, 28, 46 top, 46 bottom, 57 top, 63, 64, 66, 68 top, 68 bottom, 69, 95 top, 96 top, 97, 160, 174 bottom; MBB 43 top, 127; MoD 53 bottom, 55, 106; NDN/Brian Bradbury 166 centre; Northrop 48, 50, 51, 169 top; Panavia Aircraft 92 bottom, 93 top; Stephen P. Peltz 9 top; Photo A MD-BA 16 top, 16 bottom, 17, 39 top, 39 bottom, 40 top, 40 bottom, 41, 42, 58 bottom, 73 top, 73 bottom, 82, 149 top, 155 top; Pilatus 167; Pilatus Britten-Norman 158 bottom; RFB Rhein-Flugzeugbau/MBB 166 bottom; R.N.A.F. 185; Rockwell International 87 top, 88, 89; Rolls-Royce 56; Royal Air Force 77; Saab-Scania 10 top, 10 bottom, 18, 116 bottom, 172 centre; SEPECAT 111, 112 top; Brian M. Service 162 bottom, 172 top; Shorts 178 bottom; SIAI-Marchetti 170 top; Sikorsky 130, 141 top, 141 bottom, 142, 143, 181 bottom left; Socata 113; Swedish Air Force 80; Swiss Federal Aircraft Factory – F + W 36–7, 48–9; Tass 15 top; Transall/MBB 176 bottom; U.S. Air Force 30 bottom, 45, 99, 168 bottom; U.S. Army 180 centre, 181 bottom right; U.S. Navy 57 bottom, 79, 133, 134, 135 top, 140, 182 bottom; Valmet 162 top; Vought 47, 60, 61, 62, 94, 96 bottom, 179 top; Ryuta Watana 145 bottom; Westland Helicopters 136, 137, 138, 179 bottom, 180 top, 181 top; René Zürcher 35.

Cutaway drawings © Pilot Press

Contents

Introduction 6

1 Fighters: The Ace Makers 7

2 Fighter-Bombers: Blowing Up –
Shooting Down 32

3 Naval Fighters and Attack
Aircraft: Ship Strike 54

4 Bombers: The Deterrent 74

5 Attack Aircraft: A Bolt
from Above 90

6 Attack Helicopters: The
Cobra's Bite 119

7 Maritime Patrol and Anti-
Submarine Aircraft:
Searching the Seas 144

8 Trainers and Non-Combat
Aircraft: The Back-up
Force 160

Epilogue 187

Abbreviations 188

Index 189

Cutaway Drawings

Plate I	15-16	Plate V	137-138
Plate II	55-56	Plate VI	149-150
Plate III	83-84	Plate VII	169-170
Plate IV	99-100	Plate VIII	183-184

Introduction

In a world bulging with nuclear ballistic missiles constantly ready for launch from underground silos or mobile transporters, where under the seas heavily missile-laden submarines cruise unseen and in space satellites are able to destroy targets using lasers, it is not unreasonable to ask whether combat aircraft have any real significance as we approach the twenty-first century. The answer, of course, is that they are as important in military terms today as they have been traditionally and they will remain vital in all scenarios short of an all-enveloping nuclear war.

The definition of *fighter aircraft* or combat aircraft is always controversial, as the high cost of acquiring and using modern aircraft often dictates provision in the design for primary and secondary roles. For example, an air-superiority fighter can just as easily be armed for attack, carrying many thousands of pounds of bombs, rockets and air-to-surface missiles. Most jet trainers can perform an attack role, the British Hawk even having an emergency air-defence fighter capability when carrying Sidewinder missiles. Transport helicopters can be armed and some armed helicopters can carry troops. A recent development for the helicopter has been its adaptation to carry air-to-air missiles as an escort for troop-carrying helicopters and slower fixed-wing aircraft, and for attacking similar aircraft.

Airborne warning and control systems aircraft are not combat aircraft in the accepted sense, yet are vital for directing friendly aircraft and tracking hostile forces, some having provision for self-defence armament. As discovered as early as 1911, reconnaissance can be of very major importance and this has been reflected in the production, albeit limited, of highly specialized aircraft for this role – again not combat aircraft as such but highly significant in peace and war. Similarly, transports have actually managed to prevent war in the past by the speedy relocation of men, arms and consumables.

The recent conflict in the South Atlantic has, once again, made a reappraisal of the so-called 'numbers game' necessary, in which quantity of aircraft is seen as more important than quality. Nobody can doubt the importance of sufficient numbers of different types of aircraft and their serviceability in case of war, for modern aircraft take so long to produce that a major conflict could be won or lost before a single replacement aircraft has rolled off the production line. And this assumes that factories survive bomber and missile attack. But, as shown during the Falkland's conflict, number is not an answer in itself. The high skill of the pilots from Britain and Argentina is without question and yet a very small number of Sea Harriers managed to gain air superiority against seemingly overwhelming odds. Does this mean that air forces deploying Mirage and Skyhawk combat aircraft should be over-concerned about their own strength? Certainly not. As with the roles of military aircraft, there is no hard and fast rule to be applied to the 'numbers game'. The Sea Harriers were able to operate close to the Islands, whereas Argentine aircraft had to fly at long range, partly at low level which raised fuel consumption and undoubtedly increased pilot stress. The Sea Harrier/Harrier's ability to outmanoeuvre other aircraft using vectored thrust is unique in the world, as proven earlier in mock air combats between U.S. Marine Corps Harriers and many of the Western world's most important first-line fighters. But, it should also not be forgotten that air forces have experienced in the past situations in which outdated attack aircraft proved more useful than fast modern jets. It adds up to a situation in which planners have to make provision for many levels of possible trouble, from minor disputes to global conflict against, perhaps, an enemy with nuclear weapons at its disposal.

As can be understood, what constitutes a *fighter aircraft* or combat plane is open to interpretation. In the context of this book, *fighter aircraft* covers aircraft with actual *designed* fighting ability, and therefore includes a selection of the most important trainers with attack capability. But to balance the overall military scene, the final chapter includes some of the most significant reconnaissance, electronic counter-measures, AWACS and transport aircraft, without which an air force would be severely restricted.

1 The Ace Makers

A scene typical of the First and Second World Wars in which leather-clad pilots scramble to their neatly lined-up fighters, soon to leave the airfield in formation to engage and defeat the enemy at close quarters, is perhaps the first mental image to occur to most people on hearing the word 'fighter'. Such an image was not entirely destroyed with the deployment of jet fighters; even during the Korean War fighters fought with cannon as their primary armament. It was the development of long-range air-to-air missiles that should have finally dispelled such mental visions because these weapons allow pilots to fire at each other without visual contact. But as life has a habit of turning full circle, so the fighting in Vietnam during the 1960s and early 1970s once again showed the importance of cannon. Today most fighters are armed with cannon and either long-, medium-, or short-range dogfight missiles.

The use of *The Ace Makers* as a chapter heading is no doubt flippant, for no longer can pilots expect to become 'aces', even during fairly lengthy hostilities. Certainly they will never approach the 80 air victories credited to First World War pilot Rittmeister Manfred Freiherr von Richthofen (the so-called 'Red Baron') or the 352 victories of Major Erich Hartmann in the following World War. A modern-day pilot has not only to possess traditional flying skills but has to be expert in the use of avionics. The days when the main design emphasis was on the airframe have passed and now emphasis is on avionics and weapons.

To survive air combat in the 1980s a pilot has to put his trust as much in the sophistication and reliability of his avionics

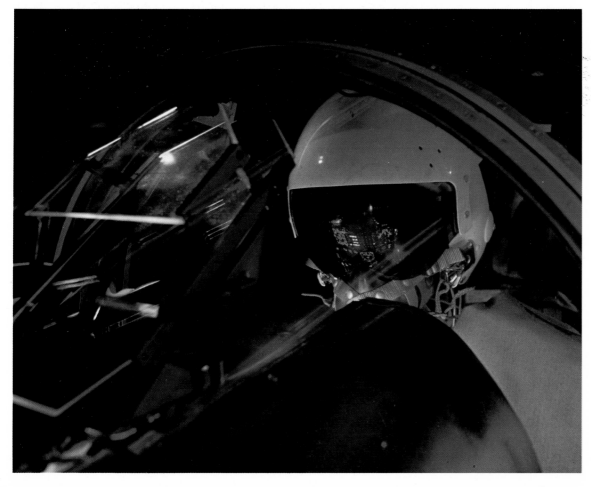

Space-age appearance of a pilot sitting in the cockpit of a modern jet fighter.

Shenyang J-6s and a single J-6Xin (second from left) of the Air Force of the People's Liberation Army.

and missiles as in his ability to manoeuvre his aircraft and outfly the enemy. In general in today's air force, he is unlikely to gain the five victories accepted to become an ace. This fact was well demonstrated during the Vietnam conflict. In the seven years of fighting that followed the first air combats between U.S. and North Vietnamese pilots in the spring of 1965, only two U.S. pilots became aces. This can be compared with 11 U.S. pilots who each gained at least 10 victories in Korea and the many aces with five or more. It should be noted that at least one pilot from North Vietnam gained sufficient victories to total double figures.

Whilst most major air forces around the world fly modern jet fighters, it is no surprise that some of the first-ever swept-wing jet fighters are still in use today with smaller forces. Interestingly, one air force still operates piston-engined F-51 Mustangs, a fighter best remembered for its role during the Second World War. These and the early jets retain fighting capability but are now designated as fighter and ground attack aircraft and, as such, appear in Chapter Two which covers fighter-bombers.

Amongst the aircraft originating in the 1950s and still in use today in its intended fighter role is the Mikoyan MiG-19. This Soviet fighter first flew as a prototype in September 1953, close on the heels of the MiG-17, and was first deployed as a day fighter in an air-defence role in 1955. Production in the Soviet Union lasted most of the decade and included versions with

limited all-weather capability. Although still widely operated by various air forces during the 1970s, the Soviet-built MiG-19 is now virtually out of use, having been superseded by the MiG-21 and MiG-23.

Despite being the first MiG fighter with true supersonic performance in level flight, the MiG-19 never achieved the acclaim of the earlier MiG-15 and MiG-17 or later MiG-21. But the MiG-19 became a favourite of China. Prior to the political separation of the U.S.S.R. and China, an agreement had been made to allow licence-production of the MiG-19 in China. As a step to full local production, many MiG-19s were delivered to China for assembly. These became Chinese fighter aircraft 6s or Jianjiji-6s, and were allocated the same *Farmer* reporting names by NATO as had been applied to Soviet-produced MiG-19s.

The first Chinese J-6s entered service with the Air Force of the People's Liberation Army (or Chung-kuo Shen Min Taie-Fang-Tsun Pu-Tai) in 1962. Such has been the enthusiasm for the aircraft that in the early 1980s production in China was still under-way at the factories located in Shenyang and Tianjin. The initial Chinese version was equivalent to the Soviet MiG-19S/SF day fighter or *Farmer-C*. Limited all-weather capability was introduced with the J-6A, armed with 30-mm NR-30 cannon and air-to-air rockets, and the J-6B, carrying semi-active radar-homing air-to-air missiles. The latter are Soviet-originated *Alkalis* (NATO name) first generation missiles with a range of 6 to 8 km ($3\frac{3}{4}$ to 5 miles) and weighing approximately 90 kg (198 lb).

The versions most recently in production have been the J-6C and J-6Xin. These fighters are each powered by two Chinese variants of the Soviet Tumansky R-9BF-811 turbojet engines, produced at Shenyang as Wopen-6s and rated with afterburning at 3 250-kg (7,165-lb)st. These bestow a maximum speed of about Mach 1.45 and a rate of climb exceeding 9 145 metres (30,000 feet) per minute. The J-6Xin is similar to the J-6A but uses Chinese-developed interception radar in place of the Soviet Izumrud type. The J-6Xin is recognizable by the conical pointed radome emerging from the divided nose air intake. The tandem two-seat operational trainer and single-seat fighter-reconnaissance versions of the J-6 carry the designations JJ-6 and JZ-6.

Armament for the J-6 versions other than that already mentioned can include the Chinese-developed CAA-1, an infra-red homing air-to-air missile similar to early versions of the U.S. Sidewinder and Soviet *Atoll*. Range is likely to be approximately 6 km ($3\frac{3}{4}$ miles). The CAA-1 is likely to be the type also supplied with the F-6, the export version of the J-6. The main user of the F-6 is the Pakistan Air Force, which has been supplied with 140 (including FT-6 two-seat operational trainers). Others have gone to Albania, Bangladesh, Egypt, Kampuchea, Tanzania and Vietnam. These are variously designated as fighters or fighter-bombers, in the latter role carrying bombs or rockets. Similarly, the J-6s that equip more than 40 Chinese air regiments are divided fairly equally into fighters and fighter-bombers. The Aviation of the People's Navy also operates J-6 fighter-bombers and JZ-6s.

The longest serving Western interceptor-fighter to remain operational in its original role in the early 1980s is the McDonnell F-101 Voodoo. The first flight of a proto-type took place in 1954. However, Canada, as the main user in recent years, began receiving McDonnell Douglas CF-18 Hornets (see Chapter Three) in October 1982 as Voodoo, Starfighter and CF-5 replacements, Voodoos going out of service initially. Those F-101s in U.S.A.F. service partly equip only two operational conversion units along with a number of Delta Darts.

Above: Currently being replaced in the Canadian Armed Forces is the McDonnell CF-101F Voodoo interceptor.

Left: Egyptian Air Force Shenyang F-6.

A two-seater powered by two 6750-kg (14,880-lb)st with afterburning Pratt & Whitney J57-P-55 turbojet engines installed side-by-side in the centre fuselage, the Voodoo possesses a maximum speed of 1963 km/h (1,220 mph) and its maximum rate of climb is 4270 metres (14,000 feet) per minute. No cannon armament is installed but air-to-air missiles can comprise two unguided Genie nuclear weapons with a 9.5km (6 mile) range and three similar range AIM-4D Falcons, the latter carried internally.

Changing shapes

The year 1955 was important for military prototypes. Currently operated fighters which first appeared then include the Swedish Saab 35 Draken and the naval carrier-based Vought F-8 Crusader. Another 1955 type was the Hawker Siddeley Gnat which, although no longer relevant, has been produced in developed form in India as the Ajeet fighter-bomber. The F-8 and Ajeet appear in following chapters.

The Draken was Saab's follow-on fighter to the Lansen. Although it had a totally revised configuration, it did continue two important Swedish traditions. Firstly, it allowed the nation's air force to continue to deploy home-produced combat aircraft, and secondly, the fighter was and is able to operate from major roads in an emergency. It has a unique 'double-delta' wing planform, designed to assist short take-offs and landings and yet leave the aircraft with good manoeuvrability and high performance.

First flown as a prototype in October 1955, J35A Draken production fighters entered Swedish Air Force service in 1960. These were followed by improved J35Bs, and from 1964 the Air Force began operating J35Ds. The 'D' represented a major improvement, not only in terms of its more powerful 7800-kg (17,195-lb)st Volvo Flygmotor R.M.6C engine but in the avionics carried. Many of the earlier

Above: Danish Draken showing clearly the 'double-delta' wing configuration and six underwing and three underfuselage attachment points.

Right: Swedish Air Force Saab Drakens, the nearest two armed with RB27 missiles.

Drakens were subsequently brought up to J35D standard, although some became two-seat operational trainers. The J35D remains one of two fighter versions of the Draken still in Swedish service. The other is the J35F, which encompasses further improvements to the fire-control system for the 30-mm Aden cannon and RB27/RB28 Falcon missiles (Swedish-built missiles similar to the U.S. AIM-26B and AIM-4D respectively).

Until recently, up to 300 Drakens were listed as operational in fighter roles with the Swedish Air Force. This figure has been reduced substantially by the delivery of Saab JA 37 Viggens from 1979, but it is expected to take until 1985 for all eight Draken fighter squadrons assigned for update to be re-equipped.

Both Denmark and Finland received examples of the export version of the Draken, produced for fighter-bomber, reconnaissance-fighter and operational training roles. Today, Denmark operates more than 30 F35 fighter-bombers and RF 35 reconnaissance-fighters alone and 12 J35BS/FS fighter-bombers are used by the Finnish Air Force. Maximum speed is 2124 km/h (1,320 mph), rate of climb is 10500 metres (34,450 feet) per minute and the increased weapon load can include two Aden cannon, two or four RB24 (Sidewinder) missiles or up to 4080 kg (9,000 lb) of bombs, rockets or other stores.

Of the fighters to enter the aviation scene in 1956, arguably the most important was the Mikoyan MiG-21. It has been in continuous production since the 1950s and is, without doubt, not only the most widely operated fighter in the world but also one of the all-time 'greats'. It can be viewed as a third-generation Soviet single-seat jet fighter, far surpassing the performance of the second generation MiG-15/-17/-19s. It is said to have been designed using all the experience gleaned from the operation of the MiG-15 in close air combat during the Korean War, with design emphasis on light weight and simplicity, good manoeuvrability and handling at transonic speed, and a punishing rate of climb. Overall size and weight were kept down to roughly those of the MiG-19, by then in service, although wing span was greatly reduced because of the MiG-21's tailed-delta configuration.

The prototype for the MiG-21 was first flown in June 1956 and on the 24th of that month, just eight days later, it appeared over Moscow during the Aviation Day flypast.

The fighter was subsequently given the reporting name *Fishbed* by NATO. The initial production version that entered Soviet service in limited number thereafter was known in the West as *Fishbed-A*. This version flew on the power of a single 5100-kg (11,244-lb)st with afterburning Tumansky R-11 and was armed with two 30-mm NR-30 cannon only.

The major variant of the first-generation MiG-21 was built as the MiG-21F, known to NATO as *Fishbed-C*. Engine thrust with afterburning was raised to 5750 kg (12,677 lb) and fuel capacity increased, but still it represented a clear-weather type. However, cannon armament was reduced to one gun to make allowance for the avionics necessary to launch two K-13 or *Atoll* (NATO name) air-to-air missiles. *Atoll* was produced as the second Soviet air-to-air missile and is equivalent to an early U.S. Sidewinder. It has a cruising speed of Mach 2.5 and range of more than 5 km (3 miles). Rocket packs were provided as alternatives to the *Atolls*. The MiG-21F is still in first-line service, having also been put into production in China as the Xian J-7 and in Czechoslovakia. The Chinese J-7 was initially the subject of only very limited production, preference instead being given to the MiG-19 derivative. J-7s entered service from the mid-1960s. Limited production resumed subsequently and as many as 280 could now be in service, compared to the original estimate of up to 80. Others have been exported to Albania (about 20) and Tanzania (one squadron), and Egypt is thought to have ordered a large number for operational training.

The second-generation MiG-21 began with the MiG-21PF or *Fishbed-D*, an all-weather fighter powered by a 5950-kg (13,120-lb)st turbojet engine. An export model has also been produced as the MiG-21FL, of which approximately 200 were built in India by Hindustan Aeronautics Limited. The many other versions of the MiG-21 that have followed have included the MiG-21PFMA or *Fishbed-J*, a multi-role combat type, a reconnaissance version of the -21PFMA with three cameras in place of the twin-barrel 23-mm GSh-23 gun, the *Fishbed-H* tactical reconnaissance versions with high standards of equipment, and the high-performance MiG-21MF or *Fishbed-J*. The latter has a 6600-kg (14,550-lb)st with afterburning Tumansky R-13-300 turbojet engine, allowing a maximum speed of Mach

Fuelling an Egyptian
Mikoyan MiG-21 MF.

2.1, and is armed with one GSh-23 gun, four *Atoll* and/or *Advanced Atoll* missiles, rockets, bombs or air-to-surface missiles.

Third-generation MiG-21s began with the MiG-21 *bis* or *Fishbed-L*. This was followed by the *Fishbed-N* with a Tumansky R-25 engine of 7500 kg (16,535 lb) st, capable of carrying *Atolls* and *Aphid* missiles, the latter with a range of 5 to 7 km (3 to $4\frac{1}{2}$ miles). Apart from several Soviet record-breaking versions of the MiG-21, specialized two-seat operational trainers have been built, known to NATO as *Mongols*. Foreign production has covered the *Fishbed-C* and the MiG-21PFM (*Fishbed-F*) produced in Czechoslovakia, and HAL has also produced examples of the MiG-21M, MF and -21 *bis* in India.

In the early 1980s the Soviet Air Forces still operate by far the largest number of MiG-21s in fighter, fighter-bomber and reconnaissance roles. However, in recent years the MiG-23 has become the prominent air-defence interceptor and fighter, with an average of about two new aircraft coming off the production lines each day. Some 33 other nations fly MiG-21s, not including the United States that flies a very small number for combat training. These U.S.A.F. MiG-21s are thought to have been received from Egypt, which is acquiring U.S. fighters.

A contemporary of the MiG-21 was the Sukhoi Su-9, a larger and more powerful all-weather single-seater that has recently been withdrawn from first-line use. An improved version became the Su-11, also known to NATO under the reporting name *Fishpot* but with a 'C' suffix. Like the Su-9, the Su-11 was delivered only to the Soviet forces and this, too, has been almost totally superseded. Power is provided by a single 10000-kg (22,046-lb)st with afterburning Lyulka AL-7F-1 turbojet engine, which gives the aircraft a maximum speed of Mach 1.8 and a rate of climb of 8200 metres (27,000 feet) per minute. Armament comprises two 16-km (10-mile) range *Anab* missiles. The Su-11's all-weather capability and large missiles made it a suitable interceptor, a role not within the capabilities of the early MiG-21.

A U.S. interceptor of very different appearance to the Sukhois, but nevertheless a contemporary and one which remains in first-line use, is the Convair F-106 Delta Dart. The second of Convair's production Delta interceptor-fighters (the first being the F-102 Delta Dagger), the first F-106A flew in December 1956. It retains the Delta Dagger's basic configuration but included in its revisions was a Hughes MA-1 guidance and control system to enable it to be used within the SAGE system. The SAGE system, standing for Semi-Automatic Ground Environment, was set up to take control of interceptors and anti-aircraft missiles in the defence of the North American continent.

Aerospace Defense Command, U.S.A.F., began receiving F-106As in 1959 and a total of 277 was produced by 1961. Sixty-three two-seat operational trainers were also produced as F-106Bs. Subsequent modification programmes have kept Delta Darts in service but these are scheduled to be replaced eventually with F-15 Eagles. In 1982 the small number of interceptors available to NORAD (North American Aerospace Defense Command) comprised mostly F-106As, 75 with five of the six regular squadrons (not including Canadian interceptors) and a similar number of aircraft and squadrons operated by the Air National Guard. A small number of Delta Darts also serve with the two operational conversion units as mentioned earlier. The maximum speed of the F-106A is 2455 km/h (1,525 mph) or Mach 2.3, and armament comprises one 20-mm M-61 Vulcan cannon and one Genie or Super Genie unguided missile and four AIM-4F or G Super Falcon missiles carried in the internal bay.

As explained at the beginning of this book, to differentiate between roles for many combat aircraft is very difficult, a problem which is highlighted by those aircraft selected for Chapter One and Chapter Two. Whereas some aircraft in Chapter Two began as fighters, their current use also in a ground-attack role labels them fighter-bombers. Yet most aircraft termed 'fighter' or 'interceptor' can carry attack armament. A precedent has been established already with the MiG-21, included in this chapter as the majority of those in use today are fighters rather than fighters with an equally important ground-attack role. Similar problems arise with the French Dassault-Breguet Mirage III and U.S. McDonnell Douglas F-4 Phantom II. Each of these is described in Chapter Two, although Britain, for one, uses the Phantom II as an interceptor-fighter.

Britain's other first-line interceptor is the Lightning, which began as the product of English Electric and is better known today as a BAC type. The first of two P.1A experimental prototype fighters flew in August 1954 and from these was developed the P.1B. The P.1B was the true Lightning

Convair F-106A Delta Dart operated by the 318th Fighter Interceptor Squadron of Aerospace Defense Command.

prototype and took to the air for the first time in April 1957. Initial production versions for the R.A.F. were the Lightning F.Mk 1 and 1A, the latter with flight refuelling capability. These were followed by the F.Mk 2/2A. None of these is in service today.

Two of the nine R.A.F. interceptor squadrons operated Lightnings in the early 1980s, comprising 24 F.Mk 3s and F.Mk 6s. A further number are in reserve. The F.Mk 3 was first flown in mid-1962 and features two Rolls-Royce Avon 301 turbojet engines. It has the capability of carrying two Firestreak or Red Top air-to-air missiles but not the Aden guns of earlier versions.

The Lightning F.Mk 6, some of which were produced by the conversion of the preceding version, is the major variant. First flown in 1964, the sweptback wings are slightly modified and the two 7420-kg (16,360-lb)st with afterburning Avon 301s installed one above the other in the rear fuselage are the same as those used in the F.Mk 3. Armament is increased to include two rocket packs (each with 24 2-in air-to-air rockets) as an option to the missiles, plus two 30-mm Aden cannon if required. The

Royal Saudi Air Force also operates 15 Lightning interceptors as F.Mk 53s (other Lightnings in reserve), these having the capability of ground attack while carrying 1,000-lb bombs, rockets or other weapons on two underwing pylons. Two-seat trainers were also built. The maximum speed of the Lightning is above Mach 2 and it has a very high rate of climb.

Two unique Soviet all-weather interceptor-fighters comprise the first of the 1960s aircraft still in service. Both are two-seaters with moderately sweptback wings. The first of these is the Tupolev Tu-28P, known to NATO by the reporting name *Fiddler*. First seen in public in 1961, it is the largest aircraft of its type ever to become operational, having a wing span and length of approximately 20 metres (65 feet 7 inches) and 26 metres (85 feet 4 inches) respectively. Weighing an incredible but estimated 45 000 kg (100,000 lb), it has a maximum speed of about Mach 1.75 on the power of two turbojet engines. These engines are each thought to be rated at about 12 250 kg (27,000 lb)st with afterburning. Four *Ash* missiles, usually a mixture of infra-red and

BAC/English Electric Lightning F.Mk 6 flown by No.5 Squadron, R.A.F., in the new NATO-approved colour scheme.

semi-active radar homing types with ranges of approximately 30 km (18½ miles), are carried. *Fiddler's* range of approximately 4 990 km (3,100 miles) makes it a formidable long-range interceptor, explaining why some 120 or so can be counted among the 2,225 to 2,500 interceptors operated for home defence by the Voyska PVO.

The second Soviet interceptor of early 1960s origin is the Yakovlev Yak-28P *Firebar*. This is just one of several combat and support aircraft to have been evolved from the basic Yak-28 – others include tactical attack and electronic countermeasures escort *Brewers* (NATO name). The Yak-28 was also first seen publicly in 1961 but it can be regarded as a less modern design, despite the fact that 200 to 300 still form part of the defence force of the Voyska PVO.

Firebar is a transonic interceptor-fighter, with a maximum speed of Mach 1.1. Its wings are swept at only 45° and the two turbojet engines, each rated at 5 950 kg (13,117 lb)st with afterburning, are carried in long underwing nacelles. Armament comprises two *Anab* missiles, with alternative infra-red or semi-active radar homing guidance systems and with an estimated range of 16 km (10 miles).

A giant leap forward

The year 1966 can be viewed as a dividing line in terms of the interceptor-fighter, by which the aircraft previously mentioned are separated from the truly modern prototypes that appeared thereafter and proved the progenitors of aircraft that entered service in the 1970s. One such prototype that appeared on the 1966 line was the French Dassault-Breguet F1. Its development was initiated as a privately financed project to produce a smaller, lighter and single-seat Mirage III replacement to rival the two-

Above: Soviet Tupolev Tu-28P armed with missiles.

Top: The tandem-seat Yakovlev Yak-28P *Firebar*, still an important Soviet interceptor.

Plate I

Dassault-Breguet Mirage 2000

cutaway drawing key

1 Pitot tube
2 Glass-fibre radome
3 Flat-plate radar scanner
4 Thomson-CSF RDM multi-rôle radar unit (initial production aircraft)
5 Cassegrain monopulse planar antenna
6 Thomson-CSF RDI pulse doppler radar unit (later production aircraft)
7 Radar altimeter aerial
8 Angle of attack probe
9 Front pressure bulkhead
10 Instrument pitot heads
11 Temperature probe
12 Fixed in-flight refuelling probe
13 Frameless windscreen panel
14 Instrument panel shroud
15 Static ports
16 Rudder pedals
17 Low voltage formation light strip
18 VHF aerial
19 Nosewheel jack door
20 Hydraulic retraction jack
21 Nose undercarriage leg strut
22 Twin nosewheels
23 Towing bracket
24 Torque scissor links
25 Landing/taxying lamps
26 Nosewheel steering jacks
27 Nose undercarriage leg doors
28 Cockpit flooring
29 Centre instrument console
30 Control column
31 Pilot's head-up display (HUD)
32 Canopy arch
33 Cockpit canopy cover
34 Starboard air intake
35 Ejection seat headrest
36 Safety harness
37 Martin-Baker Mk 10 zero-zero ejection seat
38 Engine throttle control and airbrake switch
39 Port side console panel
40 Nosewheel bay
41 Cannon muzzle blast trough
42 Electrical equipment bay
43 Port air intake
44 Intake half-cone centre body
45 Air conditioning system ram air intake
46 Cockpit rear pressure bulkhead
47 Canopy emergency release handle
48 Hydraulic canopy jack
49 Canopy hinge point
50 Starboard intake strake
51 IFF aerial
52 Radio and electronics bay

53 Boundary layer bleed air duct
54 Air conditioning plant
55 Intake centre-body screw jack
56 Cannon muzzle
57 Pressure refuelling connection
58 Port intake strake
59 Intake suction relief doors (above and below)
60 DEFA 554 30-mm cannon
61 Cannon ammunition box
62 Forward fuselage integral fuel tanks
63 Radio and electronics equipment
64 Fuel system equipment
65 Anti-collision light
66 Air system pre-cooler
67 Air exit louvres
68 Starboard wing integral fuel tank (total internal fuel capacity 835 Imp gal (3 800 l)
69 Wing pylon attachment hardpoints
70 Leading-edge slat hydraulic drive motor and control shaft
71 Slat screw jacks
72 Slat guide rails
73 Starboard wing automatic leading-edge slats
74 Matra 550 Magic "dogfight" AAM
75 Missile launch rail
76 Outboard wing pylon
77 Radar warning antenna
78 Starboard navigation light
79 Outboard elevon
80 Elevon ventral hinge fairings
81 Flight control system access panels
82 Elevon hydraulic jacks
83 Engine intake by-pass air spill duct
84 Engine compressor face
85 Hydraulic accumulator
86 Microturbo auxiliary power unit

87 Main undercarriage wheel bay
88 Hydraulic pump
89 Alternator, port and starboard
90 Accessory gearbox
91 Engine transmission unit and drive shaft
92 Machined fuselage main frames
93 SNECMA M53-5 afterburning turbofan
94 Engine igniter unit
95 Electronic engine control unit
96 Bleed air ducting
97 Engine bleed air blow-off valve spill duct
98 Fin root fillet construction
99 Leading edge ribs
100 Boron/epoxy/carbon honeycomb sandwich fin skin panels
101 Tail low voltage formation light strip
102 ECM aerial fairing

103 VOR aerial
104 Di-electric fin tip fairing
105 VHF aerial
106 Tail navigation light
107 Tail radar warning antenna
108 Honeycomb rudder construction
109 Rudder hinge
110 Fin spar attachment joints
111 Rudder hydraulic jack
112 Engine bay thermal lining
113 ECM equipment housing
114 Variable area afterburner exhaust nozzle

115 Tailpipe sealing flaps
116 Fueldraulic nozzle control jacks
117 Afterburner tailpipe
118 Engine withdrawal rail
119 Wing root extended trailing edge fillet
120 Ventral brake parachute housing
121 Rear engine mounting main frame
122 Runway emergency arrestor hook
123 Port inboard elevon

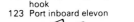

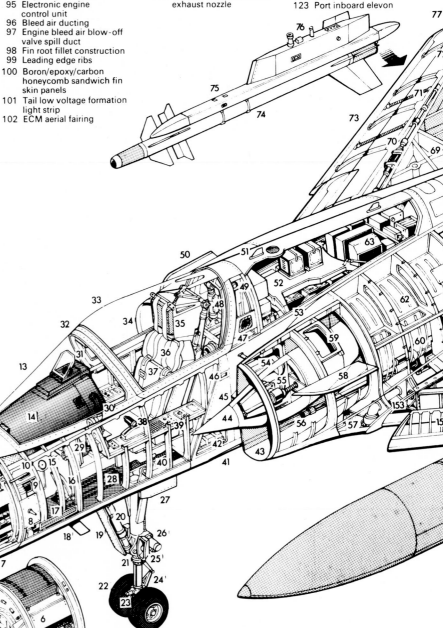

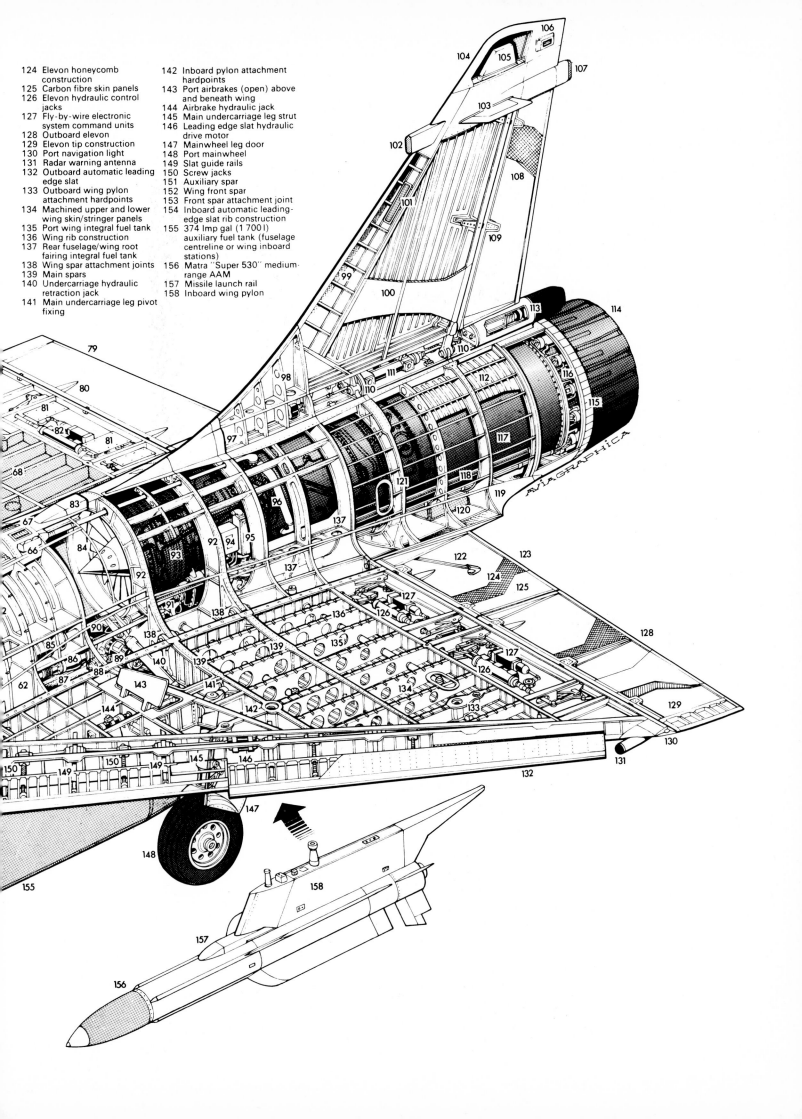

124 Elevon honeycomb
    construction
125 Carbon fibre skin panels
126 Elevon hydraulic control
    jacks
127 Fly-by-wire electronic
    system command units
128 Outboard elevon
129 Elevon tip construction
130 Port navigation light
131 Radar warning antenna
132 Outboard automatic leading
    edge slat
133 Outboard wing pylon
    attachment hardpoints
134 Machined upper and lower
    wing skin/stringer panels
135 Port wing integral fuel tank
136 Wing rib construction
137 Rear fuselage/wing root
    fairing integral fuel tank
138 Wing spar attachment joints
139 Main spars
140 Undercarriage hydraulic
    retraction jack
141 Main undercarriage leg pivot
    fixing

142 Inboard pylon attachment
    hardpoints
143 Port airbrakes (open) above
    and beneath wing
144 Airbrake hydraulic jack
145 Main undercarriage leg strut
146 Leading edge slat hydraulic
    drive motor
147 Mainwheel leg door
148 Port mainwheel
149 Slat guide rails
150 Screw jacks
151 Auxiliary spar
152 Wing front spar
153 Front spar attachment joint
154 Inboard automatic leading-
    edge slat rib construction
155 374 Imp gal (1 700 l)
    auxiliary fuel tank (fuselage
    centreline or wing inboard
    stations)
156 Matra "Super 530" medium-
    range AAM
157 Missile launch rail
158 Inboard wing pylon

seat, swept-wing F2 ordered from Dassault as a prototype by the French government. Both the F2 and F1 flew in 1966, the latter in December. The F1 exceeded Mach 2 only 15 days later during its fourth flight. The gamble paid off and the F2 was dropped.

Mirage F1s form the backbone of French air defence command or Commandement Air des Forces de la Défense Aérienne, flying alongside Mirage IIICs. By mid-1982 the French Air Force had received 252 F1-Cs, the first having been delivered in March 1973. The French 30e Escadre, comprising two squadrons based at Reims, was the first unit to become operational in the following year. Today eight squadrons fly F1-Cs, two formed as recently as 1981. An operational conversion unit flying F1-B two-seat operational trainers (with reduced fuel and cannon deleted) can also be included in the command.

Unlike all other operational Mirage combat aircraft, the F1 has shoulder-mounted sweptback wings and an all-moving tailplane. Power is provided by a

Above: French Dassault-Breguet F1 uses its non-retractable probe to take on extra fuel.

Right: Spanish Air Force Mirage F1-CEs.

16

One of five Dassault-Breguet Mirage 2000 prototypes carrying Magic missiles and bombs.

7200-kg (15,873-lb)st with afterburning SNECMA Atar 9K-50 turbojet engine. Apart from wing and fuselage fuel tanks, three jettisonable auxiliary tanks can be carried externally. Twenty-five of the French Air Force's F1-Cs have been modified to F1-C-200 standard by the installation of a permanent flight-refuelling probe. Four of these proved their long-range capability in early 1980 by flying nonstop from Corsica to Djibouti, a distance of approximately 5000 km (3,110 miles). Armament comprises two 30-mm DEFA 553 cannon carried in the forward fuselage and three Matra R.530 or Super 530 and two Matra 550 Magic or Sidewinder missiles on three of the five underfuselage/underwing pylons and two wingtip launchers. Up to 4000 kg (8,820 lb) of ground-attack weapons can be carried in this secondary role. As an interceptor, maximum speed is Mach 2.2 and maximum rate of climb is 14580 metres (47,835 feet) per minute.

Of the 678 Mirage F1s ordered for 11 air forces by mid-1982, the majority have been for export. These have included F1-Cs, F1-Bs, F1-A ground-attack aircraft with a lower standard of avionics but increased fuel capacity, and F1-E export multi-role combat aircraft for attack and interceptor duties. The only other version of the F1 is the F1-CR, a reconnaissance version which entered service with the French Air Force as a Mirage III-R/RD replacement in 1983. The air forces with the greatest number of export F1s are those of Iraq, Morocco and Spain.

The very latest single-seat interceptor and air-superiority fighter from France is the Dassault-Breguet Mirage 2000, the first examples of which are currently entering service. Reverting to the familiar delta-wing and vertical tail only configuration, it will eventually form the backbone of the Air Force's interceptor, fighter, attack and reconnaissance units. Using a single aircraft type to equip many units with differing missions is now the accepted trend. Aircraft from other countries which are used in a similar fashion include the Panavia Tornado.

The first of five prototype Mirage 2000s flew for the first time (and flew supersonically) in March 1978. The last of the prototypes was configured as a Mirage 2000B two-seat operational trainer. These and the production examples use advanced and weight-saving materials in their construction. The delta wings incorporate the latest aerodynamic features. They provide the aircraft with a large wing area to enhance manoeuvrability and performance in terms of speed (more than Mach 2.2), rate of climb (more than 18000 metres; 59,000 feet per minute), service ceiling (20000

Swedish Air Force JA 37 Viggen interceptor in latest colour scheme, armed with Sky Flash and Sidewinder missiles.

metres; 65,600 feet) and low landing speed, and yet the structure remains simple. The latest fly-by-wire control system is used. In simple terms, this is better than installing an advanced autopilot as it enables the aircraft to have excellent handling qualities throughout the flight despite the fact that the aircraft's designers might have designed it for optimum speed or other goals rather than in a shape most likely to provide the pilot with an easy-to-fly aircraft. The new aircraft handles very well by virtue of the artificial 'feel'. Power for the Mirage 2000 is provided by a 9000-kg (19,842-lb)st SNECMA M53-5 turbofan engine, but later production aircraft are likely to be fitted with a more powerful M53.

The French Air Force is likely to receive up to 200 Mirage 2000s for interceptor-fighter use, perhaps 127 initially although only 73 had been ordered up to February 1982. Perhaps the same number again might eventually be used for attack and reconnaissance roles. A further role could be undertaken by the latest Mirage 2000N, a two-seater based on the Mirage 2000B but capable of low-altitude penetration missions carrying various weapon loads including ASMP (Air-Sol Moyenne Portée) stand-off nuclear missiles. ASMP will not be available for deployment on any French aircraft until about 1985. It is a supersonic ramjet-cruising missile with an estimated range of 75 to 100 km (46 to 62 miles). Armament for the basic Mirage 2000 in an interceptor-fighter role is two 30-mm DEFA 554 cannon plus two Matra Super 530 and two Matra 550 Magic missiles or four Magics. For ground attack the weapon load will exceed 6000 kg (13,225 lb), including Exocet missiles for anti-shipping missions.

The first two foreign customers for the export Mirage 2000 are Egypt and India. Twenty have been ordered by Egypt and the first of 40 French-built aircraft will be delivered to India in 1985. A further 110 will be built under licence in India, initially using French-produced components.

In February 1967 Saab flew the first prototype of its Draken replacement, the 37 Viggen. As different in appearance to the Draken as the Draken had been to the

Lansen, it was seen as a single-seater with rear-mounted delta-type wings (incorporating compound sweep on the leading-edges), small cropped delta foreplanes and a vertical tail only. Excluding the proposed export model, the Viggen was offered in five versions as a true multi-role combat aircraft. Production of 180 Viggens for the Swedish Air Force in AJ 37 all-weather attack (with interceptor capability), SF 37 photographic-reconnaissance, SH 37 maritime-reconnaissance and SK 37 two-seat operational training versions has terminated, leaving only the JA 37 interceptor in production.

Although the JA 37 is the most important version in terms of number built or to be produced, further mention has to be made of the other models. Armament for the AJ 37, the first production version that went initially to the F7 Wing at Såtenäs in 1971, comprises the subsonic Saab-Scania RB04E 20-km ($12\frac{1}{2}$-mile)-range anti-shipping missile, or 9-km ($5\frac{1}{2}$-mile)-range supersonic RB05A or U.S. Maverick tactical air-to-surface missiles, and/or bombs, rockets and guns. It can also be used as an interceptor armed with RB28 or Sidewinder air-to-air missiles. Deliveries of the SF 37, SH 37 and SK 37 began in April 1977, June 1975 and June 1972 respectively. Both reconnaissance versions are capable of carrying air-to-air missiles for defence and the SK 37 (with a 'stepped' second cockpit) has a secondary attack role. Power plant for each of these versions is an 11800-kg (26,015-lb)st with afterburning Volvo Flygmotor RM8A turbofan engine.

The JA 37 is, as mentioned before, the single-seat interceptor version of the Viggen. It is powered by a 12750-kg (28,110-lb)st with afterburning RM8B turbofan engine, bestowing a maximum speed of more than Mach 2, and a rate of climb sufficient to allow an altitude of 10000 metres (32,800 feet) to be attained from brakes-off in 1 minute and 40 seconds. The first of the planned 149 JA 37s entered service in 1979, going to F13 Wing based at Norrköping. The JA 37 will, by 1985, have superseded Drakens in all eight designated squadrons, thereby giving the Swedish Air Force a total of 17 Viggen squadrons.

Four interceptor-fighters have gone into production in the Soviet Union since 1966. By far the most important in terms of numbers is the Mikoyan MiG-23 (NATO *Flogger*). However, a great deal of interest accompanied reports of the MiG-25, known to NATO as *Foxbat*. This was the first interceptor to go into service with a Mach 3 performance (more of this later).

Libyan Mikoyan MiG-23 *Flogger-E* carrying *Atoll* missiles.

Setting a new pace

For its follow-on to the MiG-21, Mikoyan decided to depart from the traditional style of Soviet combat aircraft (typified by the nose ram-air intake and centrebody) and produce a variable-geometry or swing-wing aircraft with side intakes. Still a single-seater with a single engine, it has since become the main Soviet home-defence interceptor (well over 800 in use) and by far the most numerous fighter with the Frontal Aviation tactical air forces (perhaps making up all but a few hundred of the 1,750 aircraft). The MiG-27 ground-attack derivative also serves in large number, as detailed in the next chapter.

First viewed in public at the 1967 Aviation Day flypast over Moscow, the MiG-23 began to enter Soviet units as early as 1970. By 1974 two Soviet regiments deploying MiG-23s had been based in East Germany and nearly a decade later production continues at an average rate of nearly two new aircraft a day. It is deployed throughout the air forces of the Warsaw Pact (with the exception of Romania) and has been exported to countries including Algeria, Cuba, Egypt, Ethiopia, India, Iraq, Libya, Syria and Vietnam.

The initial version of the MiG-23 was given the reporting name *Flogger-A* by NATO but production was very limited. Major production began with the MiG-23MF (*Flogger-B*), initially powered by a 10 200-kg (22,487-lb)st with afterburning

Tumansky R-27 turbofan engine. More recent examples of this interceptor-fighter have the 12475-kg (27,502-lb)st R-29 turbojet. This version represents a considerable redesign, the most significant change having been made to the wings, which feature fixed inboard sections and variable outer sections. Cuba is the only non-Warsaw Pact nation to have this model in use. Maximum speed is approximately Mach 2.35 and armament comprises one 23-mm GSh-23 twin-barrel cannon plus up to four *Aphid* and two much larger 33-km (20-mile)-range *Apex* air-to-air missiles.

Another interceptor-fighter version for Soviet use has been the *Flogger-G*, identifiable by its smaller-area dorsal fin. *Flogger-C* is a tandem two-seat operational trainer with the R-27 engine and *Flogger-E* is an export *Flogger-B* with reduced avionics and carrying *Atoll* missiles. All other versions of *Flogger* are ground-attack aircraft relating to the designations MiG-23 and MiG-27.

Foxbat, as mentioned earlier, has been the subject of much discussion over the years. Certainly in the early 1970s it was considered to be one of the best, if not the best, interceptor in the world. However, close examination of a *Foxbat* in 1976 brought an end to speculation. This unique opportunity presented itself in September of that year when a defecting Soviet pilot flew under Japanese radar to land at Hakodate Airport. Upon examination by Japanese and U.S. technicians, several interesting finds were made. These included an indication that the aircraft was not expected to exceed a speed of Mach 2.8 (nevertheless a very high speed) with missiles in place and that the aircraft's avionics were a mixture of old and extremely advanced technology.

Development of the fixed wing and twin-fin *Foxbat* started around the beginning of the 1960s, in an effort to produce an interceptor capable of effectively countering the North American B-70 Valkyrie Mach 3 cruise-bomber, then under development in the U.S.A. When this strategic bomber was cancelled in favour of land-based missiles, such was the potential of the MiG-25 for interceptor and reconnaissance roles that development continued. Four early MiG-25s took part in the July 1967 flypast. Prior to this, and thereafter, many world records fell to a specially prepared version of the MiG-25, known under the designation E-266.

The interceptor version of the MiG-25 is known to NATO as *Foxbat-A*. Powered by

Unusual view of a Libyan MiG-25 *Foxbat-A*, armed with *Acrid* air-to-air missiles on two of its four underwing pylons.

The first major production version of the Sukhoi Su-15 was given the name *Flagon-D* by NATO. The two-seat version is *Flagon-C*, as illustrated.

two 11 000-kg (24,251-lb)st with afterburning Tumansky R-31 turbojet engines, it has an estimated maximum speed without missiles of Mach 3.2. Maximum rate of climb from sea level is 12 480 metres (40,950 feet) per minute and service ceiling is thought to be 24 400 metres (80,000 feet). The E-266M record-breaking aircraft climbed to an altitude of 37 650 metres (123,524 feet) in 1977. Armament comprises four *Acrid*, *Apex* or *Aphid* missiles. It is believed that in the early 1980s the Soviet Voyska PVO deployed more than 300, although this figure may include a substantial number of *Foxhounds* (described later). Export *Foxbat-As* have been delivered to Algeria, Libya and Syria.

The initial reconnaissance version was the MiG-25R *Foxbat-B*, an unarmed aircraft with five camera windows and dielectric panels. Soviet Frontal Aviation tactical air forces are thought to deploy between 150 and 160 reconnaissance *Foxbats*, a total which includes a number of *Foxbat-Ds* with larger side-looking airborne radar dielectric panels but without cameras. Reconnaissance *Foxbats* also serve with the air forces of Algeria, India, Libya and Syria. Soviet-operated *Foxbat-Bs* carried out reconnaissance missions on behalf of Egypt during 1971/2 and Israeli Phantom IIs failed to intercept them after scramble. A training version of the aircraft is the tandem-cockpit MiG-25U or *Foxbat-C*.

Development of an improved MiG-25 interceptor began in the Soviet Union in the early/mid-1970s. The MiG-25M is now operational with the Voyska PVO and perhaps already makes up a third of the MiG-25s in use. This is known to NATO as *Foxhound*. It is said to be a two-seater with two engines each rated at 14 000 kg (30,865 lb)

st with afterburning; to carry four or six new missiles that, in conjunction with lookdown/shootdown pulse-Doppler radar, can be fired against extremely low-flying targets or targets at any other altitude; and to be armed also with cannon. All this suggests that its main role is that of intercepting cruise missiles of the type currently being deployed by NATO.

Even less is known in the West of the much smaller single-seat air-superiority fighter that has been under test at Ramenskoye in the Soviet Union since the late 1970s and is reportedly in production and service. Known at present as the MiG-29 and given the NATO reporting name *Fulcrum*, it is believed to have a configuration not dissimilar to the U.S. Hornet. However, its two engines are each estimated to be rated at 8 600 kg (18,960 lb)st with afterburning, making it more powerful. This would be consistent with reports that the aircraft's maximum speed is in the high Mach 2 class. Manoeuvrability is said to be very good. Early production examples have probably joined the Voyska PVO.

A U.S. reconnaissance satellite is also undoubtedly responsible for the identification of a second interceptor-fighter under test at Ramenskoye. Believed to be a product of the Sukhoi bureau and given the designation Su-27 (NATO *Flanker*), it is thought to be in the class of the U.S. F-15 Eagle. No further information is currently available other than it is a larger aircraft than the F-15.

An earlier Sukhoi that forms a substantial part of the Soviet Voyska PVO interceptor force is the Su-15. This is known to NATO as *Flagon*. However, with the increasing number of *Flogger/Foxbat/Foxhounds* available to that force, the number of Su-15s has

Israel Defence Force IAI
Kfirs in camouflage.

gone down from more than 900 to between 700 and 750. The Soviet Air Force has been the only user.

First seen in public during the July 1967 flypast, *Flagon* is a single-seat all-weather interceptor powered in *Flagon-F* form by two 7200-kg (15,873-lb)st with afterburning Tumansky R-13 turbojet engines. It is considerably larger than the earlier Su-11 and carries two *Anab* missiles. Provision is made for other weapons. Maximum speed while carrying missiles is believed to be Mach 2.3.

Apart from the *Flagon-C* two-seat operational trainer, it appears that all production versions of *Flagon* are used in first-line service with the exception of the initial *Flagon-A*. The latter can be regarded as a version used by development squadrons and differed considerably from aircraft produced later. *Flagon-D* was the first major version, with engines less powerful than those provided for subsequent interceptor versions. *Flagon-E* was produced in the greatest numbers, with 6600-kg (14,551-lb)st with afterburning engines and improved avionics. Deliveries began in about 1973. *Flagon-F* has the most powerful engines and a larger nose radome.

Israel's entry into fighter production was necessitated by the French government's refusal to allow delivery of Dassault-Breguet Mirage 5s to that country. Rapidly, Israel Aircraft Industries set about producing its own spare parts for Mirage IIIs already operational and began the design of a fighter of its own. The outcome was the Nesher (Eagle). Flown as a prototype in 1969 (only two years after IAI had been formed from the Bedek Aircraft Company), it was based on a modified Mirage III-type airframe. Power was provided by a SNECMA Atar 9C engine and the aircraft's avionics and other equipment were of Israeli origin. The Nesher entered service from 1972 and it is believed that about 40 were used during the 1973 Yom Kippur War. Missile armament probably comprised the Israeli Shafrir dogfight missile.

The Argentine Air Force received Neshers from Israel, 26 being available for use during the Falkland Islands conflict. The loss of Argentine aircraft of several types during the conflict does not allow an estimate to be made of the number of Neshers still in first-line use.

Even before the use of the Nesher in battle in 1973, IAI had begun the development of a much more ambitious combat aircraft which became the Kfir (Lion Cub). This first flew as a prototype in 1973. The selection of the General Electric J79 turbojet as the power plant necessitated major revisions to the Mirage-type airframe of the Nesher. These included a redesigned rear fuselage of reduced length but increased diameter and a flatter underfuselage. The undercarriage was strengthened because of the increased all-up weight and various other changes were made. For its air-defence role, selected armament was two 30-mm DEFA cannon and two Shafrir missiles. In ground-attack configuration, weapons included the TV-guided Luz-1 air-to-surface tactical missile.

Production of the Kfir was undertaken but only two Israeli squadrons received the type. Already by 1974 a further revision had produced the Kfir-C2, now Israel's most numerous fighter. First displayed in 1976, it was seen to have detachable foreplanes forward of and above the main delta wings, the latter themselves having been modified by the extension of the outer leading-edges. Other changes had also been made. As a result of these modifications, the Kfir's performance at take-off and landing, and its manoeuvrability at lower speeds, are enhanced. The modified aircraft became the main variant and a programme was initiated to bring earlier C1s up to this standard. Further improvements to the Kfir-C2 have been introduced during production. By early 1982 more than 200 Kfir-C1/C2s had been built, including a number of Kfir-TC2 two-seat operational trainers. Kfir-C2s have been exported to Colombia, which ordered 12.

The Kfir-C2 is equally suited to interceptor, fighter and ground-attack roles. As an interceptor-fighter armament comprises the fixed 30-mm Israeli-built DEFA 552 cannon plus two Shafrir 2 missiles. Up to 5 775 kg (12,730 lb) of ground-attack weapons can be carried alternatively, including Luz-1, Hobos, Maverick or Shrike missiles, bombs, rockets, etc. The 8 120-kg (17,901-lb)st General Electric J79-J1E turbojet engine allows a maximum speed of more than Mach 2.3 and a rate of climb of 14 000 metres (45,950 feet) per minute. Interestingly, a new combat aircraft to replace several Israel Defence Force types in the 1990s, including the Kfir-C2, is currently under development as the small and

The Nesher preceded the Kfir as Israel's first home-produced fighter.

lightweight Lavi (Young Lion). This too will have rear-mounted main wings and foreplanes.

During the early years of the last decade, development of a new fighter of advanced design was initiated in China at the Shenyang works. This has the Chinese name Jianjiji-8 but is better known in the West simply as the Shenyang J-8. Its NATO reporting name is *Finback*. Little has been reported of this aircraft, despite the fact that several Americans viewed a prototype in 1980. Its development was assisted by the receipt of at least one ex-Egyptian MiG-23 in 1976. However, it is believed that *Finback's* configuration is nearer that of the latest French delta. It is also thought that

production is being delayed by the lack of a suitable engine, the Chinese-built Tumansky R-11 probably proving inadequate for this aircraft which is undoubtedly larger and heavier than the Xian J-7. The maximum speed of a production J-8 is likely to be more than Mach 2.

In Europe a formidable interceptor has been produced as just one variant of the Panavia Tornado. Details of the development of the Tornado are given in the chapter dealing with attack aircraft. The Tornado ADV (Air Defence Variant) has been designed to British requirements as a Lightning and Phantom II replacement and indeed the R.A.F. will be its sole user. Carrying the R.A.F. designation Tornado

Kfir-C2 as flown by the Israel Defence Force, in its latest colour scheme.

F.Mk 2, it is a variable-geometry or swing-wing two-seater, powered by two uprated Turbo-Union R.B.199-34R turbofan engines mounted side by side in the rear fuselage. Armament consists of one 27-mm IWKA-Mauser cannon plus two AIM-9L Sidewinder missiles carried under the wings and four Sky Flash missiles carried under the fuselage. By virtue of its Foxhunter track-while-scan pulse-Doppler interception radar, the Tornado F.Mk 2 can locate targets at a range of more than 185 km (115 miles) and track several at any one time. Compared to the Tornado IDS, the ADV is longer, with a more pointed nose radome, and the fixed inboard wing panels are of longer chord.

The R.A.F. is expected to receive a total of 165 Tornado F.Mk 2s. The maximum speed of each will be above Mach 2. The first prototype ADV flew initially in October 1979. The first production Tornado F.Mk 2 flew in 1983 and the first aircraft are scheduled to become operational by late 1984. Most Tornado F.Mk 2s are likely to be

stationed in the United Kingdom, with the role of protecting NATO's northern and western approaches and for the air defence of the U.K. Others will be based in Europe.

The aircraft currently replacing the F-106A Delta Dart as the main interceptor of the North American Aerospace Defense Command (NORAD) is the McDonnell Douglas F-15 Eagle. The first air defence squadron to be so equipped was the 48th Fighter Interceptor Squadron, stationed at Langley Air Force Base in Virginia, with 20 aircraft. But most of the 779 Eagles delivered to the U.S.A.F. by February 1983 have gone to tactical combat squadrons, including 68 to the 1st Tactical Fighter Wing of the Rapid Deployment Force. In addition, 14 Eagles have been built for Japan, to be included in a total of 88 single-seat F-15Js and 12 two-seat operational training F-15DJs being acquired for the Japan Air Self-Defence Force. The remainder of the 100 Eagles are being built under licence in Japan by Mitsubishi. The first J.A.S.D.F. unit to be equipped with the Eagle was formed in 1981. Twenty-five

Third prototype Panavia Tornado F.Mk 2 in the new colour scheme, carrying four Sky Flash and two Sidewinder missiles and drop-tanks.

McDonnell Douglas
F-15C Eagle in U.S.A.F.
service carrying a full
load of Sparrow and
Sidewinder missiles.

F-15A and F-15B Eagles have also been delivered to Israel, these being the first to see combat, and more Eagles are expected to join the Israel Defence Force. The first Eagles of an order for 62 from Saudi Arabia were delivered in 1981.

The F-15 Eagle was the McDonnell Douglas follow-up air-superiority fighter and fighter-bomber to its F-4 Phantom II, and it set new standards in performance and capability. Initial funding for a new fighter was requested by the U.S.A.F. in the mid-1960s and subsequently McDonnell Douglas was asked to produce 20 research and development prototypes. Of these, two were configured as two-seat trainers and all were subsequently taken into service. These are included in the total number of Eagles previously given. The first prototype of an F-15A single-seater flew initially in July 1972 but it was an F-15B two-seater that first went into U.S.A.F. service in 1974.

By 1979, when production switched to the single-seat F-15C and two-seat F-15D, 382

F-15As and 60 F-15Bs had been completed. The F-15A and C, and the F-15B and D, are generally similar. Each has shoulder-mounted fixed wings, a large and angular two-dimensional air intake on each side of the fuselage, a twin fin and rudder tail unit and a high-positioned cockpit canopy affording the pilot excellent all-round vision. Power is provided by two Pratt & Whitney F100-PW-100 turbofan engines, each rated at about 10854 kg (23,930 lb)st with afterburning, giving the single-seaters a maximum speed of more than Mach 2.5, and extremely high rate of climb and service ceiling. The rate of climb was amply demonstrated in 1975 when a specially prepared F-15 named *Streak Eagle* captured eight world time-to-height records. These achievements ranged from taking 27.57 seconds to reach an altitude of 3000 metres (approx. 9,800 feet) to taking 3 minutes and 27.8 seconds to reach 30000 metres (over 98,000 feet). Of the eight, the two highest were quickly recaptured by the Soviet Union with its Mikoyan E-266M, which also set a new record by attaining 35000 metres (almost 115,000 feet) in 4 minutes and 11.7 seconds. The E-266M's time to 30000 metres was a mere 3 minutes and 9.85 seconds.

In 1979 the F-15C and F-15D became the production versions, differing from the earlier Eagles mainly in respect of the fuel carried. Apart from a greater internal fuel capacity, each has the ability to be fitted with FAST (Fuel And Sensor Tactical) packs. Developed for the Eagle, FAST packs comprise two pallets of streamlined shape that can be attached one each side of the fuselage to the air intakes. These are quickly removable but do not limit the aircraft's ability to fly at twice the speed of sound. Each pack contains extra fuel and desired operational equipment including reconnaissance cameras or sensors, a laser designator, low-light-level TV or perhaps radar detection and ECM equipment. Even with these packs fitted the Eagle can be fully armed for an air-superiority fighter role, carrying four AIM-7F Sparrow and a similar number of AIM-9L Sidewinder missiles plus a 20-mm M61A1 multi-barrel cannon. Although McDonnell Douglas has produced a specialized ground-attack version of the Eagle, known as the F-15E Enhanced Eagle, the fighter versions can themselves carry a massive 7257 kg (16,000 lb) of weapons in a secondary attack role. Naturally the F-15C is a heavier aircraft than the F-15A, the 'C' having a maximum take-off weight with FAST packs attached of 30845 kg (68,000 lb).

The U.S. Navy's equivalent of the U.S.A.F.'s Eagle is the F-14 Tomcat, although this has variable-geometry or swing-wings and is a carrier-borne fighter. Detailed in the appropriate chapter covering naval fighters and attack aircraft, it is also operated by the Iranian Islamic Revolutionary Air Force as a land-based fighter. Iran received a total of 80 F-14A Tomcats in the latter 1970s before the Islamic Republic was formed in 1979, but the majority of these are probably now unserviceable.

J.A.S.D.F. F-15J with three external fuel tanks and its fuselage speed-brake in the up position.

U.S.A.F. two-seat
training Eagle.

Return of the lightweights

The last fighter to be mentioned in this chapter is the General Dynamics F-16 Fighting Falcon, a combat aircraft that made the 'lightweight fighter' attractive to a number of air forces. It had been designed originally as a contender in the U.S.A.F.'s Lightweight Fighter (LWF) programme. The first of two YF-16 prototypes made its maiden flight in February 1974. Having been selected for further development in 1975, work also began under a U.S.A.F. directive to increase the aircraft's day-fighting role to encompass some all-weather capability and a secondary ground-attack role.

Pre-production aircraft comprised six F-16A single-seat air-superiority fighters and two two-seat operational trainers designated F-16Bs. The first of these, an F-16A,

first flew in December 1976. By the time of writing, the U.S.A.F. had announced its intention of procuring no fewer than 1,985 F-16s. These will comprise mostly single-seaters but with more than 200 two-seaters included. Of this overall total, more than 1,000 had been ordered by the spring of 1982. Production is at a rate of one F-16 every three days on average.

The F-16A Fighting Falcon was first delivered to the U.S.A.F.'s 388th Tactical Fighter Wing, stationed at Hill Air Force Base in Utah, in early 1979. Today U.S.A.F. F-16s are based in the U.S.A., Europe and South Korea. F-16s have also begun entering service with the U.S. Air National Guard and will be followed shortly by the first for the U.S. Air Force Reserve.

Soon after the F-16 had been selected for further development, in 1975, it was announced that Belgium, Denmark, the Netherlands and Norway had decided to deploy the fighter as a replacement for their ageing F-104 Starfighters. It had been chosen in the face of stiff competition from the Saab Viggen and Dassault-Breguet Mirage F1-E, and at the time there was great debate as to whether the correct choice had been made in view of the F-16's day-fighter restrictions. It was argued that front-line European air forces required a fighter that could cope in adverse weather conditions at least. It was too much to hope that an attack would begin on a clear sunny day and end before nightfall. Of course there would still be heavy all-weather fighters stationed in Europe to back up the F-16s but the overall impression was that the forces would be weakened. Fortunately, the increased capabilities worked into the F-16 thereafter, including the provision of radar and all-weather navigation avionics, resolved this problem. The F-16 is, without doubt, one of the most formidable fighters in service today, perhaps on a level slightly below that of the latest 'heavies' of the F-15 class. Nevertheless it is highly manoeuvrable, fast climbing and has a maximum speed of more than Mach 2 on the power of its single Pratt & Whitney F100-PW-200 turbofan engine. This is rated at about 11 340-kg (25,000-lb)st with after-burning. Take-off weight of the F-16A in a fighter role is up to 10 800 kg (23,810 lb), when not carrying drop-tanks to increase fuel capacity.

F-16s for Europe are produced under an agreement which permits final assembly of those destined for the air forces of Belgium and Denmark to be undertaken by SABCA and Sonaca in Belgium. Those for the

General Dynamics F-16A Fighting Falcon lightweight fighters in U.S.A.F. markings.

Netherlands and Norway are assembled by Fokker in the former country. Various components for F-16s are also of European manufacture. The air forces of Belgium and the Netherlands received their first F-16s in 1979, the first of 116 and 142 ordered so far respectively. In the following year the forces of Denmark and Norway received initial examples of the 58 and 72 ordered respectively. Initial operational deployment was made by the Belgium and Royal Danish Air Forces in 1981.

The F-16 Fighting Falcon has also received wide acceptance outside NATO. In 1977 Israel declared its intention to acquire an initial 75 F-16s, all of which had been delivered from the U.S.A. by 1982. Eight of these became the first F-16s to see action, when, in the company of F-15 Eagles, they attacked Iraq's Osirak nuclear reactor then under construction. Egypt is in the process of receiving 40 F-16s and 24, 40 and 36 are to join the air forces of Venezuela, Pakistan and South Korea respectively.

As part of a continuing F-16 improvement programme initiated by the U.S.A.F., Fighting Falcons completed from late 1981

Above: Final assembly of F-16 Fighting Falcons for European air forces at Fokker's Schiphol plant.

Right: U.S.A.F. F-16B two-seater operated by the 388th TFW. It carries three external fuel tanks for a ferry flight to Egypt to take part in the joint U.S./Egyptian exercise, Bright Star 82.

have provision for advanced avionics to allow for their future use (in F-16C and F-16D forms) in specialized interception and attack roles. Future armament for air-to-air combat will include the AMRAAM, a medium-range missile under development by Hughes as a Sparrow replacement, possessing the so-called 'launch and leave' capability. In the meantime, armament includes a 20-mm General Electric M61A1 multi-barrel cannon and up to six AIM-9J or L Sidewinders, Sparrow or Sky Flash air-to-air missiles. In a secondary ground-attack role, up to 9276 kg (20,450 lb) of weapons can be carried, including air-to-surface missiles, rockets, guns, etc.

General Dynamics has also produced an example of its F-16/79, proposed to fulfil a U.S. government requirement for an air-defence fighter with secondary roles that could be exported to countries that have little use for an aircraft of U.S.A.F. service

calibre. By the installation of an 8165-kg (18,000-lb)st with afterburning General Electric J79-GE-119 turbojet engine, the cost of each unit is lowered at the expense of an increase in weight and some reduction in performance.

Another F-16 derivative produced by General Dynamics is the new F-16XL. With U.S.A.F. assistance, two development aircraft have been produced, the first of which flew initially in July 1982. The most obvious external changes are to the wing and tail configurations. The F-16's normal short-chord cropped-delta wings, that blend into the fuselage shape, and its all-moving tailplane are replaced by a new wing described as having a cranked-arrow planform. This new configuration reduces the aircraft's take-off and landing distances and allows many more weapons to be carried. Fuel capacity is also greatly increased.

F-16XL advanced technology Fighting Falcon with the new 'cranked arrow' wing.

2 Blowing Up – Shooting Down

A fighter-bomber is an aircraft with the designed roles of fighter and attack on tactical surface targets both in the battle area and behind enemy lines. The term can also be applied to aircraft assigned these joint roles as their air-to-air capabilities have diminished with age.

The oldest aircraft in this chapter, and the only one to be piston-engined, is the North American F-51D Mustang. It was designed and used during the Second World War and as late as the 1970s it could still be found in the inventories of several South American air forces and that of Indonesia. By the early 1980s only the Dominican Republic still operated the F-51D as a first-line aircraft, perhaps 10 being flown by a single squadron.

Powered by a 1,695-hp Packard V-1650-7 engine, the F-51D has a maximum speed of about 703 km/h (437 mph). It is armed with six 0.50-in cannon in the wings and eight underwing attachment points allow for two 1,000-lb bombs and rockets.

The development and deployment of the Soviet Mikoyan-Gurevich MiG-15, and its subsequent use during the Korean War of the early 1950s, proved two points of significance. The first was that Soviet fighter design was as good as any in the world, and the second was that in combat MiG-15s were at least as good as the Western fighters opposing them. In both single-seat fighter and two-seat training versions, the MiG-15 was operated by a great many nations. But, today, it is most commonly used in the MiG-15UTI training form. However, a small and diminishing number are still listed as fighter-bombers, due mainly to the adoption of the aircraft for new production in China many years ago.

Chinese production centred on the MiG-15*bis*, known as the Shenyang F-2. This, and the MiG-15UTI derivative, were the first turbojet-powered aircraft to be built in China. Today, apart from the MiG-15UTI, the Soviet MiG-15 and the Chinese F-2 are listed as fighter-bombers with Albania and the Congo Republic, while the small number of single-seaters in service in Czechoslovakia can be so used but are more likely operated as advanced trainers.

Far more significant today are the MiG-17 and J-5/F-5. The MiG-17 was the follow-on Soviet fighter to the MiG-15 and in many ways was more successful than the later MiG-19. It represented an attempt to produce a supersonic fighter based on the MiG-15 layout, incorporating new wings

Dominican Republic F-51D Mustang.

with greater sweepback and a lengthened fuselage. Initially, a turbojet engine similar to that found in the MiG-15*bis* was used (a 2 700-kg; 5,950-lb st VK-1), but this was subsequently superseded by a 3 170-kg (6,990-lb)st with afterburning Klimov VK-1A.

In the early 1980s it is believed that no fewer than 19 air forces operate MiG-17s in two main forms. These are the MiG-17F (NATO *Fresco-C*) day fighter and the MiG-17PF (*Fresco-D*) limited all-weather version. Poland was one of three countries that produced MiG-17s, and examples of its LiM-6 remain in major use. China was another country that produced its own versions from about 1956, having J-5 designations for home use and F-5 for those exported. It is thought that the Air Force of the People's Liberation Army still includes approximately 1,000 J-5as and J-5 Jia/J-5As (relating to *Fresco-C* and *D* respectively) and the Aviation of the People's Navy has some 300. F-5s are also flown by the air forces of Albania, Kampuchea, the Sudan and Vietnam. The maximum speed of the *Fresco-C* is 1 145 km/h (711 mph), its rate of climb is approximately 3 900 metres (12,800 feet) per

minute and its armament comprises one 37-mm and one 23-mm cannon plus rockets or bombs carried under the wings.

Time has not been so kind to the American equivalent of the MiG-15, the North American F-86 Sabre. First flown in 1947, it showed its paces during the Korean War and was for many years a standard fighter of the U.S.A.F. and many NATO and other countries. Even as recently as the late 1970s 10 air forces still operated American-, Australian- or Canadian-produced Sabres. But, today, operators have been reduced to just South Korea, Honduras and Venezuela.

Above: The Mikoyan-Gurevich MiG-17 still plays an important role as a fighter-bomber with the Egyptian Air Force.

Top: One of the few remaining North American Sabres is this one, operated by the Honduran Air Force.

Four squadrons of the Republic of Korea Air Force deploy F-86Fs, each powered by a 2 708-kg (5,970-lb)st General Electric J47-GE-27 turbojet engine. Maximum speed is 1 105 km/h (687 mph) and armament comprises six 0.50-in machine-guns in the nose and either two Sidewinder missiles, two 1,000-lb bombs or rockets under the wings. Venezuelan F-86Ks have more powerful engines with afterburning, increased wing span and four 20-mm cannon instead of machine-guns.

Greater longevity has been attained by the F-100 Super Sabre, North America's follow-up fighter to the Sabre. First flown in 1953, it was the first of the U.S.A.F.'s so-called Century Series fighters. This aircraft represented a totally new design and one with supersonic performance. The U.S.A.F. no longer operates the Super Sabre. Of those other air forces that received the type, Denmark, Taiwan and Turkey are currently the only users. Versions in service are: the F-100C single-seat fighter-bomber with strengthened wings, in-flight refuelling capability and eight attachment points for up to 3 400 kg (7,500 lb) of weapons; the F-100D, similarly powered to the 'C' with a 7 710-kg (17,000-lb)st with afterburning Pratt & Whitney J57-P-21A turbojet engine but having a taller tailfin; and the F-100F two-seat operational trainer and attack aircraft. The maximum speed of the F-100D is 1 390 km/h (864 mph) and its armament includes four 20-mm cannon and four Sidewinder missiles or up to 3 400 kg (7,500 lb) of bombs, rockets, etc.

The Swiss Air Force has long been served by fighter-bombers of British origin, although the oldest of these, the de Havilland Vampire, has fairly recently been withdrawn. Only Zimbabwe is believed to retain any Vampires as fighter-bombers, but even this deployment must be regarded as doubtful. An update of the Vampire by

Above: North American F-100 Super Sabre.

Right: Swiss Hawker Hunter F.Mk 58 operating from a main road during a training exercise.

de Havilland produced the Venom of 1949, another straight-winged single-seater, with the 2 200-kg (4,850-lb)st de Havilland Ghost 103 turbojet engine exhausting between twin booms. Apart from British production for the R.A.F. (long since out of service), production was also undertaken under licence in Switzerland. Today the Swiss Air Force retains three squadrons of Venom FB.Mk 50s with improved avionics in a modified nose. Maximum speed is 1030 km/h (640 mph) and armament comprises four 20-mm cannon in the nose and underwing attachment points for up to 907 kg (2,000 lb) of attack weapons.

Switzerland is also the operator of the greatest number of Hawker Hunters. First flown as a prototype in 1951 and entering R.A.F. service from 1954, the Hunter is still widely flown as a combat aircraft, although not by British forces. It is, incredibly, still a much sought-after aircraft.

The Hunter is in service in a combat role with the air forces of Chile, India, Iraq, Lebanon, Oman, Qatar, Singapore, Switzerland, the United Arab Emirates and Zimbabwe. By far the largest number with a single air force are the 140 F.Mk 58s of the Swiss Air Force, operated alongside eight trainers by nine of its 12 fighter-bomber squadrons. Sixty of these were refurbished in Switzerland by the Swiss Federal Aircraft Factory (F + W), a government aircraft establishment that is currently involved in the assembly of Northrop F-5E/F Tiger IIs.

The Hunter F.Mk 58 is basically similar to the F.Mk 6 and Mk 56, as used by India and Lebanon and powered by the Rolls-Royce Avon 203 turbojet engine. The FGA.Mk 9 ground-attack aircraft, and the generally similar Mks 57, 59, 71 and 73, are flown by the forces of Chile, Iraq, Lebanon, Oman and Zimbabwe. Power is provided by a 4540-kg (10,000-lb)st Rolls-Royce Avon 207 turbojet engine. Maximum speed is 1142 km/h (710 mph), maximum rate of climb is about 2440 metres (8,000 feet) per minute, and armament includes four 30-mm cannon carried in the nose as well as two 1,000-lb bombs, rocket packs or other weapons.

Soon after Hunters began entering R.A.F. service, the first flight took place of what became known as the Hawker Siddeley Gnat. This had been designed as a single-seat lightweight fighter. Gnat Mk 1 production

A Swiss-refurbished
Hunter follows a Swiss-
assembled F-5E and two
Mirage IIIs.

aircraft flew on the power of a single 2050-kg (4,520-lb)st Bristol Siddeley Orpheus 701 turbojet engine. Maximum take-off weight was up to 4020 kg (8,885 lb) and a speed of 1118 km/h (695 mph) was attainable. Armament was two 30-mm Aden cannon supplemented by two 500-lb bombs or other weapons.

The Gnat Mk 1 was not adopted by the R.A.F. as a combat aircraft, although T. Mk 1 two-seat trainers did enter service. Trainers are best remembered as the former mounts of the R.A.F. Red Arrows aerobatic team. However, Gnat Mk 1s did enter service with the Indian Air Force, with licence-production in India being undertaken from 1962 until 1973. The final two Indian Gnats were converted into prototypes of a Mk 2 version, subsequently named Ajeet (Invincible) by Hindustan Aeronautics Limited (HAL). The first took to the air in March 1975.

spring of 1982, when production continued. Some Gnats have also been modified to Ajeet standard.

Indian Air Force HAL Ajeet, developed from the British Gnat.

Prior to the construction of Gnats or Ajeets, HAL had already flown the prototype of its HF-24 Marut single-seat fighter. Powered also by the Orpheus, in this instance two 2200-kg (4,850-lb)st Orpheus 703s, the Marut Mk 1 production model proved to have supersonic performance (Mach 1.02) and entered service from 1964. Three Indian Air Force squadrons were so equipped but the Ajeet is currently replacing the Marut with the two remaining Marut squadrons assigned to fighter-bomber missions. Armament comprises four 30-mm cannon and 48 air-to-air rockets carried in a pack that retracts into the fuselage. Underwing weapons can include four 1,000-lb bombs.

Like the Gnat, the prototype French Dassault Super Mystère B-2 first flew as a prototype in 1955. Today only Honduras counts the Super Mystère B-2 among its aircraft, these coming from Israel during the latter 1970s. All 12 aircraft have a 4218-kg (9,300-lb)st Pratt & Whitney J52-P-8A turbojet engine installed in place of the former SNECMA Atar 101G, a lengthened fuselage and uprated avionics. Maximum speed is just supersonic and armament comprises two 30-mm DEFA cannon plus air-to-air missiles or ground-attack weapons. Refurbishing had been undertaken in Israel.

Powered by a 2041-kg (4,500-lb)st Orpheus 701-01 turbojet engine, the Ajeet has improved communications and navigation avionics, better longitudinal control and can be armed with two 30-mm Aden cannon and underwing weapons in addition to drop-tanks. Maximum take-off weight has been increased and its maximum speed is reported to be 1152 km/h (716 mph). A training version is also built. The Indian Air Force had taken delivery of 80 Ajeets by the

Dassault Super Mystère B2, prior to service with the Honduran Air Force.

Tailless deltas and manned missiles

Undoubtedly the best known of all modern French-built combat aircraft is Dassault-Breguet's celebrated tailless delta, the Mirage III. It has been successfully winning French Air Force and foreign orders for more than two decades. The prototype single-seat Mirage III first flew in November 1956 and 10 Mirage III-As were quickly followed by the first major version, the Mirage III-C. From the beginning Mirage aircraft could operate from semi-prepared strips. The first III-C took to the air in October 1960 and eventually 95 were delivered to the French Air Force for use in interceptor and attack roles. In the early 1980s two squadrons remained operational as interceptors with the French Air Defence Command, comprising some 30 aircraft. Others were exported to Israel, South Africa and Switzerland, the former two today deploying sufficient numbers for one squadron each. Power is provided by one SNECMA Atar 9B.

Two-seat trainers were produced as Mirage III-Bs and III-Ds, followed alphabetically by the Mirage III-E. The latter has proved to be the most important of all versions of the delta and first appeared in 1961. Production had totalled more than

530 by the spring of 1982. Designated a long-range fighter-bomber and intruder aircraft, the Mirage III-E is powered by a single 6 200-kg (13,669-lb)st with afterburning SNECMA Atar 9C turbojet engine. Its maximum take-off weight is 13 700 kg (30,200 lb) and its maximum speed is Mach 2.2. As for other versions, a jettisonable rocket motor is available to boost power. Armament varies according to role but can comprise two 30-mm DEFA cannon and either one Matra R.530 and two Sidewinder air-to-air missiles or ground-attack weapons including the AS.30 missile and 1,000-lb bombs or rockets. The 30 Mirage III-Es flown by the two strike squadrons of 4e Escadre, French Air Force, also carry AN 52 tactical nuclear weapons, but the majority of French III-Es and those exported do not. The Australian Government Aircraft Factories (GAF) licence-built Mirage III-Os for the R.A.A.F.; the III-O is similar to the Mirage III-E but is used in either a fighter or an attack role. The R.A.A.F. III-Os are in service with three first-line squadrons and one operational conversion unit. Several reconnaissance versions of the Mirage III have been produced, with provision for armament.

A new and advanced version of the Mirage III is currently under development

Left: Mirage III-R
reconnaissance derivative
of the III-E.

Dassault-Breguet Mirage
III-E long-range fighter-
bomber and intruder,
flown by the French Air
Force and armed with
an air-to-surface missile.

as the Mirage III NG (new generation). Intended as an export fighter, it will have a fly-by-wire control system, as used in the Mirage 2000, and foreplanes. A prototype was scheduled to fly in 1982.

A specialized ground-attack version of the Mirage III-E has been built as the Mirage 5. Basic changes include provision for greater flexibility in the weapons carried, increased internal fuel capacity, and a lower standard of avionics but with the choice of upgrading. The Mirage 5 is also fully capable of a secondary interceptor-fighter role. The French Air Force has two operational Mirage 5 squadrons but most of the 428 aircraft ordered by early 1982 were for export to 10 countries.

A multi-role Mirage delta, suitable for interceptor, fighter, ground-attack and reconnaissance roles, is the Mirage 50, first

Mirage 5-BD two-seat operational trainer in Belgian markings.

Pakistan Air Force Mirage 5-PA.

flown in 1979. Largely due to a 7200-kg (15,873-lb)st with afterburning SNECMA Atar 9K-50 turbojet engine, but aided by a maximum take-off weight no greater than that for the Mirage III-E, the Mirage 50 has the highest acceleration and rate of climb of the Mirage III/5/50 series. Manoeuvrability is also improved. Maximum speed remains at Mach 2.2 but the maximum rate of climb is 11 100 metres (36,400 feet) per minute.

The Chilean Air Force ordered 16, some of which equip one of the force's four fighter and fighter-bomber squadrons.

A more formidable single-seat multi-role combat aircraft is the new Super Mirage 4000, the prototype of which flew for the first time in March 1979. Developed as a private venture as a very high performance interceptor and low-level penetration-attack aircraft, it has a maximum speed of more than Mach 2.3 and the incredible rate of climb of 18300 metres (60,000 feet) per minute. Unlike all other Mirage fighter aircraft, it is powered by two engines, in this case 9700-kg (21,385-lb)st with afterburning SNECMA M53 turbofans. The typical Mirage wing and tail configuration is retained but with the control and some other surfaces constructed from advanced materials. Sweptback foreplanes are fitted to the air intakes forward of and above the wings, and the blister cockpit canopy is more typical of U.S. fighters than Mirages. A fly-by-wire control system is employed. Armament in an interceptor role could be the two 30-mm DEFA cannon plus up to 14 air-to-air missiles. The attack weapon load of more than 8000 kg (17,635 lb) can include four air-to-surface missiles.

When Lockheed produced its Model 83 and took it on its first flight in February 1954, it was seen by the chosen few as a fighter the like of which had never been seen before. Officially designated F-104 by the U.S.A.F.,

as one aircraft in the so-called Century Series of fighters, it appeared that its name, Starfighter, was an accurate description. The stars were the limit. Its fuselage was long and slender with a needle nose, a T-tail was mounted at the extreme rear, and the biconvex supersonic section wings were extremely short. Indeed, the Starfighter resembled a manned missile and had the performance to match.

Initial versions of the Starfighter were built as interceptors and fighters, but in limited number for Air Defense Command and tactical units of the U.S.A.F. This service no longer deploys any operationally. Large-scale deployment came with the development of the F-104G, a single-seat multi-mission combat aircraft with a 7167-kg (15,800-lb)st with afterburning General Electric J79-GE-11A turbojet engine. The airframe had also been strengthened and an ejection seat was provided for the pilot that took him 'upwards' out of the aircraft. This became the main version and was met with

Dassault-Breguet Mirage 50.

Super Mirage 4000 carrying various pods, laser-guided bombs under the fuselage, drop-tanks, AS 30 Laser and Magic missiles.

approval in Europe. As a result, Belgium, West Germany, Italy and the Netherlands selected the type for operational service, setting up assembly lines in these countries to produce F-104Gs under licence. Outside Europe, both Canada and Japan undertook their own production.

Eventually European assembly of the F-104G totalled 1,027 aircraft. Production by Lockheed in the United States provided many more for Germany and for overseas use under the Military Assistance Program (MAP), plus other single-seat and two-seat training Starfighters. Today the air forces of Belgium, Canada, Denmark, West Germany, Greece, Italy, Japan, the Netherlands, Norway, Taiwan and Turkey operate Starfighters. Of these, Belgium, Denmark, the Netherlands and Norway are re-equipping with F-16 Fighting Falcons. Canada will eventually re-equip with CF-18 Hornets (these replacing CF-104s after CF-101s), and West Germany and

Italy are in the process of receiving replacement Tornados.

Both Italy and Turkey operate another version of the Starfighter, manufactured in Italy. Known as the F-104S, this was the last version to be built and is not due for replacement. The F-104S was based on the F-104G but with an uprated 8120-kg (17,900-lb)st General Electric J79-GE-19 turbojet engine. Maximum speed is 2330 km/h (1,450 mph). Normal armament is one 20-mm M61 cannon and two Sparrow air-to-air missiles, but four Sidewinders can be carried. For attack missions, the nine external stations can carry bombs, rockets, etc. Aeritalia produced 246 in Italy up to 1979, 40 going to Turkey and the remainder into Italian service. Today, most Turkish F-104S Starfighters are operated by three interceptor squadrons, while seven Italian Air Force Wings operate F-104Ss as interceptors and fighter-bombers. Aeritalia is continuing with development and is

Left: German Marineflieger Lockheed F-104G Starfighter armed with a Kormoran anti-shipping missile.

Below: Italian Air Force F-104S.

now working towards enhancing both the weapon system and the mission capability of the F-104S, mainly by the proposed installation of advanced avionics.

The Republic F-105 Thunderchief was produced as another aircraft of the so-called Century Series of fighters and was first flown as a prototype in October 1955. Production F-105s were built with forward-swept air intakes at the wing roots. Several versions were produced for the U.S.A.F., comprising the initial production single-seat F-105B, the F-105D major production version of which 600 were produced, and the F-105F two-seat operational trainer. The F-105D and F were deployed widely during the Vietnam conflict, their avionics updated to enable greater operational use. Some 30 F-105Ds were modified to carry the T-Stick II bombing system, but more important were the F-105Fs modified into F-105Gs under the Wild Weasel programme. Each F-105G carries electronic countermeasures pods on the fuselage below the wings and is armed with either four Shrike or two Standard ARM anti-radiation missiles. With these missiles, F-105Gs attacked anti-aircraft missile sites in Vietnam, knocking out guidance radars.

Although F-105Gs were still in first-line service with two U.S.A.F. squadrons in the late 1970s, they have since been superseded by F-4Gs. Instead, the F-105G has joined the F-105B, D and F versions still operated by Air National Guard and Air Force Reserve squadrons. The maximum speed of the F-105D tactical fighter-bomber is 2230 km/h (1,385 mph) at height or 1375 km/h (855 mph) at sea level. Armament comprises a 20-mm M61 multi-barrel cannon plus Sidewinder air-to-air missiles and drop-tanks, or various arrangements of ground-attack weapons up to a total weight of more than 6350 kg (14,000 lb).

Republic F-105D Thunderchief with a 450 U.S. gallon fuel tank under each wing.

McDonnell's incredible Phantom

Under the military designation XF4H-1, the first prototype McDonnell Phantom II flew for the first time in May 1958. Its design had been initiated many years earlier as a naval two-seat attack aircraft but this original specification had been enlarged subsequently to incorporate air-to-air missile armament. Twenty-three years after this first flight, the very last Phantom II was delivered, last of 138 built under licence by Mitsubishi in Japan for the J.A.S.D.F.

The Phantom II is, without question, one of the all-time 'great' aircraft to come from the United States. Over the years it has been built in thousands, has formed the backbone of NATO and other air forces and has given good account of itself in battle from land bases and aircraft carriers. It was as a naval carrier-based missile fighter that it first went into production under the designation F4H-1F. Just 45 pre-production and production examples of the F4H-1F were built. U.S. Navy Squadron VF-121 became the first unit anywhere to receive the Phantom II, just before the end of 1960. Shortly

thereafter, the aircraft's designation was changed to F-4A. Power was provided by two General Electric J79-GE-2 turbojets, carried in the centre fuselage and exhausting below the anhedral tailplane. The wings were of unusual form, with the outer panels possessing marked dihedral. The crew of two sat in tandem.

The first major production version of the Phantom II was the F-4B. This all-weather fighter for the U.S. Navy and Marine Corps, together with other naval versions, is detailed in the following chapter. U.S.A.F. interest in the Phantom II, following trials to establish its ground-attack capabilities, resulted in the production of the F-4C. Powered by J79-GE-15 turbojets, this was basically a land version of the Navy's F-4B, with the carrier arrester gear and folding wings retained. Production of 583 was undertaken between 1963 and 1966, including 36 which were delivered to the Spanish Air Force. Spanish F-4Cs still equip two interceptor squadrons, although the F-4C was built primarily as a close-support and attack aircraft.

F-4Cs were the first Phantom IIs used by the Europe and Pacific commands of the

U.S.A.F. and Egyptian Air Force McDonnell Douglas F-4E Phantom IIs fly together close to the pyramids of Giza during the Bright Star 82 exercise.

U.S.A.F. and the Air National Guard. Some F-4Cs were modified under the EF-4C Wild Weasel programme, as detailed previously, but these have been eclipsed by the F-4G Advanced Wild Weasels that first entered service with the 35th Tactical Fighter Wing in 1978.

The F-4D followed the F-4C into production for the U.S.A.F. It was designed as an improved version with upgraded avionics. A total of 825 was built, including

small numbers for Iran and South Korea. Massive overseas acceptance of the Phantom II came with the production of the F-4E. First flown in 1967, the F-4E uses two 8120-kg (17,900-lb)st with afterburning J79-GE-17A turbojet engines, which bestow a maximum speed of more than Mach 2. Armament comprises one M61A-1 cannon and usually up to eight Sparrow and Sidewinder missiles as a fighter or up to 7250 kg (16,000 lb) of ground-attack weapons for interdiction and close air-support roles. Bombs can include those of conventional or tactical nuclear type. The U.S.A.F. received nearly 950 F-4Es, a large number of which were supplied to other air forces under MAP. A version of the 'E' was also built under licence in Japan by Mitsubishi (total, 127 F-4EJs).

Having received 10 F-4Es, West Germany ordered 175 F-4F fighters. These were delivered between 1973 and 1976. The Royal Navy received 52 F-4Ks, and they first became operational with No. 892 Squadron in March 1969. Basically a development of the F-4B, the F-4Ks have been in service with the R.A.F. since the Royal Navy decommissioned HMS *Ark Royal*. The R.A.F. was, by then, already an operator of the Phantom II, having itself received a total of 118 F-4Ms from 1968. In service, these are designated

Above: U.S.A.F. Phantom II fires a Sparrow air-to-air missile.

Right: Mitsubishi-produced RF-4EJ Phantom II.

Phantom FGR. Mk 2s. Today the R.A.F. has five squadrons of Phantom FGR. Mk 2 and two of FG. Mk 1 (ex-Royal Navy) interceptors, plus others with operational conversion units. In addition, since deploying Phantom IIs in the Falkland Islands on a permanent basis, it has been announced that another Phantom squadron is to be formed.

Not including those produced in Japan (mentioned earlier), 5,057 Phantom IIs have been built. This figure is made up of 2,597 aircraft for the U.S.A.F. (including RF-4C reconnaissance aircraft), U.S. Navy and U.S.M.C. aircraft, and 1,196 for use by other air forces. The latter number includes RF-4E reconnaissance aircraft used by six foreign air forces. The Phantom IIs of the U.S. forces were operated widely in Vietnam. Captain Richard S. Ritchie of the 555th Squadron, the U.S.A.F.'s only 'ace'

fighter pilot of the war, flew a Phantom II. Aircraft of the Israel Defence Force and Iranian Islamic Revolutionary Air Force are also among those which have seen action.

Another fighter used in carrier and land-based forms is the Vought F-8 Crusader. This is detailed in the following chapter but mention has to be made here of the F-8H version. This is a modernized F-8D and 24 are operated by one squadron of the Philippine Air Force as land-based fighter-bombers. All are ex-U.S. aircraft; delivery took place in 1978.

For air defence, the Philippine Air Force operates Northrop F-5As and Bs. These are the original single-seat combat and two-seat operational training versions of the highly successful F-5 supersonic light tactical fighter. Design of the F-5 began in the mid 1950s. The prototype F-5 flew for the first

One of the 24 Vought F-8H Crusaders flown by the Philippine Air Force.

Canadair-built Northrop NF-5A for the Netherlands (right) and similar aircraft for the Canadian Armed Forces.

time in July 1959 and a large number was built thereafter to orders placed by the U.S. Department of Defense and foreign contract. Department of Defense (DoD) aircraft were mainly for supplying foreign air forces under MAP; recipients were Ethiopia, Greece, Iran, Libya, Morocco, Pakistan, the Philippines, South Korea, South Vietnam, Taiwan, Thailand and Turkey. Norway purchased single- and two-seaters, plus reconnaissance examples, and licence production was undertaken in Canada by Canadair for the Canadian Armed Forces and the Royal Netherlands Air Force under CF and NF designations respectively. Production for the Spanish Air Force was undertaken by CASA. Maximum speed of the F-5A is Mach 1.4 on the power of two 1850-kg (4,080-lb)st with afterburning General Electric J85-GE-13 turbojets. The rate of climb is 8750 metres (28,700 feet) per minute and armament comprises two 20-mm cannon plus two Sidewinder missiles as an interceptor, up to four Sidewinders as a fighter or ground-attack weapons.

The success of the F-5A as a light tactical fighter for foreign use prompted the U.S. government to look for a successor. In 1970 Northrop was announced winner of the IFA (International Fighter Aircraft) competition with its F-5E Tiger II. Changes from the F-5A include two 2268-kg (5,000-lb)st with afterburning J85-GE-21B turbojet engines, a wider fuselage and larger-area low-mounted wings incorporating auto-

matically or manually operated manoeuvring flaps. As a result, its maximum speed is Mach 1.64 and its rate of climb is 10516 metres (34,500 feet) per minute. Manoeuvrability is also greatly enhanced and up to 3175 kg (7,000 lb) of weapons can be carried.

The first F-5E single-seaters were delivered to the 425th Tactical Fighter Squadron, U.S.A.F., in 1973. These were

employed to train foreign users prior to delivery of their aircraft. By early 1982 no fewer than 1,104 F-5Es and nearly 200 two-seat F-5F Tiger IIs had been ordered for use by the air forces of 31 nations. These include several European air forces and even the Republic of Viet-Nam. The U.S.A.F. and U.S. Navy are also users, but in the novel role of 'aggressor'. These simulate enemy aircraft at training schools and 'attack' operational units when least expected. Swiss Air Force Tiger IIs have been assembled at the Federal Aircraft Factory (F + W), with 72 F-5E/Fs delivered and 38 following, and AIDC is producing 248 F-5E/Fs for the Chinese Nationalist Air Force.

In 1979 Northrop flew, for the first time, a specialized reconnaissance version of its Tiger II, known as the Tigereye. It incorporates modifications to the airframe

F-5E Tiger II assembled by the Swiss Federal Aircraft Factory.

49

Northrop F-5G
Tigershark prototype
makes its first flight,
lasting 40 minutes, from
Edwards Air Force Base.

and carries specialized equipment to fulfil its
new role, but can also be armed with cannon
and Sidewinders for self-defence.

In August 1982 the first flight took place of
a further-advanced version of the F-5, this
time designated F-5G Tigershark. It
includes several airframe modifications but,
most importantly, it is powered by a single
7710-kg (17,000-lb)st-class with afterburning General Electric F404-GE-100
turbofan engine. This allows a maximum
speed of more than Mach 2 and a maximum
rate of climb of 16490 metres (54,100 feet)
per minute, performance far higher than is
obtainable from earlier F-5s. Armament in
a fighter role could be two 20-mm M39
cannon plus six Sidewinders. Bahrain is
reportedly the first interested nation.

The F/A-18A Hornet, ordered for the
U.S. Navy, U.S.M.C., Canadian Armed
Forces, R.A.A.F. and Spanish Air Force,

and detailed in Chapter Three, has a land-
based-only derivative known simply as the
F/A-18L. Its prime contractor is Northrop,
which is not surprising as both the F/A-18L
and Hornet were developed from the YF-17,
a lightweight fighter produced by Northrop
to rival the General Dynamics YF-16 for
possible U.S.A.F. contracts.

Powered by two 7257-kg (16,000-lb)st-
class with afterburning General Electric
F404-GE-400 turbofan engines, the F/A-18L
is a single-seat strike fighter, its designation
indicating Fighter/Attack roles. It has a
lighter empty weight than the Hornet and
can carry extra equipment if required in
the space made available by the use of a
simplified undercarriage. Armament can
include the usual selection of air-to-air
and ground-attack weapons, up to a
maximum of 9072 kg (20,000 lb), with
provision for the British Sky Flash and other

advanced missiles. Maximum speed is about Mach 2 and maximum rate of climb is estimated to be in the 18 290 metres (60,000 feet) per minute class.

At the 1967 Soviet Aviation Day display, what appeared to be a modern derivative of the Sukhoi Su-7B was seen for the first time. This new aircraft, too, was a single-seater powered by a single engine, but differed most obviously by having new wings. These seemed to be a compromise between the Su-7B's fixed wings and new-technology variable-geometry or swing-wings, with only the outer panels able to vary the angle of sweepback. Not surprisingly the aircraft on view was considered in the West to be no more than a development type. By the early 1970s this assumption had been proved incorrect. Already production aircraft were in service with the Soviet tactical air forces.

It was subsequently discovered to be the Su-17, powered by an 11 200-kg (24,692-lb)st with afterburning Lyulka AL-21F-3 turbojet engine. Compared to the Su-7B, it has a much higher performance, greater weapon-carrying capability and longer range. It is believed that about 800 to 850 are operated by the Soviet Air Force and 35 to 40 by Soviet Naval Aviation units in an anti-shipping role. Export versions are the Su-20 and Su-22.

The initial production version of the Su-17 was given the reporting name *Fitter-C* by NATO. (The use of the name *Fitter* indicates the aircraft's overall similarity to the Su-7B *Fitter-A*.) *Fitter-C* has a maximum speed of Mach 2.17, a maximum rate of climb of about 13 800 metres (45,275 feet) per minute and the ability to carry up to 4000 kg (8,818 lb) of weapons in addition to its two 30-mm NR-30 cannon.

Other Soviet-operated single-seaters are the longer and better equipped *Fitter-D* and the longer-range and improved *Fitter-H*. Two-seaters are *Fitter-E* and *G*, both of which are used for training and carry one cannon each, the latter with increased operational capability.

It is probable that the most combat-efficient of the exported Su-17 derivatives is

The prototype for the Northrop F/A-18L flies over southern California.

Polish Air Force Sukhoi Su-20s (*Fitter-Cs*) taxi out, carrying 800-litre drop-tanks on outer wing pylons.

the Su-20. This is believed to be powered by a Lyulka turbojet engine but has a lower standard of avionics compared to the Su-17. Algeria, Egypt, Iraq and Viet-Nam, plus the Warsaw Pact nations of Czechoslovakia and Poland, deploy this version. Libya, North Yemen, Peru, South Yemen and Syria operate the Su-22, thought to have been produced in two versions as *Fitter-F* (relating to the *Fitter-D*) and *Fitter-J* (relating to *Fitter-H*) but with lower standards of avionics and powered by the 11500-kg (25,353-lb)st with afterburning Tumansky R-29B turbojet engine. Libya operates by far the largest number of Su-22s, with more than 100 in service.

Although over the years the J.A.S.D.F. has relied fairly heavily on locally produced versions of U.S. fighters, a decision made in the early 1970s was responsible for the ultimate deployment of an all-Japanese combat aircraft. This is the Mitsubishi F-1, a single-seat close-support fighter based on the company's T-2 supersonic trainer and powered by two Rolls-Royce/Turboméca Adour turbofan engines. It has a maximum speed of about Mach 1.6 and has a fixed 20-mm J M61 multi-barrel cannon. For a fighter role, armament is four Sidewinder missiles. For attack, a total weapon load of 2722 kg (6,000 lb) can be carried, later to include two Mitsubishi ASM-1 anti-shipping missiles. Delivery of the F-1 to the J.A.S.D.F. began in September 1977 and by the spring of 1982 more than 60 had entered service. A total of 80 F-1s is likely to be delivered.

Left: Mitsubishi F-1 close-support fighters in squadron service with the J.A.S.D.F.

Below: Soviet Sukhoi Su-17 (*Fitter-C*), with wings spread at approximately 62°.

3 Ship Strike

As a direct result of the fighting over the Falkland Islands, it is probably true to say that the British Aerospace Sea Harrier is the best known of all carrier-based combat aircraft. Those persons that advocated the commissioning of light aircraft carriers with V/STOL combat aircraft to supersede the conventional carriers of HMS *Ark Royal* type have been exonerated, but none could have guessed that their decision would be put to the test so quickly. Never since the end of the Second World War had a new combat aircraft been subjected to such an immediate trial of strength.

On 5 April 1982 the main element of the British Task Force left Portsmouth for the South Atlantic. Included in the number were the Royal Navy carriers old and new, namely HMS *Hermes* and HMS *Invincible*. *Hermes* had been commissioned in 1959. In 1971 its provision to launch and retrieve fixed-wing aircraft had been deleted during a conversion into a commando carrier. At a cost of more than £25 million, *Hermes* rejoined the Navy in its new role in 1973. Three and a half years later it again joined the fleet after conversion to fulfil a new anti-submarine carrier role. The final conversions were undertaken thereafter, when a so-called 'ski-jump' was fitted for use by Sea Harriers.

The original proposal for a 'ski-jump' dates back to 1977, when it was first suggested that a launching ramp for vectored-thrust aircraft would allow a much greater load to be carried under short take-off conditions. As a matter of continuous reappraisal, the angle of the 'ski-jump' has gradually increased. Today, the Royal Navy operates HMS *Invincible* and its sister ship

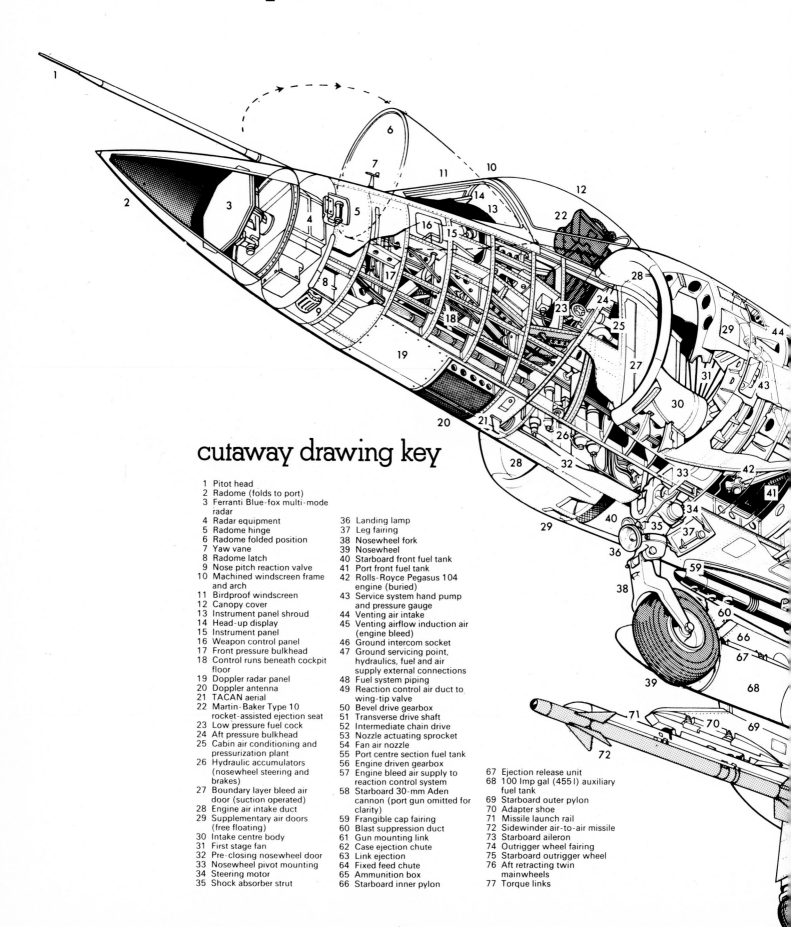

Plate II

British Aerospace Sea Harrier FRS Mk1

cutaway drawing key

1 Pitot head
2 Radome (folds to port)
3 Ferranti Blue-fox multi-mode radar
4 Radar equipment
5 Radome hinge
6 Radome folded position
7 Yaw vane
8 Radome latch
9 Nose pitch reaction valve
10 Machined windscreen frame and arch
11 Birdproof windscreen
12 Canopy cover
13 Instrument panel shroud
14 Head-up display
15 Instrument panel
16 Weapon control panel
17 Front pressure bulkhead
18 Control runs beneath cockpit floor
19 Doppler radar panel
20 Doppler antenna
21 TACAN aerial
22 Martin-Baker Type 10 rocket-assisted ejection seat
23 Low pressure fuel cock
24 Aft pressure bulkhead
25 Cabin air conditioning and pressurization plant
26 Hydraulic accumulators (nosewheel steering and brakes)
27 Boundary layer bleed air door (suction operated)
28 Engine air intake duct
29 Supplementary air doors (free floating)
30 Intake centre body
31 First stage fan
32 Pre-closing nosewheel door
33 Nosewheel pivot mounting
34 Steering motor
35 Shock absorber strut

36 Landing lamp
37 Leg fairing
38 Nosewheel fork
39 Nosewheel
40 Starboard front fuel tank
41 Port front fuel tank
42 Rolls-Royce Pegasus 104 engine (buried)
43 Service system hand pump and pressure gauge
44 Venting air intake
45 Venting airflow induction air (engine bleed)
46 Ground intercom socket
47 Ground servicing point, hydraulics, fuel and air supply external connections
48 Fuel system piping
49 Reaction control air duct to wing-tip valve
50 Bevel drive gearbox
51 Transverse drive shaft
52 Intermediate chain drive
53 Nozzle actuating sprocket
54 Fan air nozzle
55 Port centre section fuel tank
56 Engine driven gearbox
57 Engine bleed air supply to reaction control system
58 Starboard 30-mm Aden cannon (port gun omitted for clarity)
59 Frangible cap fairing
60 Blast suppression duct
61 Gun mounting link
62 Case ejection chute
63 Link ejection
64 Fixed feed chute
65 Ammunition box
66 Starboard inner pylon

67 Ejection release unit
68 100 Imp gal (455 l) auxiliary fuel tank
69 Starboard outer pylon
70 Adapter shoe
71 Missile launch rail
72 Sidewinder air-to-air missile
73 Starboard aileron
74 Outrigger wheel fairing
75 Starboard outrigger wheel
76 Aft retracting twin mainwheels
77 Torque links

78 Shock absorber strut
79 Mainwheel leg fairing
80 Pre-closing mainwheel doors
81 Rear exhaust nozzle
82 Nozzle drive chain and
    sprocket
83 Transverse drive shaft
84 Pressure refuelling point and
    control panel
85 Hydraulic reservoir
86 Wing front attachment point
87 Centre spar attachment
88 Aft attaching link
89 Machined skin planks
90 Wing front spar
91 Intermediate centre spar
92 Wing fuel tank
93 Rear spar web
94 Tank pressurizing air
95 Fuel/air valves
96 Inner pylon fitting
97 Leading edge dog tooth
98 Leading edge wing fence

 99 Aileron control rod
100 Reaction control air duct
101 Tandem aileron jack and
     autostabiliser
102 Aileron hinge
103 Bonded aluminium
     honeycomb flap structure
104 Port aileron, bonded
     aluminium honeycomb
     structure
105 Roll reaction control valve
106 Outer pylon fitting
107 Navigation light
108 Wing tip
109 Outrigger wheel fairing
110 Hydraulic retraction jack
111 Leg fairing (upper section)
112 Port outrigger wheel
113 Leg fairing (lower section)
114 Torque links
115 VHF aerial
116 ECM fairing
117 Fin structure

118 Bonded aluminium
     honeycomb rudder structure
119 Fuselage efflux shield
120 Ventral fin
121 Fuselage rear fuel tank
122 Lox container (1·1 lmp
     gal/5 l)
123 Avionics equipment bay
124 Airbrake (extended)
125 Avionics bay air conditioning
     system
126 Standby UHF aerial
127 Radar altimeter aerials
128 Starboard all-moving
     tailplane
129 Tandem tailplane jack
130 Port all-moving tailplane
131 Tailplane structure
132 Bonded aluminium
     honeycomb trailing edge
133 Pitch and yaw reaction
     valves
134 Tail warning radar

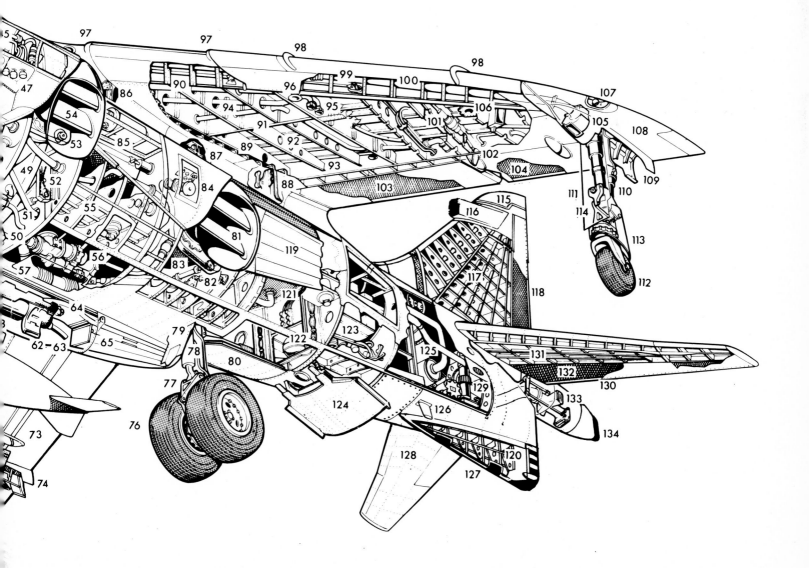

Three U.S. Marine Corps AV-8A Harriers in Okinawa.

HMS *Illustrious* with 7° 'ski-jumps', while HMS *Hermes* now has a 12° 'jump'. HMS *Ark Royal*, the new light carrier of the *Invincible* class, yet to be commissioned, will also have a 12° 'jump'.

On 28 April 1982 it was announced that the British government would impose an air blockade around the Falkland Islands in 48 hours. On 1 May Sea Harriers attacked the airfields at Port Stanley and Goose Green, following an earlier raid by an R.A.F. Vulcan on Port Stanley airfield. The same day a Sea Harrier shot down a Mirage IIIEA fighter-bomber with a Sidewinder missile. During the course of the conflict, which lasted until 14 June, the 28 Sea Harriers carried out 2,380 sorties and were responsible for the destruction of a sizeable number of aircraft in air-to-air combat. A total of 2,680 flying hours was logged and no Sea Harrier was lost in air-to-air combat, although a few were lost to ground fire and accidents claimed others. A Sea Harrier pilot was the only British prisoner of war.

The Sea Harrier itself dates from 1975, when it was announced that a maritime version of the Harrier was to be developed. The first Sea Harrier, designated FRS.Mk 1 by the Royal Navy as a fighter, reconnaissance and strike aircraft, took to the air for its first flight in August 1978. Number 700A Squadron, the Naval Intensive Flying Trials Unit, was commissioned in September 1979 and two months later trials on board HMS *Hermes* began. This unit became subsequently No.899 HQ Squadron. The original order for 34 Sea Harrier FRS.Mk 1s has been increased to cover the purchase of 48 aircraft. Of these, 32 had been delivered by the beginning of the Falkland's fighting. Apart from No.899 HQ Squadron, which is shore-based, the Royal Navy has three first-line Sea Harrier squadrons with five aircraft each.

The Sea Harrier is powered by a 9752-kg (21,500-lb)st Rolls-Royce Pegasus Mk 104 vectored-thrust turbofan engine. This exhausts through four rotatable nozzles which direct the engine efflux at angles of up to 98° from the full-aft horizontal flying position, so as to achieve backward, vertical, hovering or forward flight. Bleed air is used for the jet reaction control system. Provision is made in the design for an in-flight refuelling probe and this flight refuelling capability was used to get more Sea Harriers and Harriers to the Falkland Islands via Ascension Island. These reinforcements left Britain and arrived at Ascension on 8 May. The Sea Harriers within the group are included in the overall total of 28 such aircraft operated during the conflict.

Compared to the R.A.F.'s Harrier, the Sea Harrier has a raised cockpit for the pilot, has a pointed nose containing a multi-mode Ferranti radar instead of the GR.Mk 3's 'thimble' nose containing a laser ranger and marked target seeker, its airframe has no component parts of magnesium construction, and it has changes to the avionics. Armament comprises (optionally) 30-mm Aden cannon and AIM-9L Sidewinder missiles for its role as an interceptor-fighter or various attack weapons up to a total weight of 3 630 kg (8,000 lb), including Sea Eagle anti-shipping missiles. Maximum speed is Mach 1.25 and it is reported that it can be flying 55 km (35 miles) from base in

less than six minutes from the order to scramble.

The Indian Navy is the second operator of the Sea Harrier, its six FRS.Mk 51s having replaced Hawker Siddeley Sea Hawks on board its ex-British *Majestic* class carrier *Vikrant*. This carrier had been laid down in 1943 and launched in September 1945, but work was ended in 1946 as the Royal Navy had no need for a new ship of this type.

This development AV-8B Harrier incorporates the new leading-edge root extensions (LERX) that will be standard on production examples.

Left: An early example of the Soviet Yakovlev Yak-36MP *Forger-A* prepares to land on the *Kiev*. (See page 60.)

Having been purchased by India in 1957, *Vikrant* was completed and commissioned in 1961. Although it is a large aircraft carrier, a 'ski-jump' is not planned as this would prevent the use of the Navy's Breguet Alizé anti-submarine aircraft.

During the Falklands conflict R.A.F. Harrier GR.Mk 3s were also flown from the British carriers, but this was an unusual act for an unusual situation. However, the United States Marine Corps is an operator of the Harrier, as its no-runway operating capability fits in nicely with the U.S.M.C.'s traditional amphibious assault operations. A much smaller number, in fact a total of 11 single-seat AV-8S and two two-seat operational-training TAV-8S Matadors, are flown by the Spanish Navy, mostly from the ex-U.S. *Independence* class aircraft carrier *Dédalo*. A new aircraft carrier will replace the *Dédalo* around 1984, from which the Matadors will then operate using, perhaps, a 'ski-jump'.

The Harrier Mk 50 for the U.S.M.C, or AV-8A as it is known to that service, is used basically for the roles of close support and reconnaissance. However, provision has been included from the beginning for the optional use of Sidewinder air-to-air missiles. None has the laser ranger and marked target seeker of R.A.F. Harriers. The first AV-8A, of what became an eventual total of 102 single-seaters and eight TAV-8A trainers, was delivered in early 1971. Of the U.S.M.C.'s 14 close-support squadrons, three operate AV-8s. These are VMA 231, 513 and 542.

Starting in 1979, 47 U.S.M.C. AV-8As have been modified to the new AV-8C standard, the AV-8B designation having been reserved for the Harrier II as described in detail hereafter. Changes include the installation of forward-looking passive radar warning avionics and tail warning radar, and devices to enhance lift at take-off.

AV-8B is the U.S.M.C. designation of the new Harrier II, which also carries the R.A.F. designation Harrier GR.Mk 5. It has been developed as an advanced Harrier, taking over from earlier British and U.S. projects.

Above: *Forger-B*, with tandem seats for its training role.

Right: Dassault-Breguet Super Etendard on board the French carrier *Clemenceau*, carrying an Exocet anti-ship missile. (*See page 61.*)

Vought F-8E (FN) with its wing in high-incidence position for take-off. (*See page 61.*)

Indeed, after Britain pulled out of a joint U.K./U.S. project of the early 1970s, both Hawker Siddeley and McDonnell Douglas continued work independently. Fortunately, the split was not permanent and the best features from each project have been incorporated into the Harrier II.

The main aim of the Harrier II programme is to produce a follow-on to the standard Harrier which incorporates sufficient aerodynamic and other improvements to allow a very substantial rise in weapon-carrying capability and/or range. This can be judged by a maximum stores load for the Harrier II of 4173 kg (9,200 lb) and an increase in the internal fuel capacity from 2295 kg (5,060 lb) to 3402 kg (7,500 lb). Four of the six underwing pylons can carry drop-tanks.

Two AV-8B prototypes were produced by modification of AV-8As. These can be identified from actual AV-8B development aircraft by their lack of raised bubble-type canopies. The first prototype flew initially in November 1978. Both proved highly successful during trials. Four full-scale development aircraft followed, all flown between November 1981 and mid-1982. It is reported that the U.S.M.C. requires a total of 257 AV-8Bs initially, perhaps reaching

336 eventually. These will be used to re-equip three present Harrier squadrons and to replace Skyhawks with another five. However, operational deployment is not expected before mid-1985, with the last of the eight units becoming operational by 1989. The 60 Harrier GR.Mk 5s for the R.A.F. will enter service in the latter half of 1986.

Construction of components for the Harrier II is undertaken by both McDonnell Douglas in the U.S.A. and British Aerospace in the U.K., with assembly of U.S.M.C. and R.A.F. aircraft in the U.S.A. and U.K. respectively. The 9979-kg (22,000-lb)st Rolls-Royce Pegasus 11-21 turbofan engine for most Harrier IIs is being produced in the U.K., although Pratt & Whitney in the U.S.A. has a manufacturing agreement covering engines to one-quarter of the total overall value. Maximum speed of the Harrier II at sea level is approximately 1083 km/h (673 mph). Gun armament comprises two General Electric five-barrel 25-mm cannon or two 30-mm Aden cannon on U.S.M.C. and R.A.F. Harrier IIs respectively.

The Harrier, Sea Harrier and Harrier II are without doubt the most formidable vertical take-off combat aircraft in the

Vought A-7E Corsair IIs press home a mock attack. (*See page 64.*)

world, possessing the ability to operate from large or small ships and to support land forces without the need of a runway. They can greatly increase their weapon load by using the short take-off technique rather than vertical take-off, and possess the proven capability of outmanoeuvring many of the world's finest conventional fighters using thrust-vectoring in forward flight. The world's only other fixed-wing vertical take-off combat aircraft, the Soviet Yakovlev Yak-36MP, known to NATO as *Forger*, appears not to be so versatile on board ship and is unlikely to be capable of improving manoeuvrability by thrust-vectoring.

The Yak-36MP was developed for use with the Soviet Navy on board its first aircraft carriers, those of the *Kiev* class. The first such vessel, the *Kiev*, was commissioned in May 1975 and was first seen at sea in the following year. It is a 42,000-ton carrier capable of accommodating 12 single-seat *Forger-As*, perhaps a two-seat *Forger-B*

trainer and 19 Kamov Ka-25 (NATO *Hormone*) anti-submarine and missile-targeting helicopters. The second ship, the *Minsk*, was commissioned in 1978 and at least one other carrier of the class has been completed. Another is about to follow on. At least one nuclear-powered aircraft carrier of much larger size is also reported to be under construction in the Soviet Union, perhaps equivalent in size to the U.S. Navy's *Nimitz* class. However, although *Forgers* could be flown from this new carrier, it is more likely that variable-geometry or swing-wing attack aircraft and fighters will be deployed. These could be new types or navalized versions of the Sukhoi Su-24 and Mikoyan MiG-23, remembering that in the 1960s the U.S. Navy planned to acquire the General Dynamics F-111B, which is roughly equivalent to the Su-24.

The *Forger* has shown itself to be capable of precise landings on carrier decks and is believed to have a maximum speed of about

60

Mach 1.1. Armament is thought to include various combinations of a 23-mm GSh-23 cannon, air-to-air or air-to-surface missiles, bombs and rockets, up to an estimated total weight of 1360 kg (2,998 lb). These weapons would be consistent with the roles of anti-submarine, anti-surface ship, land strike and air defence; reconnaissance must also be within its tasks. Its main limitation comes with its believed inability to make short take-offs on board ship to increase its weapon load or fuel capacity. The fact that *Kiev* class vessels lack a 'ski-jump' of any type perhaps confirms this. This inability comes from its engine layout, comprising a large turbojet engine exhausting through two vectoring nozzles to the rear of the mid-mounted wings and two lift-jets exhausting downward. The lift-jets are installed to the rear of the pilot's cockpit, with doors above and below that open during operation. However, even without STOL capability, *Forger* is a most competent strike aircraft, giving the Soviet Navy its first capability to deploy rapidly a strong combat aeroplane force off the coast of a potential trouble spot.

Apart from VTOLs

The French Navy operates two aircraft carriers for fixed-wing aircraft, namely the *Clemenceau* and *Foch*. Both will eventually be replaced by nuclear-powered carriers but this is unlikely before the 1990s. Each has a fully-loaded displacement of 32,780 tons. However, as an economy measure, only the *Clemenceau* deploys fixed-wing aircraft, although *Foch's* helicopters can be supplemented in an emergency.

Not including helicopters, each French carrier can accommodate 20 Dassault-Breguet Super Etendard strike fighters, Vought F-8E(FN) Crusader fighters and Breguet Alizé anti-submarine aircraft. Total aircraft strength for each vessel is 40. Apart from the French Navy, the Argentine Navy has also received Super Etendards; eight of the 14 ordered had been delivered from France by the outbreak of fighting over the Falkland Islands. As on French Navy Super Etendards, the 2100-kg (4,630-lb) total weapon load can include a French AM39 Exocet anti-shipping missile. The Argentine

A-7E of VA-46 operating from USS *John F. Kennedy*. (*See page 64*.)

Facing page: McDonnell Douglas A-4M Skyhawk II, flown by VMA-331, U.S.M.C. (*See page 65.*)

Navy used Exocets to good effect during the hostilities. On 4 May 1982, an Argentine Super Etendard launched an Exocet at long range and this struck the Royal Navy Type 42 destroyer HMS *Sheffield* with devastating effect. Further Super Etendard attacks were carried out thereafter.

The Super Etendard was developed as an improved version of the Etendard IV-M carrier-based fighter and IV-P reconnaissance and tanker aircraft. The original prototype Etendard had flown as long ago as 1958, and today the French Navy still counts at least 20 IV-Ms and IV-Ps in service use with operational conversion and reconnaissance squadrons. Power for each of these is provided by a 4400-kg (9,700-lb)st SNECMA Atar 8B turbojet engine, bestowing a maximum speed of 1085 km/h (674 mph), a rate of climb of 6000 metres (19,700 feet) per minute, and the ability to carry up to 1360 kg (3,000 lb) of weapons (by the IV-M). These can include air-to-air or air-to-surface missiles.

The first flight of a Super Etendard prototype took place in October 1974 and delivery of production aircraft began in mid-

1978. The original plan to equip the French Navy with 100 aircraft was subsequently revised and this figure now stands at 71. All but 10 of these had been delivered by May 1982. This version differs from the previous Etendard IV-M by having much improved avionics, modified sweptback wings, a 5000-kg (11,023-lb)st SNECMA Atar 8K-50 turbojet, and a heavier weapon load as mentioned earlier. In addition to bombs, Exocet or Magic missiles, French Navy Super Etendards can carry tactical nuclear weapons. Maximum speed is about Mach 1.

The French Navy is now the only navy to fly the Vought F-8 Crusader fighter from aircraft carriers. The U.S. Navy no longer has the Crusader in its fighter strength and those flown by the Philippine Air Force are land-based fighter-bombers. It was in 1955 that the Crusader prototype first flew. Several production versions followed for the U.S. Navy, plus a number of modernized versions. The F-8E was an improved all-weather version with an 8165-kg (18,000-lb)st with afterburning Pratt & Whitney J57-P-20 turbojet engine, bestowing a maximum speed of nearly 2127 km/h

Three Navy TA-7C two-seat trainers of VA-174 demonstrate their combat capability.

TA-4J Skyhawk two-seat
trainer, operated by
U.S. Navy operational
conversion units, with its
arrester hook lowered for
a carrier landing.

(1,322 mph). The F-8E(FN) was the export
version of the F-8E for France, with blown
flaps and provision for R.530 missiles carried
each side of the front fuselage plus
Sidewinders. One French Navy squadron is
currently operational with the F-8E(FN)
Crusader, an aircraft remarkable for having
a variable-incidence high wing to allow the
wing incidence to be increased without
raising the fuselage for low-speed take-offs
and landings.

To a U.S. Navy requirement, Vought
produced a single-seat light attack aircraft
based on the Crusader. This was given the
Navy designation A-7 and the name Corsair
II. The prototype flew for the first time in
September 1965 and this was clearly a very
different aircraft. Although retaining some
of the Crusader's features, its wings were of

greater span and were not variable in
incidence, the fuselage was shorter and
power was provided by a turbofan engine. A
very heavy weapon load could be carried.

Initial production versions were the A-7A,
B and C, 60 Bs and Cs re-entering service in
1978 after modification into TA-7C two-seat
operational trainers. Power for the A-7B (in
reserve) and TA-7C is provided by a 6078-
kg (13,400-lb)st Pratt & Whitney TF30-P-
408 turbofan engine. The U.S. Navy's main
version of the Corsair II is the A-7E, basically
similar to the A-7C but with a 6800-kg
(15,000-lb)st Allison TF41-A-2 turbofan
replacing the 5534-kg (12,200-lb)st Pratt &
Whitney TF30-P-8 used for the 67 A-7Cs.

A-7Es entered Navy service from 1969
and were almost immediately used in
action during the fierce fighting in Vietnam.

The final A-7E was delivered in 1981, bringing the total number built to 596. Each can carry, in addition to its 20-mm M61A1 Vulcan cannon, more than 6800 kg (15,000 lb) of weapons, including air-to-air and air-to-surface missiles and tactical nuclear weapons. Maximum speed is 1112 km/h (691 mph).

A version of the A-7E with improved night attack capability was first delivered to the U.S. Navy in 1978. This is known as the A-7E FLIR and carries special avionics to aid target recognition and attack. All other versions of the A-7 Corsair II are land-based.

Even older than the Crusader and Corsair is the McDonnell Douglas A-4 Skyhawk, a single-seat carrier-borne light attack bomber that remained in production for an amazing 26 years. Over this period 2,960 Skyhawks were built. The prototype for the U.S. Navy flew for the first time in June 1954. This single aircraft was followed by 19 service evaluation YA4D-1s and 146 initial production A-4As.

Today several navies and air forces continue to fly the Skyhawk, its impressive capabilities being demonstrated during the recent conflict over the Falkland Islands. Argentine Skyhawks pressed home many attacks on the British Task Force, including that of 25 May when bombs destroyed the Type 42 destroyer HMS *Coventry*.

Skyhawks operated from land by air forces are detailed in a later chapter. Today the navies of Argentina and Australia and the U.S. Marine Corps fly Skyhawks, in A-4Q, A-4G and mainly A-4M Skyhawk II/OA-4M versions respectively. The A-4Q represents the main combat strength on board the Argentine aircraft carrier *Veinticinco de Mayo*, in early 1982 numbering 15. The Fleet Air Arm of the Royal Australian Navy normally operates eight A-4G Skyhawks. These have been equipped to carry Sidewinder missiles as well as attack weapons and operate from the aircraft carrier *Melbourne*.

The main U.S.M.C. version is the improved A-4M Skyhawk II. This is powered by a 5080 kg (11,200 lb)st Pratt & Whitney J52-P-408A turbojet engine and has a maximum speed of 1038 km/h (645 mph) with a 1814-kg (4,000-lb) load. However, the maximum total load is 4535 kg (10,000 lb), which can include a very wide range of attack weapons including nuclear. Like Australian Skyhawks, A-4Ms can launch Sidewinders. It was an A-4M that ended Skyhawk production. The final U.S.M.C. version of the Skyhawk was delivered from 1979 as the OA-4M. Twenty-three were produced by converting TA-4F two-seat trainers for forward air control duties.

Royal Australian Navy CAC/Aermacchi MB 326H trainer accompanies an A-4G Skyhawk.

Combat aircraft for 'supercarriers'

The early history of the McDonnell Douglas F-4 Phantom II has been detailed in the previous chapter. Today's U.S. Navy relies more on the Grumman F-14A Tomcat as a fleet fighter than the Phantom II, and yet an impressive number still serve with operational and reserve squadrons. The closely related U.S. Marine Corps still depends on the Phantom II as its main fighter.

The first major production version of the Phantom II was the F-4B for the U.S. Navy and Marine Corps. The three main versions of the Phantom II in service with these forces today are all directly related to the 'B'. The F-4J is primarily an interceptor but it has equal ability to serve in a ground-attack role. Power is provided by two General Electric J79-GE-10 turbojets and this version uses a

Lear Siegler AJB-7 bombing system. The F-4N is basically an update of the F-4B; 227 were so modified. The final naval combat version, the F-4S, is another modification, this time of the F-4J. Changes include a strengthened structure to extend the aircraft's operational life, new wing leading-edge flaps, and improvements to the electrical and weapon control systems. The first F-4S Phantom IIs re-entered service in 1978.

Because of Grumman's long tradition with the U.S. Navy, going back to the years before the outbreak of the Second World War, it is perhaps fitting that this company should produce the main fighter to replace the long-serving naval Phantom II. The Grumman F-14 Tomcat is the U.S. Navy's first variable-geometry aircraft and so far the only swing-wing aircraft to serve on an aircraft carrier anywhere in the world. A

Phantom IIs of VF-96 from USS *America*.

prototype of this two-seat multi-role fighter flew for the first time in December 1970. Twelve research and development F-14s followed. Trials on board an aircraft carrier began in mid-1972 and by the second half of 1974 two U.S. Navy squadrons were operational on board the nuclear-powered aircraft carrier USS *Enterprise*. The Tomcat has proved a fitting fighter for the U.S. Navy's new *Nimitz* class nuclear-powered carriers that have been commissioned since 1975, their displacement of 81,600 tons and length of 333 metres (1,092 feet) only slightly less than those of *Enterprise*. At present the U.S. Navy has four nuclear-powered and 10 conventionally powered aircraft carriers, with a further six in reserve.

By 1983, 447 F-14A Tomcats had been delivered by Grumman. Continuing construction at a rate of some 24 a year will mean that the F-14 could still be in production in

Above: Wings spread for take-off, this F-14A is about to thunder from USS *Constellation*.

Left: U.S. Navy Grumman F-14A Tomcat armed with four Phoenix long-range missiles, two Sparrows and two Sidewinders.

the mid-1990s. In addition to U.S. Navy aircraft, 80 land-based Tomcats were delivered to Iran (as detailed in Chapter One). Forty-nine Navy F-14s have received reconnaissance pods which are carried under the fuselage.

From late 1983, production of the Tomcat switched from the F-14A to the F-14C, the latest version introducing two Pratt & Whitney TF30-P-414A turbofan engines, in place of the F-14A's 9480-kg (20,900-lb)st TF30-P-412As, and much improved avionics. Maximum speed of the F-14A is Mach 2.4 and armament comprises one M61A-1 Vulcan cannon plus either six Phoenix Mach 4 air-to-air missiles with a range of 200 km (124 miles) and two Sidewinders, or four Phoenix and four Sidewinders, or four Phoenix, two Sparrows and two Sidewinders. For attack, a weapon load of 6577 kg (14,500 lb) is possible.

Becoming operational at the time of writing is the U.S. Navy/U.S.M.C. McDonnell

Above: The first McDonnell Douglas CF-18 Hornet for Canada is rolled out, July 1982. To its right stands a CF-101 Voodoo.

Facing page: U.S. Marine Corps Hornet in the markings of VFA-125, the first development squadron.

Right: A TF/A-18A two-seat training Hornet flies alongside a single-seater.

Douglas F/A-18 Hornet. Of the 1,377 aircraft expected to join these services by the 1990s in F/A-18A single-seat strike fighter and TF/A-18A two-seat operational trainer forms, 40 had been delivered by August 1982. A reconnaissance version is currently being evaluated as the RF-18. In addition, the Canadian Armed Forces is receiving 114 single-seat and 24 two-seat CF-18s to replace Voodoos, Starfighters and CF-5s as land-based aircraft; the Royal Australian Air Force is replacing its Mirage III-Os with land-based F/A-18As from 1984; and the Spanish Air Force will eventually receive perhaps 84 land-based F/A-18As.

As the designation F/A implies, the Hornet has the joint roles of fighter and attack. Like Northrop's F/A-18L, it was developed from Northrop's YF-17 light-weight fighter following U.S. Navy interest in a multi-mission lightweight fighter to replace some Phantom IIs, Skyhawks and Corsair IIs. It is suited to carrier-based and land-based operations, but, as most of those to be built are for the U.S. Navy and closely integrated Marine Corps, it is detailed in this chapter. The prototype Hornet first took to the air in November 1978

and carrier trials were completed the following year.

Power for the Hornet is provided by two 7257-kg (16,000-lb)st General Electric F404-GE-400 turbofan engines carried side-by-side in the rear fuselage. Like other modern U.S. combat aircraft, it has twin outward-canted fins and rudders. Armament comprises an M61 cannon plus up to six Sidewinder and two Sparrow missiles or four of each in a fighter role, or up to 7710 kg (17,000 lb) of external stores for attack. Maximum speed of the Hornet is more than Mach 1.8.

Grumman, previously mentioned as the manufacturer of the Tomcat, has several other aircraft in service with the U.S. Navy for carrier operations. These include the E-2 Hawkeye early-warning aircraft, the C-2A Greyhound carrier on-board delivery (COD) aircraft to transport supplies and passengers to carriers at sea, the EA-6B Prowler electronic countermeasures aircraft, and the Intruder. Some of these are illustrated in the final chapter. The latter, in its latest A-6E form, is a standard attack bomber, equipped to carry out attacks on targets in all weathers, by day or night, at all

Grumman Intruder armed with two Standard ARMs (anti-radiation missiles).

Above: A-6E Intruders
of VA-42.

Left: A-6E/TRAM
Intruder flown by VA-
65 Tiger Squadron, U.S.
Navy.

Lockheed S-3A Viking anti-submarine aircraft, surrounded by a Prowler, Intruders and Corsair IIs.

Facing page, top: Breguet Alizé, as delivered to the Indian Navy, with its radome retracted into the rear fuselage.

Facing page, bottom: French Navy Breguet Alizé anti-submarine aircraft.

ranges. It has a formidable weapon-carrying capacity of up to 8 165 kg (18,000 lb), which can comprise 30 500-lb bombs. Its maximum speed on the power of its two forward fuselage-mounted 4 218-kg (9,300-lb)st Pratt & Whitney J52-P-8B turbojet engines is 1 037 km/h (644 mph) at sea level. The pilot and bombardier/navigator sit in slightly staggered side-by-side seats.

The original Intruder was the A-6A, the prototype of which first flew in 1960. Other early production versions followed, of which EA-6A electronic countermeasures aircraft and KA-6D flight-refuelling tanker conversions of 62 A-6As remain in use. Currently the U.S. Navy has 12 first-line squadrons with A-6Es and tankers and the U.S.M.C. has a further five. The A-6E represents a major improvement with new avionics. This version has been in service since 1972. Production of more than 300 A-6Es has been undertaken, with the latest completed in FY 1983. Since 1979 those delivered have been of the A-6E/TRAM type (Target Recognition and Attack Multisensor), indicating that a further improvement has been made in avionics to enhance the detection of targets in bad weather conditions and their

attack. All A-6Es will be converted to TRAM standard. A number of Intruders, perhaps 50, are also being equipped to carry six Harpoon anti-shipping missiles each.

The final two aircraft are both carrier-borne anti-submarine types. The oldest of these is the French Breguet Alizé, which first flew as a prototype in 1956. Currently operated by the navies of France and India, the Alizé is powered by a 2,100-ehp Rolls-Royce Dart RDa 7 Mk 21 turboprop engine. This bestows a maximum speed of 470 km/h (292 mph). Weapons carried in the internal bay can be three depth charges or a torpedo. Underwing racks provide for an additional two depth charges and two AS.12 missiles or six air-to-surface rockets.

The second of these is the U.S. Navy's Lockheed S-3 Viking. First flown as a prototype in January 1972, it is a four-seat aircraft with high-mounted wings and is powered by two 4 207-kg (9,275-lb)st General Electric TF34-GE-2 turbofan engines, pod-mounted below the wings. Maximum speed is 834 km/h (518 mph) and its range is over 3 700 km (2,300 miles). Split fuselage bays can house four torpedoes, up to four depth charges, four destructors, or a similar number of bombs or mines. Further armament carried under the wings can include rockets.

When production of the S-3A ended in 1978, the U.S. Navy had received 187 examples. USS *John F. Kennedy* was the first aircraft carrier to carry Vikings operationally, from July 1975. Work currently underway to produce S-3B prototypes by conversion may eventually lead to the modification of 160 S-3As to this standard, each aircraft then having improved weapon system avionics and the ability to carry and launch the Harpoon anti-shipping missile. Carrier on-board delivery and tanker versions of the Viking have also been flown in prototype form as S-3A modifications. At least three further US-3A transport conversions have been undertaken.

4 The Deterrent

A discovery of the First World War was that aircraft used to destroy the enemy's manufacturing capability, its communications network and defence installations were every bit as usefully deployed as those engaged in actual air combat at the fronts. More sinister was the use of airships and aeroplanes to bomb towns and cities in an attempt to break the will of the populus to continue the war. There have been occasions since that first world war whereby a policy of bombing civilians has had this result, but these have been few and far between. The bombing of Britain, for example, during the First World War achieved only a cry for retribution. Amidst the rubble of the Second World War, British and American bombers gradually took the war to the aggressor until a day-and-night round-the-clock offensive was achieved and sustained. Yet, although this offensive destroyed much of the enemy's capacity to produce new military weapons, and thereby shortened the war, it took an invasion by land to bring an end to all hostilities.

In more recent years the role of the bomber has changed. Today it is assumed that should there ever be an all-out world war, nuclear weapons could destroy military and civilian areas alike. It is beyond reason to suppose that such an engagement would benefit either side. The current policy of the super-powers is to use the triad system. The triad gives the ability to launch a nuclear attack from land, sea and air, in an attempt to keep the peace through deterrent and is able, at the same time, to strike back after an unprovoked nuclear attack.

Land-based missiles and nuclear missile-armed submarines have little use beyond that of deterrent, which is important in itself if it can be proved to maintain peace. However, the bomber can also be conventionally armed and thereby engage in limited hostilities anywhere in the world, or can be used in a strategic role during a major war with only conventional bombs on board. It is unrealistic to suppose that one side in a major war could bomb with conventional weapons while the other used nuclear weapons. It is to restrain either side from first using nuclear weapons of any type that the bomber's operational flexibility is so useful.

The bomber

In the early 1980s only China, the U.S.S.R. and the U.S.A. still operate strategic bombers in the traditional role. Of these, the Soviet Union has by far the most modern bomber force, resulting from a sustained programme of development. Of the other nations around the world that continue to deploy tactical and medium bombers, the majority of aircraft are of Soviet origin. One such aircraft is the straight-winged Ilyushin Il-28. Although the Il-28 is the oldest aircraft in current use as a bomber in terms of its first appearance, its users include Afghanistan, Algeria, China, Iraq, North Korea, Viet-Nam and South Yemen. Furthermore, several hundred were built in China as Hongzhaji-5s or Harbin H-5s and these continue in service with the Air Force of the People's Liberation Army and the Aviation of the People's Navy. Albania also received H-5s.

Development of the Il-28, later known to NATO as *Beagle*, began in 1946 and a Soviet version of the Rolls-Royce Nene turbojet engine (the RD-45) was used to power the prototype that flew in 1948. Following a large number of pre-production aircraft, production proper got underway and several thousand were produced over the next decade in the Soviet Union and Czechoslovakia. Of these, it is believed that some 1,000 were acquired by other air forces, at least half going to China. Production Il-28s were each given two 2700-kg (5,952-lb)st. Klimov VK-1A turbojet engines, representing developed RD-45s. Maximum speed at an altitude of 4500 metres (14,765 feet) is 902 km/h (560 mph). Armament comprises four 23-mm cannon in fixed nose and movable tail-gun positions, plus up to

3000 kg (6,614 lb) of weapons carried in the bomb-bay.

Following the political split between China and the U.S.S.R., China put several aircraft of Soviet origin into production for its own forces. One was the Il-28, built at the Harbin works. Not including Il-28U/HJ-5 two-seat operational training aircraft, it is believed that the air force currently operates well over 500 three-seat Il-28s and H-5s and the navy operates a further 100 or so as torpedo- and bomb-carrying attack aircraft. As many as 12 air regiments of the air force may be so equipped.

Although operational in much smaller number, the Air Force of the People's Liberation Army depends on a derivative of another Soviet bomber for its main strategic capability. This is the Hongzhaji-6 or Xian H-6, Chinese version of the Tupolev Tu-16.

One of five Ilyushin Il-28s operated by the Egyptian Air Force.

Chinese Xian H-6.

Right: Tupolev Tu-16 *Badger-C* modified carrying a Kingfish missile, photographed by the Royal Danish Air Force.

Egyptian Tupolev Tu-16 *Badger-G* carrying a *Kelt* stand-off missile (with a range of more than 160 km; 100 miles) under its wing.

It is thought that up to 120 H-6s could be in service and production continues. H-6s can carry conventional or nuclear weapons. Indeed several of the nuclear weapons dropped at the Lop Nur test area in 1980 were released from aircraft of this type. China also supports the small number of Tu-16s operated by Egypt, probably now the only nation currently to use the bomber outside the U.S.S.R. and China.

The Tu-16, itself, first went into Soviet operational service in the mid-1950s and as many as 2,000 might have been built. The first version was that known to NATO as *Badger-A*, a strategic bomber with swept wings and two 8750-kg (19,290-lb)st Mikulin AM-3 turbojet engines installed in nacelles on the fuselage sides. From the earliest opportunity this aircraft was given the capability of carrying nuclear or conventional bombs. *Badger-B*, however, was the first to deploy large air-to-surface missiles, but this capability has been deleted from currently used examples. Instead it can carry up to 9000 kg (19,840 lb) of conventional bombs. *Badger-A* and *B* have seven 23-mm cannon for self-defence.

Of the 10 or so versions of the Tu-16 that have been identified, half are bombers. The remainder are operated in other roles. The Soviet Dalnaya Aviatsiya or long-range air force and Soviet Naval Aviation use a total of approximately 800 *Badgers*. Of these, the main D.A. versions are the *Badger-A* and *G*. The latter can carry bombs internally but its main armament is either two conventionally armed *Kelt* or the more modern *Kingfish* nuclear or conventional air-to-surface stand-off missiles. Naval Aviation operates *Badger-As*, *Cs* and *Gs*, *Badger-C* being an anti-shipping version with *Kipper* nuclear missiles or *Kingfish*. The D.A.'s other 125 *Badgers* and Naval Aviation's 110 comprise maritime and electronic reconnaissance, photographic reconnaissance, tanker and electronic countermeasures aircraft. The newer *Badgers* are powered by 9500-kg (20,944-lb)st

Mikulin RD-3M turbojet engines. The maximum speed of the *Badger-A* is approximately 992 km/h (616 mph) and its range with less than half the maximum possible bomb load is 4800 km (2,980 miles).

One of two older style long-range strategic bombers still operated by the Soviet Dalnaya Aviatsiya is the Myasishchev M-4. Known to NATO as *Bison*, it was the first Soviet four-turbojet bomber to go into production and service, although not that nation's first four-jet bomber. *Bison-A* is believed to be the only remaining version in first-line service, having been operational since the 1950s. It is a huge swept-wing bomber with a span of 50.5 metres (165 feet 7 inches) and an overall length of 47.2 metres (154 feet 10 inches). Four 8700-kg (19,180-lb)st Mikulin AM-3D turbojet engines are carried in pairs in the wing roots, but these proved insufficient to give the bomber the specified performance. Its maximum speed is thought to be 1000 km/h (620 mph) but its range is only 8000 km (4,971 miles) while carrying a 5500-kg (12,125-lb) warload of nuclear or conventional bombs. Service ceiling is also low, dictating the need for

A Soviet Myasishchev M-4 *Bison-B* is escorted by an R.A.F. Lightning.

defensive armament of 10 23-mm cannon. Today, the strategic bomber force is believed to use 45 *Bison-As*, while another 35 are probably occupied as hose-reel type flight-refuelling tankers.

The other old-style bomber in D.A. service is the Tupolev Tu-95, known to NATO under the reporting name *Bear*. Although it is true that *Bear* first came onto the aviation scene during the 1950s, it is now known that limited production was still being undertaken in the early 1980s to make good any losses through normal operational attrition.

A contemporary of *Bison*, the Tu-95 looks more antiquated because of its contra-rotating propellers. However, these are driven by the most powerful turboprop engines ever built, namely four 12,000-ehp

Kuznetsov NK-12MVs. These provide the bomber with outstanding performance and the ability to carry a heavy nuclear or conventional weapon load. Its maximum speed is 925 km/h (575 mph) at height and its maximum range while carrying 11 340 kg (25,000 lb) of weapons is an impressive 12 550 km (7,800 miles). This makes the Tu-95 the Soviet equivalent of the U.S.'s B-52 Stratofortress.

In the early 1980s it is believed that the Soviet strategic bomber force includes approximately 109 Tu-95s and that Naval Aviation operates a further 95 as anti-submarine and reconnaissance aircraft under the separate designation Tu-142. Naval *Bears* are often detected flying close to the coasts of NATO and other countries and they also overfly U.S. Navy and other naval forces during exercises.

Bear-A is the NATO reporting name for the initial long-range bomber version of the Tu-95. Despite a much better performance than *Bison*, it still carries twin 23-mm cannon in dorsal and ventral turrets as well as the usual tail position. *Bear-B* is flown by the D.A. and Naval Aviation as a strategic bomber and maritime reconnaissance-bomber respectively. Bombers can be armed with either *Kangaroo* or *Kitchen* air-to-surface stand-off missiles plus internally carried nuclear or conventional bombs. The missiles can have either nuclear or high-explosive warheads fitted.

Bear-C is another version carrying *Kangaroo* missiles, leaving *Bear-F* as the only other combat version. The latter is a much modified and more sophisticated anti-submarine aircraft, first seen by Western observers in 1973. The remaining two versions of *Bear* are naval aircraft and comprise *Bear-D*, which is used to detect and give the exact position of targets to distant missile-armed aircraft and ships, and the maritime reconnaissance *Bear-E*.

The Soviet Union goes supersonic

The Soviet Union's first supersonic bomber was first seen in 1961 as the twin-engined and swept-wing Tupolev Tu-22. Roughly equivalent to the U.S.A.F.'s former Convair B-58 Hustler, although considerably slower, the three-crew Tu-22 is believed to have proved a disappointment and production was restricted to approximately 250 aircraft. These comprised the NATO named *Blinder-A* reconnaissance-bomber, possessing a maximum speed of about Mach 1.4 and capable of reaching targets up to 3 100 km (1,926 miles) from base carrying free-fall bombs; *Blinder-B* with the added capability of launching the *Kitchen* air-to-surface missile; *Blinder-C* naval maritime reconnaissance aircraft; and the *Blinder-D* trainer with stepped tandem cockpits for the pilot and instructor.

In the early 1980s it is believed that some 125 *Blinder-As* and *Bs* remain operational as bombers, and a small number in a reconnaissance role. Naval Aviation operates a further 40 *Blinder-Cs* for maritime reconnaissance and specialist electronic roles. Each *Blinder* is powered by two 12 250-kg (27,006-lb)st with afterburning turbojet

Facing page, top: Tupolev *Bear-D* photographed over the North Sea by an R.A.F. aircraft.

Facing page, bottom: *Bear-F* anti-submarine bomber photographed by the Royal Norwegian Air Force.

Tupolev Tu-22 *Blinder-Bs* in Libyan Air Force markings are investigated by a U.S. Navy Phantom II.

79

engines, carried one each side of the vertical tail. Small numbers also serve with the air forces of Iraq and Libya.

As a truly modern replacement for many D.A. and Naval Aviation bombers and maritime aircraft, Tupolev has been delivering examples of its Tu-22M *Backfire* since the early 1970s. This is the world's first large variable-geometry or swing-wing bomber, estimated to be capable of a maximum speed of more than Mach 2. Unrefuelled, it can range over Europe and the Atlantic carrying Mach 2 *Kitchen* nuclear or high-explosive missiles or up to 12000 kg (26,455 lb) of conventional bombs or, with flight refuelling, it could reach targets in the United States and elsewhere.

The first prototype Tu-22M probably flew initially in 1969/70 and, following a number of development aircraft, production for the Soviet Dalnaya Aviatsiya began with the NATO-named *Backfire-A*. This version was produced in very small number and was quickly followed by the much refined *Backfire-B*. This is the standard version and well over 200 are in service as bombers with the D.A. and as maritime reconnaissance and attack bombers with Naval Aviation. Production is thought to add at least 30 new *Backfires* each year. Power is provided by two large turbofan engines installed side-by-side in the rear fuselage. The usual tail defence cannon are carried.

In addition to a new and more advanced version of *Backfire*, Tupolev is also responsible for another new variable-geometry bomber that has been seen in prototype form since 1981. This has been named *Blackjack* by NATO and it is believed that operational deployment could begin in the mid-1980s. It has been reported to be nearly half as big again as *Backfire*, with an equal increase in weapon load which could include cruise missiles, although it has been suggested that a separate cruise missile carrier could be under development. Its maximum speed could be as high as Mach 2.3 and its range, without in-flight refuelling (though this would undoubtedly be possible), could be 13500 km (8,390 miles), making *Blackjack* by far the most formidable Soviet bomber.

Britain's last bombers

By the summer of 1982 it had been expected that the Vulcan would finally be out of R.A.F. service as a medium attack and tactical support bomber. The last of Britain's former V-bomber series, its withdrawal was to end the R.A.F.'s tradition of deploying a bomber capable of strategic attacks. No longer would such capability be available to the R.A.F. and British government. But, in May 1982, the Vulcan was suddenly needed once more and some aircraft from the three remaining squadrons were sent off hastily to Ascension Island. From there a small number carried out the longest-range bombing missions ever performed by any air force, flying for up to 16 hours to crater the airfield at Port Stanley on the Falkland Islands and attack warning and ground defence radars.

These attacks, though reported at the time, masked some very remarkable facts. Perhaps the most interesting of these is that for many years prior to the Falklands crisis, Vulcans and their crews had not undertaken a high-altitude bombing role or used in-flight refuelling. Yet for the airfield attacks both were employed. The two raids on the radar installations were also firsts for the Vulcan, the Shrike missiles having been fitted to newly prepared underwing pylons and the crews trained in their use only as a result of the crisis. The future for the Vulcan as a bomber is unsure but trials have been conducted using modified Vulcans as flight-refuelling tankers.

The prototype Vulcan flew for the first time in 1952 and the currently used bomber version is the B.Mk 2. This easily identifiable delta is powered by four 9072-kg (20,000-lb)st Rolls-Royce Bristol Olympus Mk 301 turbojet engines. These bestow a maximum cruising speed of more than 1005 km/h (625 mph) and the capability of attacking targets more than 3700 km (2,300 miles)

The formidable Tupolev Tu-22M *Backfire* variable-geometry bomber, photographed by the Swedish Air Force while carrying a *Kitchen* missile. The nose refuelling probe has been removed.

Above: The Vulcan B.Mk 2 undertook the longest-range bombing missions of all time during the conflict over the Falkland Islands.

Left: Canberra B.Mk 82, one of about 20 Canberras operated by the Venezuelan Air Force.

French Air Force
Dassault-Breguet Mirage
IV-A delta-winged
bomber in camouflage.

from base without in-flight refuelling. Normal weapon load, as used against Port Stanley airfield, is 21 1,000-lb conventional high-explosive bombs.

While the Vulcan represents Britain's last operational bomber, the nation's first-ever jet bomber was the English Electric Canberra. As the A.1, the prototype Canberra flew for the first time in May 1949 and several three-seat tactical light bomber versions entered service thereafter. Today the Canberra no longer fulfils this role with the R.A.F., the few remaining aircraft serving in various training and radar/radio calibration roles. A similar fate has overtaken the Martin B-57, a variant of the Canberra, built under licence in the United States and no longer in service as a light bomber or night interdictor with the U.S.A.F.

In the early 1980s the air forces of several other countries still had combat versions of the Canberra in their strengths. These include Canberras flown by Argentina, Ecuador, India, Peru, South Africa, Venezuela and Zimbabwe. Martin B-57Bs are still operated by the Pakistan Air Force. The Canberra B. Mk 6, powered by two 3357-kg (7,400-lb)st Rolls-Royce Avon 109 turbojet engines installed in wing nacelles, has a maximum speed of 930 km/h (580 mph). Range is an impressive 6100 km (3,790 miles) and the weapon load carried can total 3629 kg (8,000 lb).

A Mirage for all roles

France is still served by its first and only supersonic bomber, the Dassault Mirage IV-A. This was developed to provide France with an aircraft capable of fulfilling a nuclear deterrent role, carrying one AN-22 weapon semi-recessed under the fuselage, or of serving in a non-nuclear capacity, carrying 16 1,000-lb bombs. The prototype flew for the first time in mid-1959 and was clearly a scaled-up Mirage III accommodating a crew of two. From 1963 the French Air Force received 62 aircraft, each powered by two 7200-kg (15,873-lb)st with afterburning SNECMA Atar 9K-50 turbojet engines installed in the rear fuselage. Maximum speed is 2340 km/h (1,454 mph) and a target 1240 km (770 miles) from base can be attacked.

With the basing of French-built land ballistic missiles and the commissioning of ballistic missile submarines, the role of the Mirage IV-A has changed to that of low-level tactical strike. However, the 34 Mirage IV-As currently in first-line service can still carry their original weapon loads or four Martel air-to-surface missiles, although 15 will be modified to deliver the ASMP (Air-Sol Moyenne Portée) supersonic theatre missile from about 1985. A further six bombers are in reserve, together with six Mirage IV-As converted for strategic reconnaissance.

NATO's bombers

The backbone of the U.S.'s strategic bomber force, and the country's and NATO's only heavy bomber, is the Boeing B-52 Stratofortress. As the Boeing Model 464 (U.S.A.F. designated YB-52), the first prototype Stratofortress took to the air for the first time in April 1952. Although Boeing had originally envisaged a straight-winged bomber powered by turboprop engines, the design had been revised several times before a prototype appeared, partly as a result of a visit to postwar Germany by Boeing technicians.

The first production B-52A was completed in 1954 and the Stratofortress entered U.S.A.F. service the following year as an eight-engined long-range heavy strategic bomber. Production totalled 744, 1962 marking the end of production. In the two

The Boeing B-52D Stratofortress, 78 of which remain in U.S.A.F. service.

Plate III

Boeing B-52G Stratofortress

cutaway drawing key

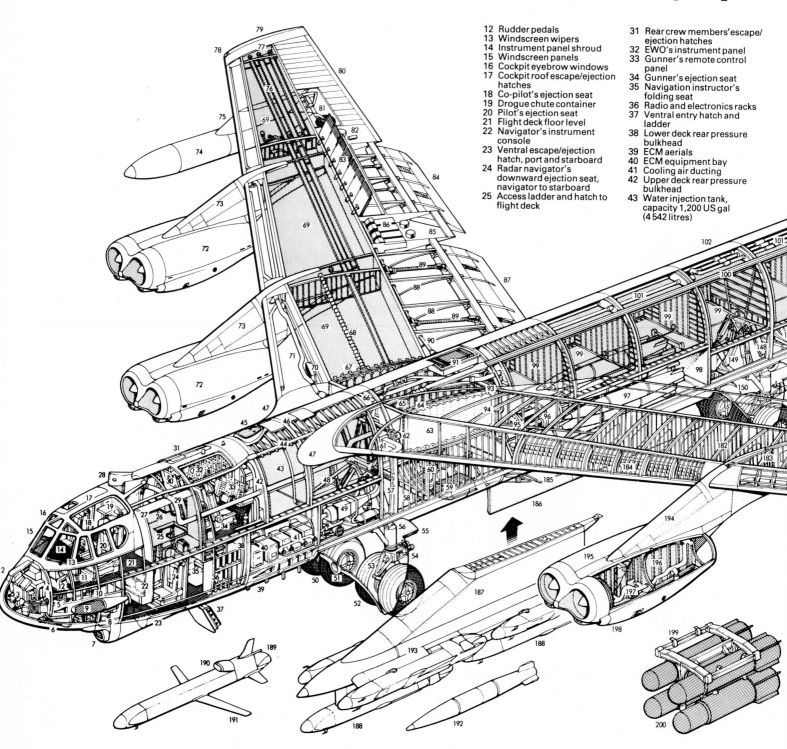

12 Rudder pedals
13 Windscreen wipers
14 Instrument panel shroud
15 Windscreen panels
16 Cockpit eyebrow windows
17 Cockpit roof escape/ejection hatches
18 Co-pilot's ejection seat
19 Drogue chute container
20 Pilot's ejection seat
21 Flight deck floor level
22 Navigator's instrument console
23 Ventral escape/ejection hatch, port and starboard
24 Radar navigator's downward ejection seat, navigator to starboard
25 Access ladder and hatch to flight deck

31 Rear crew members' escape/ejection hatches
32 EWO's instrument panel
33 Gunner's remote control panel
34 Gunner's ejection seat
35 Navigation instructor's folding seat
36 Radio and electronics racks
37 Ventral entry hatch and ladder
38 Lower deck rear pressure bulkhead
39 ECM aerials
40 ECM equipment bay
41 Cooling air ducting
42 Upper deck rear pressure bulkhead
43 Water injection tank, capacity 1,200 US gal (4 542 litres)

1 Nose radome
2 ALT 28 ECM antenna
3 Electronic countermeasures (ECM) equipment bay
4 Front pressure bulkhead
5 Electronics cooling air intake
6 Bombing radar

7 Low-light television scanner turret (EVS system), infra-red on starboard side
8 Television camera unit
9 ALQ 117 radar warning antenna
10 Underfloor control runs
11 Control column

26 EWO instructor's folding seat
27 Electronics equipment rack
28 In-flight refuelling receptacle, open
29 Refuelling delivery line
30 Electronic warfare officer's (EWO) ejection seat

44 Fuselage upper longeron
45 Astro navigation antenna
46 Tank access hatches
47 Leading edge 'strakelets' fitted to identify cruise missile carriers
48 Forward fuselage fuel tank
49 Air conditioning plant

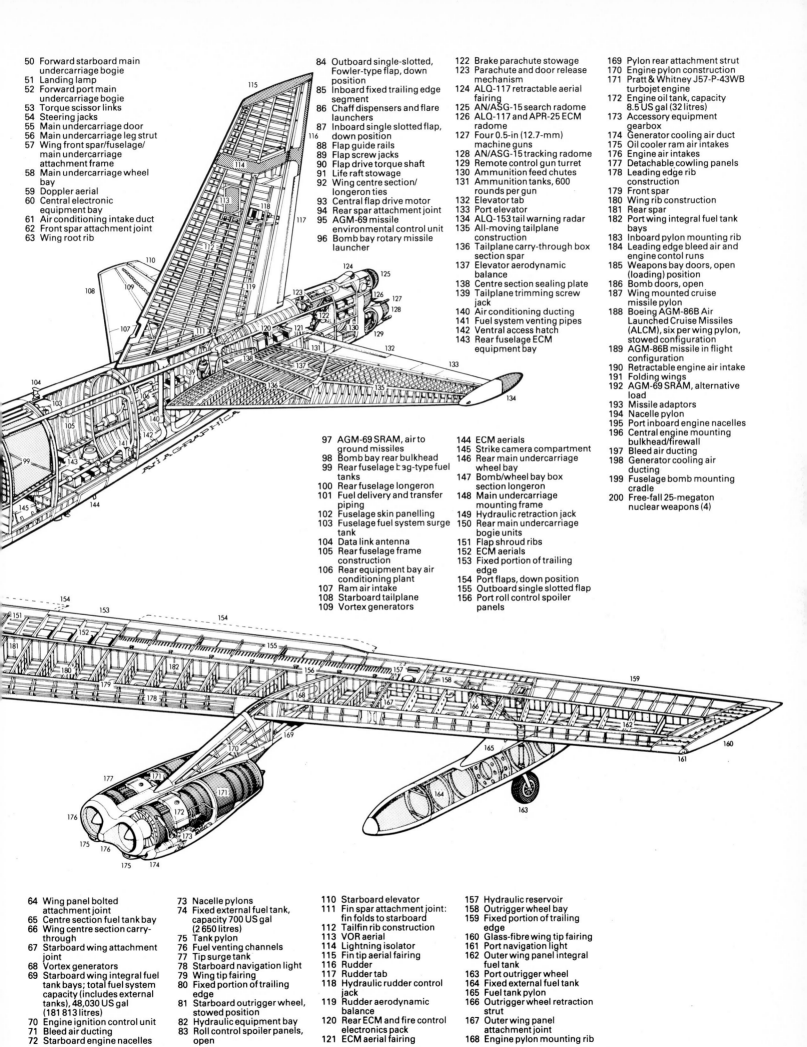

50 Forward starboard main undercarriage bogie
51 Landing lamp
52 Forward port main undercarriage bogie
53 Torque scissor links
54 Steering jacks
55 Main undercarriage door
56 Main undercarriage leg strut
57 Wing front spar/fuselage/main undercarriage attachment frame
58 Main undercarriage wheel bay
59 Doppler aerial
60 Central electronic equipment bay
61 Air conditioning intake duct
62 Front spar attachment joint
63 Wing root rib

84 Outboard single-slotted, Fowler-type flap, down position
85 Inboard fixed trailing edge segment
86 Chaff dispensers and flare launchers
87 Inboard single slotted flap, down position
88 Flap guide rails
89 Flap screw jacks
90 Flap drive torque shaft
91 Life raft stowage
92 Wing centre section/longeron ties
93 Central flap drive motor
94 Rear spar attachment joint
95 AGM-69 missile environmental control unit
96 Bomb bay rotary missile launcher

97 AGM-69 SRAM, air to ground missiles
98 Bomb bay rear bulkhead
99 Rear fuselage bag-type fuel tanks
100 Rear fuselage longeron
101 Fuel delivery and transfer piping
102 Fuselage skin panelling
103 Fuselage fuel system surge tank
104 Data link antenna
105 Rear fuselage frame construction
106 Rear equipment bay air conditioning plant
107 Ram air intake
108 Starboard tailplane
109 Vortex generators

122 Brake parachute stowage
123 Parachute and door release mechanism
124 ALQ-117 retractable aerial fairing
125 AN/ASG-15 search radome
126 ALQ-117 and APR-25 ECM radome
127 Four 0.5-in (12.7-mm) machine guns
128 AN/ASG-15 tracking radome
129 Remote control gun turret
130 Ammunition feed chutes
131 Ammunition tanks, 600 rounds per gun
132 Elevator tab
133 Port elevator
134 ALQ-153 tail warning radar
135 All-moving tailplane construction
136 Tailplane carry-through box section spar
137 Elevator aerodynamic balance
138 Centre section sealing plate
139 Tailplane trimming screw jack
140 Air conditioning ducting
141 Fuel system venting pipes
142 Ventral access hatch
143 Rear fuselage ECM equipment bay

144 ECM aerials
145 Strike camera compartment
146 Rear main undercarriage wheel bay
147 Bomb/wheel bay box section longeron
148 Main undercarriage mounting frame
149 Hydraulic retraction jack
150 Rear main undercarriage bogie units
151 Flap shroud ribs
152 ECM aerials
153 Fixed portion of trailing edge
154 Port flaps, down position
155 Outboard single slotted flap
156 Port roll control spoiler panels

169 Pylon rear attachment strut
170 Engine pylon construction
171 Pratt & Whitney J57-P-43WB turbojet engine
172 Engine oil tank, capacity 8.5 US gal (32 litres)
173 Accessory equipment gearbox
174 Generator cooling air duct
175 Oil cooler ram air intakes
176 Engine air intakes
177 Detachable cowling panels
178 Leading edge rib construction
179 Front spar
180 Wing rib construction
181 Rear spar
182 Port wing integral fuel tank bays
183 Inboard pylon mounting rib
184 Leading edge bleed air and engine contol runs
185 Weapons bay doors, open (loading) position
186 Bomb doors, open
187 Wing mounted cruise missile pylon
188 Boeing AGM-86B Air Launched Cruise Missiles (ALCM), six per wing pylon, stowed configuration
189 AGM-86B missile in flight configuration
190 Retractable engine air intake
191 Folding wings
192 AGM-69 SRAM, alternative load
193 Missile adaptors
194 Nacelle pylon
195 Port inboard engine nacelles
196 Central engine mounting bulkhead/firewall
197 Bleed air ducting
198 Generator cooling air ducting
199 Fuselage bomb mounting cradle
200 Free-fall 25-megaton nuclear weapons (4)

64 Wing panel bolted attachment joint
65 Centre section fuel tank bay
66 Wing centre section carry-through
67 Starboard wing attachment joint
68 Vortex generators
69 Starboard wing integral fuel tank bays; total fuel system capacity (includes external tanks), 48,030 US gal (181 813 litres)
70 Engine ignition control unit
71 Bleed air ducting
72 Starboard engine nacelles

73 Nacelle pylons
74 Fixed external fuel tank, capacity 700 US gal (2 650 litres)
75 Tank pylon
76 Fuel venting channels
77 Tip surge tank
78 Starboard navigation light
79 Wing tip fairing
80 Fixed portion of trailing edge
81 Starboard outrigger wheel, stowed position
82 Hydraulic equipment bay
83 Roll control spoiler panels, open

110 Starboard elevator
111 Fin spar attachment joint: fin folds to starboard
112 Tailfin rib construction
113 VOR aerial
114 Lightning isolator
115 Fin tip aerial fairing
116 Rudder
117 Rudder tab
118 Hydraulic rudder control jack
119 Rudder aerodynamic balance
120 Rear ECM and fire control electronics pack
121 ECM aerial fairing

157 Hydraulic reservoir
158 Outrigger wheel bay
159 Fixed portion of trailing edge
160 Glass-fibre wing tip fairing
161 Port navigation light
162 Outer wing panel integral fuel tank
163 Port outrigger wheel
164 Fixed external fuel tank
165 Fuel tank pylon
166 Outrigger wheel retraction strut
167 Outer wing panel attachment joint
168 Engine pylon mounting rib

decades that have followed, not one single production heavy bomber of any type has been built in the United States.

In 1982 the U.S.A.F. had an operational B-52 strength of 347 aircraft. These comprised 269 of the missile and bomb-carrying and much improved B-52Gs and Hs, plus 78 B-52Ds that can each be armed with 84 500-lb bombs in the weapons bay and 24 750-lb bombs carried under the wings. Every B-52 carries either four 0.50-in guns or a 20-mm Vulcan multi-barrel cannon (B-52H only) in the tail for defence against aircraft approaching from the rear. A further 187 various Stratofortress bombers are 'mothballed' in case of an emergency.

Two very modern types of supersonic bomber were produced as prototypes of possible production aircraft to supersede the Stratofortress, with maximum speeds of Mach 3 and Mach 2 respectively. The first of these was a giant delta. In each case

financial and political restrictions prevented production, with the result that the B-52 is likely to be with the U.S.A.F. for many years to come. Some say it could even be the first heavy bomber to endure more than 40 years from prototype to phase-out. Its future will depend, to some extent, on the future production of the B-1B.

It has been important to the U.S.A.F. to maintain operational capability, especially in view of the fact that B-52s flown from Thailand during the Vietnam conflict were attacked successfully on several occasions. Therefore several modification programmes have been aimed at improving the bomber's weapons, avionics, equipment and surviv-ability. The first major improvement came during the early 1970s when 281 B-52Gs and Hs were each modified to carry 20 SRAMs (Short-Range Attack Missiles) plus bombs to supersede Hound Dog missiles. From 1974 B-52Gs and Hs were given new avionics

A B-52G refuels from a KC-135 Stratotanker.

Left: A close-up of a B-52H shows the two Electro-optical Viewing Systems (EVS) undernose turrets, added to enhance low-level penetration.

to enhance their low-level penetration capability, and other electronic updates followed. Current programmes cover the uprating of the navigation and weapons delivery systems of these two versions and the modification of 173 B-52Gs to carry AGM-86B cruise missiles. The first B-52G cruise missile carriers were expected to become operational from December 1982, each armed with 12 AGM-86Bs, eight internally carried SRAMs and bombs. A subsequent programme will allow these aircraft to carry cruise missiles internally in place of the SRAMs. A number of B-52Hs may also be modified to carry cruise missiles. Future programmes could include a change of power plant for the B-52G cruise missile carriers from the standard eight 6237-kg (13,750-lb)st Pratt & Whitney J57-P-43WB turbojets to PW2037 turbofans installed in airliner-type pods. The B-52H already uses turbofan engines, in the form of eight TF33-P-3s. The maximum speed of the B-52G is 957 km/h (595 mph) and its range without in-flight refuelling is more than 12070 km (7,500 miles). The B-52H without having to refuel can cover 16093 km (10,000 miles) or more.

The B-52G is the main carrier of the AGM-86B air-launched cruise missile; 12 are attached to the inboard wing pylons.

The U.S.A.F.'s only supersonic strategic bomber is the General Dynamics FB-111A, here carrying SRAMs.

The U.S.A.F.'s only other strategic bomber is the small General Dynamics FB-111A, 60 of which remain in service with Strategic Air Command. Developed from the F-111, details of which appear in the next chapter, the first of two prototypes flew in July 1967. Meanwhile, it had been announced by the Secretary of Defense that the U.S.A.F. would receive 210 FB-111s to supersede the much larger B-52C and F Stratofortress heavy bombers and the supersonic B-58 Hustler. The first production-built FB-111A took to the air for the first time in July 1968, but in March of the following year the Secretary announced that production would be restricted to just 76 aircraft. The 340th Bomb Group (a training unit of Strategic Air Command) at Carswell Air Force Base, Texas, became the first to receive FB-111As, from October 1969. Four squadrons became operational thereafter, with the 509th Bomb Wing and 380th Strategic Aerospace Wing. In the early 1980s the U.S.A.F. uses 60 FB-111As as operational medium-range bombers and a further three aircraft are in reserve.

The FB-111A was developed from the F-111A, the first production examples having the same TF30-P-3 turbofan engines of the tactical fighter. These engines, however, were temporary only and the standard power plant became two 9230-kg (20,350-lb)st with afterburning Pratt & Whitney TF30-P-7 turbofan engines installed side-by-side in the rear fuselage. The wing span when fully spread was increased from 19.2 metres (63 feet) for the F-111A to 21.34 metres (70 feet). Avionics are of more advanced type and the undercarriage is strengthened to allow for a greater maximum take-off weight. Armament comprises either up to 14288 kg (31,500 lb) of conventional weapons carried in the fuselage bay and on eight underwing attachment points, or two SRAMs in the bay and four under the wings, or a similar number of nuclear bombs. The maximum speed is 2655 km/h (1,650 mph) and the range is 6437 km (4,000 miles).

The aircraft expected to represent the next generation of U.S. strategic bomber is the Rockwell International B-1B. This is a

Left: Rockwell International B-1 with wings in fully spread position.

A U.S.A.F. pilot climbs into the cockpit of an FB-111A to prepare for a simulated combat mission over ranges near Plattsburgh, New York.

multi-role bomber to follow the original B-1, the latter having been cancelled by President Carter in 1977 just as production was expected to begin on 244 to replace the B-52s. President Carter had not proposed a replacement for the B-1 but instead backed the development of the cruise missile. If the B-1 had not been cancelled, the U.S.A.F. would have received all 244 by 1981.

As discussed earlier, both the U.S.S.R. and U.S.A. rely on triad strategic forces. For a very long time the Stratofortress has represented the air component of the U.S. triad defence system. This has proved the only component with sufficient flexibility of operation to allow major use in a conventional conflict, in Vietnam. The so-called AMSA requirement of 1965 was formulated to start development of an Advanced Manned Strategic Aircraft to replace the B-52, although not to the same performance requirements that had produced the earlier prototype North American XB-70 Valkyrie Mach 3 cruise bomber. Arguably, the Valkyrie was potentially the most formidable bomber ever built by any nation. Further details of this aircraft can be found in the first chapter.

Requests for proposals were issued to the U.S. aircraft industry in 1969 and in the following year the Los Angeles Division of North American Rockwell was awarded the contract to produce the airframe and

develop the bomber. General Electric was awarded contracts to produce the power plant. It had been intended originally to produce five flying prototypes and two static airframes plus 40 F101 turbofan engines, but to save cost the numbers were reduced to three, one and 27 respectively. However, a fourth B-1 was later flown, this representing a pre-production standard aircraft.

The first B-1 prototype flew for the first time in December 1974. The second aircraft to fly was actually the third prototype, fitted for its role as the testbed for the advanced avionics. This flew in March 1976. The last of the four flew in February 1979 and carried offensive and defensive avionics. By this time, however, the B-1 had been ordered into production and then cancelled, although continued research and development had been permitted in case of future requirements. The development of cruise missiles made the Department of Defense consider carrier aircraft in addition to the B-52. In 1979 the U.S.A.F. asked Rockwell to give thought to a B-1 derivative for this role.

Rockwell also gave consideration to the concept of a less expensive B-1 bomber which could fulfil cruise missile requirements and other more conventional bombing roles. This study proved most fortunate, as it reflected the conclusions of the Air Force Scientific Advisory Board, which recommended that any future U.S.A.F. bomber should be capable of various bombing roles.

When President Reagan was elected to office, he fulfilled his election pledge by ordering 100 B-1B multi-role bombers and continue the M-X land-based missile programme. The first B-1B prototype, in fact

From the B-1 is being developed the B-1B multi-role strategic bomber for the U.S.A.F.

the second B-1 prototype modified to the new standard, flew in early 1983. Delivery of production B-1Bs is expected to begin in 1985 and continue until mid-1988, with the first squadron becoming operational in August 1986.

Unlike the original Mach 2 B-1 bomber, the B-1B has fixed engine inlets and other changes which reduce its maximum speed to about Mach 1.25. The B-1B has a higher maximum take-off weight, at approximately 216365 kg (477,000 lb), and therefore a strengthened structure. Very high-technology avionics are used for its major role of high-subsonic low-level penetration and to ensure that it has the best chances of surviving attacks made on heavily defended areas. The inclusion of low observable

technology means that the B-1B will give off a radar signature 100 times smaller than that currently given by the Stratofortress. Like the original B-1, the B-1B employs variable-geometry or swing wings, spread for optimum take-off and landing performances and swept for high-speed flight. Power is provided by four 13608-kg (30,000-lb)st-class General Electric F101-GE-102 augmented turbofan engines, carried in pairs under the fixed centre-section of the wings. Armament, carried in the three fuselage bays and on a further eight underfuselage attachment points, will include up to 22 AGM-86B cruise missiles, or 38 SRAMs or nuclear bombs. For a conventional bombing role, up to 128 500-lb or 38 2,000-lb conventional bombs can be carried.

B-1 with its wings fully swept at 67° 30′.

5   A Bolt from Above

Attack aircraft are used to strike at tactical targets, to perform close-support missions to back up land forces in the battlefield, or to attack non-strategic targets behind enemy lines in an interdiction role. They can be purpose-built, like the Fairchild Republic A-10A Thunderbolt, or can be one version of a multi-role aircraft.

There are more aircraft types in this category of U.S. origin than of any other nation. It would be a mistake to assume from this, however, that U.S. types comprise the greatest number of attack aircraft in use around the world. The three most formidable aircraft covered in this chapter are, arguably, the U.S. General Dynamics F-111, the Soviet Sukhoi Su-24 and the European Panavia Tornado.

Swinging wings

The F-111 was developed by General Dynamics under the TFX tactical fighter programme. The initial contract covered the production of 18 F-111As for the U.S.A.F. and five similar development aircraft for the U.S. Navy as carrier-based F-111Bs. Each was to be a two-seater, the crew sitting side by side under a glazed canopy. The first F-111 to fly was an F-111A, which became airborne for the first time in December 1964. This represented the first application of variable-geometry or swing-wings on a production aircraft and, indeed, the development of the technology involved in swinging the wings during flight caused General Dynamics many problems. Power for all F-111 versions is provided by two Pratt & Whitney TF30 turbofan engines installed in the rear fuselage, although progressively more powerful versions of the engine were used as production continued.

The F-111A development aircraft were each powered by two TF30-P-1 turbofans and first went to the 4,480th Tactical Fighter Training Group in July 1967. Operational deployment of production-standard F-111As with TF30-P-3 engines

began with the 474th Tactical Fighter Wing. Altogether, 141 production F-111As were completed. These have a maximum speed of Mach 2.2, slightly lower than the specified maximum speed of Mach 2.5. Other specified requirements included supersonic speed at sea level and the ability to fly to any airfield in the world in a single day.

The U.S. Navy's F-111B was cancelled by Congress after the development and two production aircraft had been built, and the British government cancelled the 50 F-111Ks ordered for the R.A.F. Export success was attained with the 24 F-111C strike aircraft for Australia, of which 16 remain in use and four are currently employed as reconnaissance aircraft.

The F-111E was the next U.S.A.F. version. Ninety-four were built, serving with the 20th Tactical Fighter Wing, U.S.A.F.E., in England and with the 474th TFW. Modifications to the engine air intakes give this version a higher maximum speed. Next came the F-111D, of which 96 were delivered to the 27th TFW. Uprated avionics and TF30-P-9 engines represented the major improvements. The final production version was the F-111F, combining F-111E/FB-111A avionics and two 11385-kg (25,100-lb)st with afterburning TF30-P-100 turbofan engines. This version gave the U.S.A.F. its required Mach 2.5 performance and allowed a heavier weapon load. The latter comprises one 20-mm M61 multi-barrel cannon and perhaps two bombs in the internal bay plus other weapons on six underwing pylons. One hundred and six were completed. F-111Fs were first deployed in the U.K. in 1977.

The Soviet equivalent of the F-111 is the Sukhoi Su-24, known to NATO as *Fencer*. It has a slightly smaller wing span (when the variable-geometry wings are fully spread) and a shorter length than the F-111. Power is provided by two engines carried in the rear fuselage and accommodation is the same as on its U.S. equivalent. Maximum speed is clearly above Mach 2 and armament

Above: This aircraft
taking-off was the final
production F-111F for
the U.S.A.F.

Left: F-111 carrying two
GBU-15 cruciform-wing,
TV-guided glide-bombs
for pinpoint attacks on
ground targets.

comprises a cannon plus up to about 8000 kg (17,635 lb) of weapons carried on eight underfuselage and underwing stations.

Fencer has greatly strengthened Soviet Frontal Aviation forces in Europe. It is said to incorporate terrain-avoidance radar. Its very capable weapon system avionics, coupled with a laser rangefinder and marked target seeker, makes the delivery of weapons very accurate in all weathers. More than 400 *Fencers*, perhaps as many as 550, are believed to be already in Soviet service. Some are now based in East Germany.

The European Panavia Tornado is an advanced tandem two-seat multi-purpose combat aircraft, but is smaller than the

F-111 and Su-24 and very much lighter. Maximum speed is also above Mach 2 but the distance it can fly with a heavy weapon load is considerably shorter. It has been developed for the air forces of the U.K., West Germany and Italy and the German Navy (Marineflieger), to replace the Vulcan and the land strike version of the Buccaneer, the Lockheed F-104G, the F-104G and G91R, and the F-104G respectively. British Aerospace, MBB and Aeritalia represent the three nations in the Panavia Tornado programme. The air-defence variant of the Tornado has been detailed previously.

The Tornado is a variable-geometry or swing-wing aircraft capable of performing all the roles mentioned at the beginning of this chapter plus those of naval strike and reconnaissance. It is powered by two 7257-kg (16,000-lb)st with afterburning Turbo-Union RB.199-34R Mk 101 turbofan engines and, in addition to its two fixed 27-mm IWKA-Mauser cannon, it can carry a heavy load of non-nuclear weapons on three underfuselage and four underwing stations, up to a total of 8165 kg (18,000 lb). Weapons available can include various types of bombs, air-to-surface and anti-shipping missiles, Sidewinders, and a munitions dispenser which scatters small bombs or mines.

Soviet Sukhoi Su-24 *Fencer*, carrying two 800-litre drop-tanks.

A Panavia Tornado GR.Mk 1 sweeps low over hazardous terrain. Drop-tanks and electronic countermeasures pods are carried under the wings.

Left: The first production Tornado for Marinefliegergeschwader 1 of the Federal German Naval Air Arm arrives in Jagel.

German, Italian and R.A.F. Tornados, operated from the Tri-national Tornado Training Establishment at R.A.F. Cottesmore.

The first of nine flying prototypes took off for the first time in August 1974. These were followed by six pre-production Tornados and the initial production aircraft. The first of 220 Tornado GR.Mk 1s for the R.A.F. were delivered to No. 9 Squadron in early 1982 as Vulcan replacements. This squadron became operational mid-year. The famous 'Dam Busters' squadron, No. 617, was the R.A.F.'s second operational squadron. When all Tornados have been delivered, it will be the first time in the R.A.F.'s long history that a single type of aircraft will have formed some two-thirds of its combat force.

The German Luftwaffe also began operational deployment of the Tornado in 1982, using the first of its 212 aircraft. The German Marineflieger is receiving 112 for over-sea strike missions against surface vessels and coastal targets and for maritime reconnaissance. The first Italian Air Force unit to operate Tornados is the 154° Gruppo of 6° Stormo, and this air force will eventually have 54 in first-line use. A further 12 are being delivered as dual-control trainers with operational capability and 34 will be placed in store. As well as being used for ground attack, Italian Tornados will be operated in reconnaissance and fighter roles, although those aircraft used for air-superiority duties will not be of the R.A.F.'s ADV (air defence variant) type but IDS (interdictor strike) aircraft. Production of the Tornado to fulfil present requirements will not be completed until 1989. Tri-national training is undertaken at R.A.F. Cottesmore.

American aircraft dominate the scene

Two modified versions of standard production fighters are expected to be in competition for U.S.A.F. orders as strike fighters. As many as 400 could be required in the long term by the Air Force, each aircraft having all-weather interdiction capability in addition to that of fighter. The General Dynamics F-16XL has been detailed in the first chapter. The second aircraft is the McDonnell Douglas F-15E Enhanced Eagle, formerly known as the Strike Eagle. It has avionics changes compatible with its new role, including a synthetic aperture radar (SAR) modification to the pulse-Doppler radar. The latter makes it possible for the specialist officer in the rear cockpit of the aircraft to locate small targets at night or in bad-weather conditions at ranges up to about 32 km (20 miles). A weapon load of 10885 kg (24,000 lb) can include the latest air-to-surface and anti-shipping missiles, and Sparrow air-to-air defence missiles can be carried on FAST Packs (detailed in Chapter One).

Land-based versions of the Vought A-7 Corsair II are flown by the U.S. Air National Guard (U.S.A.N.G.) and the Hellenic Air Force. A.N.G. units deploy 375 A-7Ds as close air support and interdiction aircraft,

each powered by a 6577-kg (14,500-lb)st Allison TF41-A-1 turbofan engine. Armament is one 20-mm M61A1 Vulcan multibarrel cannon plus 6805 kg (15,000 lb) of attack weapons. Air-to-air missiles can be carried.

In early 1981 A.N.G. units began receiving the A-7K Corsair II. This is a two-seat training version of the A-7D but with operational capability. The engine remains the same but the fuselage is longer by 0.86 metres (2 feet 10 inches). One A-7K is assigned to each of the 14 A.N.G. A-7 units and 16 to the 162nd Tactical Fighter Training Group. A land-based version of the A-7E is operated by the Hellenic Air Force, which has three squadrons of A-7Hs and a small number of two-seat TA-7H trainers with Allison TF41-A-400 engines.

The McDonnell Douglas A-4 Skyhawk is another naval aircraft type also operated on land by air forces. Undoubtedly the best known operator is the Argentine Air Force, which used its A-4Ps with devastating effect against British Task Force vessels during the conflict over the Falkland Islands. The Israel Defence Force includes six squadrons of A-4Es, Hs, Ms and Ns, plus trainers. Kuwait has two squadrons with a total of 30 A-4KUs, New Zealand has nine A-4Ks plus trainers, and Singapore operates 32 A-4D Skyhawks and five trainers.

A-7H single-seater, flown by the Hellenic Air Force.

Left: McDonnell Douglas F-15 Enhanced Eagle demonstrator, fitted with FAST packs containing auxiliary fuel and armed with 22 500-lb bombs.

Below: U.S.A.F. Vought A-7D Corsair II, about to take-off with eight napalm bombs.

Right: McDonnell Douglas A-4H Skyhawk, distinctive because of the angular top to its tailfin.

Below: A-7K Corsair II lengthened two-seat operational trainer, flown by a U.S. Air National Guard unit.

A purpose-designed close-support aircraft is the Fairchild Republic A-10A Thunderbolt II. Reviving the name Thunderbolt for this aircraft was a stroke of genius, for few aircraft can deliver such a massive blow in this role. The heart of the A-10A is its huge General Electric GAU-8/A Avenger 30-mm seven-barrel cannon, carried in the nose. It has 1,174 rounds of ammunition which can be fired at the very high rate of 2,100 or 4,200 rounds per minute, although obviously in short bursts. The Avenger gun has the main task of crippling armoured vehicles. Underfuselage and underwing stations allow for a total weapon load of 7250 kg (16,000 lb), including conventional and laser-guided bombs, air-to-surface missiles and gun pods. Electronic countermeasures or other electronic jammer pods can be carried to enhance survivability in the battlefield and drop-tanks can extend its range.

The single-seat A-10A has an unusual configuration, with straight wings, a twin fin and rudder tail unit, and two 4112-kg (9,065-lb)st General Electric TF34-GE-100 turbofan engines carried in pods one each side of the upper rear fuselage. It was selected for production in 1973, nearly a year after the prototype had flown for the first time, having previously won the evaluation trials against the Northrop A-9A. The first production A-10A took to the air in October 1975 and the 354th Tactical Fighter Wing began receiving A-10As in March 1977, to become the first operational A-10A wing. European deployment started in early 1979, with the 81st TFW based in England. Others are now stationed in West Germany and South Korea.

By 1982, when production was continuing, a total of more than 580 A-10As had been delivered to the U.S.A.F. More than

One of the Argentine Air Force's A-4P Skyhawks, probably prior to delivery, with U.S.A.F. B-52 bombers to the rear.

97

Right: Close support took on new meaning with the U.S.A.F.'s deployment of the Fairchild Republic A-10A Thunderbolt II.

Below: Sweeping low to make a surprise attack, an A-10A can devastate armour.

Facing page: An A-10A of the 353rd Tactical Fighter Squadron. The nose Avenger seven-barrel cannon heads its armoury.

720 will have been completed by the end of planned production, including a small number of two-seat operational trainers. While carrying six 500-lb bombs, the A-10A has a speed of 704 km/h (438 mph). It is intended to operate in support of U.S. and NATO ground forces, specifically to fly low and make surprise attacks on tanks and other ground targets that are close in. These attacks would be co-ordinated with the firepower and movement of the friendly ground forces.

Another form of attack aircraft is the counter-insurgent (COIN), used against guerrilla forces, for light attack or to escort helicopters. Those in use today include armed versions of the T-33A Shooting Star two-seat trainer, known as the AT-33A. The single-seat Shooting Star was the first U.S. operational jet fighter and the T-33A two-seat training derivative became widely used in the United States and some 30 other countries. Typical of the countries that operate small numbers of AT-33As are Burma and Colombia.

Back in 1964, North American (now part of Rockwell International) was announced the winner of a design competition organized by the U.S. Navy to provide the U.S. Marine Corps with a light, armed, reconnaissance

Plate IV

FMA IA.58 Pucará

cutaway drawing key

1 Nose compartment cowling
2 Cockpit ventilating intake
3 Cockpit air system
4 Nosewheel housing
5 Forward fuselage construction
6 Cannon muzzle blast trough
7 Nosewheel doors
8 Nose undercarriage leg
9 Steering mechanism
10 Nosewheel forks
11 Nosewheel
12 Pitot tube
13 Windscreen
14 Windscreen wiper
15 Instrument panel shroud
16 Rudder pedals
17 Control column
18 Cockpit floor
19 Throttles
20 Machine gun muzzle blast troughs
21 Safety harness
22 Pilot's Martin-Baker Mk 6A zero-zero ejection seat
23 Seat firing handle
24 Canopy breaker
25 Cockpit canopy cover
26 Starboard engine cowlings
27 Engine reduction gearbox
28 Propeller spinner
29 Three-bladed Hamilton Standard 23LF propeller
30 Auxiliary drop tank (86 Imp gal/300 l capacity)
31 Starboard Aero 20A1 wing pylon
32 Outboard wing panel
33 Starboard navigation light
34 Starboard wing tip fairing
35 Static discharge wicks
36 Starboard aileron
37 Aileron tab
38 Starboard wing self-sealing fuel tank (50 Imp gal/230 l capacity)
39 Flap
40 Cockpit canopy arch frame
41 Rear instrument panel shroud
42 Co-pilot's Martin-Baker Mk 6A zero-zero ejection seat
43 Safety harness
44 Machine gun barrels
45 FN-Browning 7,62-mm machine guns (900 rpg)
46 Ammunition feed chutes
47 Hispano HS-804 20-mm cannon (270 rpg)
48 Cockpit rear bulkhead
49 Canopy hinges
50 Fuselage main frame construction
51 Fuselage fuel tanks (two) with total capacity of 176 Imp gal/800 l
52 Fuel filler cap
53 Rear fuselage frame construction
54 Tailplane control rods
55 Air bottle
56 Radio and electronics rack
57 VHF aerial cable
58 Fin root fairing
59 Tailcone stringer joint
60 Fin construction
61 Elevator control rod
62 VOR aerial
63 Starboard tailplane
64 Starboard elevator

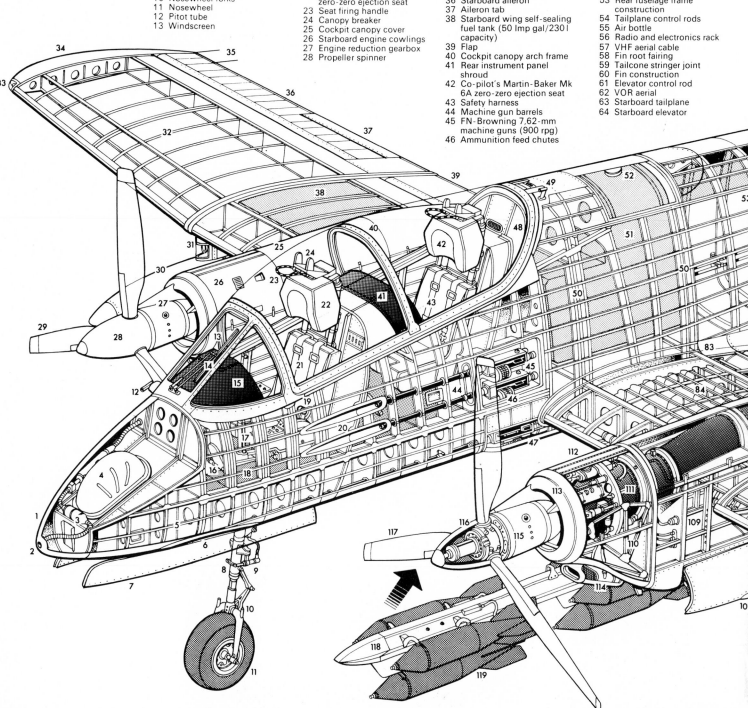

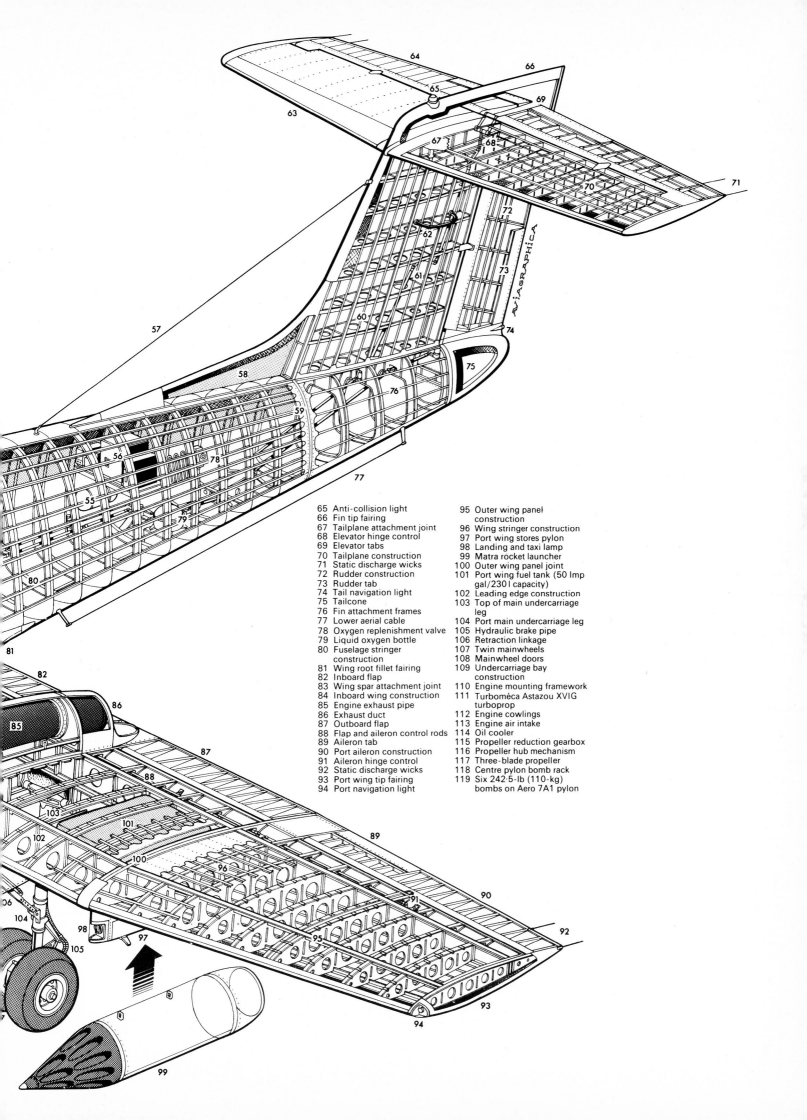

65 Anti-collision light
66 Fin tip fairing
67 Tailplane attachment joint
68 Elevator hinge control
69 Elevator tabs
70 Tailplane construction
71 Static discharge wicks
72 Rudder construction
73 Rudder tab
74 Tail navigation light
75 Tailcone
76 Fin attachment frames
77 Lower aerial cable
78 Oxygen replenishment valve
79 Liquid oxygen bottle
80 Fuselage stringer
   construction
81 Wing root fillet fairing
82 Inboard flap
83 Wing spar attachment joint
84 Inboard wing construction
85 Engine exhaust pipe
86 Exhaust duct
87 Outboard flap
88 Flap and aileron control rods
89 Aileron tab
90 Port aileron construction
91 Aileron hinge control
92 Static discharge wicks
93 Port wing tip fairing
94 Port navigation light

95 Outer wing panel
   construction
96 Wing stringer construction
97 Port wing stores pylon
98 Landing and taxi lamp
99 Matra rocket launcher
100 Outer wing panel joint
101 Port wing fuel tank (50 Imp
    gal/230 l capacity)
102 Leading edge construction
103 Top of main undercarriage
    leg
104 Port main undercarriage leg
105 Hydraulic brake pipe
106 Retraction linkage
107 Twin mainwheels
108 Mainwheel doors
109 Undercarriage bay
    construction
110 Engine mounting framework
111 Turboméca Astazou XVIG
    turboprop
112 Engine cowlings
113 Engine air intake
114 Oil cooler
115 Propeller reduction gearbox
116 Propeller hub mechanism
117 Three-blade propeller
118 Centre pylon bomb rack
119 Six 242·5-lb (110-kg)
    bombs on Aero 7A1 pylon

aircraft suited also to COIN duties. The first YOV-10A Bronco prototype made its maiden flight in July of the following year. It was a two-seat aircraft, with the crew seated in tandem in a fuselage pod. Below the constant-chord shoulder-mounted wings were carried two turboprop engines, housed in the forward portions of twin tail booms that ended with twin fins and rudders and a joining fixed-incidence tailplane.

The first production version was the OV-10A for the U.S.M.C. and U.S.A.F., the latter using the aircraft mainly for forward air control duties. Power for the OV-10A is provided by two 715-ehp Garrett T76-G-416 or 417 turboprop engines, which bestow a maximum speed of 452 km/h (281 mph). Armament for U.S.M.C. aircraft can comprise two 7.62-mm machine-guns fixed in the sponsons plus up to 1 633 kg (3,600 lb) of other weapons including two Sidewinders for self-defence or for use during escort duties. Six were subsequently acquired by Morocco, of which four are currently operated. The West German government received 18 similar aircraft as OV-10Bs and OV-10B(Z)s for non-combat duties; 40 were built as OV-10Cs for COIN duties with the Royal Thai Air Force; and the air forces of Indonesia and Venezuela each received 16 similar OV-10Fs and OV-10Es respectively. One squadron of the Republic of Korea Air Force also deploys Broncos.

The U.S. Army currently operates Broncos, mainly for observation but also for light attack roles. Observation is also important to the U.S.M.C., which also received 17 OV-10Ds (conversions of OV-10As). These are specially equipped night observation and surveillance aircraft with more powerful engines. They retain weapon-carrying capability on fuselage and underwing stations. A turreted 20-mm cannon can be carried under the fuselage.

A similar type of aircraft to the Bronco is the FMA Pucará, a product of Argentina. The Pucará's configuration is, however, entirely different. This counter-insurgency, close air support and reconnaissance aircraft has low-mounted wings with dihedral on the outer panels. It has a conventional fuselage, accommodating a crew of two in tandem under a single canopy and supporting a T-tail. Power for the initial production version is provided by two 988-shp Turboméca Astazou XVI G turboprops. Maximum speed is 500 km/h (310 mph).

Having flown prototypes, the first of which made its maiden flight in August 1969, production began with the IA 58A Pucará. The Argentine Air Force received approximately 45 and the Uruguayan Air Force acquired export examples. Argentine aircraft were first used in action in 1976, when they were used to attack rebels within the country. They were also expected to make a good account of themselves during the conflict over the Falkland Islands, especially in support of the ground forces on the Islands. Perhaps as many as 20 of these were lost, however, as a result of the British Task Force action that followed.

The designation IA 58B was given to an improved version of the Pucará, with avionics changes and the fixed armament upgraded from two 20-mm Hispano cannon in the fuselage to a similar number of 30-mm DEFA 553 cannon. Both versions have a further four fixed 7.62-mm FN-Browning machine-guns within the fuselage. The maximum weight of attack weapons that can be carried externally has also been increased, from 1 620 kg (3,571 lb) to 1 686 kg (3,717 lb). However, in 1980 a new version of the Pucará appeared under the designation IA 66. The main difference is the use of 1,000-shp Garrett TPE331-11-601W turboprop engines. The 40 IA 58Bs ordered for the Argentine Air Force prior to the Falklands conflict could now include IA 66s.

Small size is the common factor of the remaining aircraft of United States origin to be included in this chapter. A light attack version of the Cessna T-37 trainer is the A-37 Dragonfly, which was produced initially for service with the U.S.A.F. in Vietnam. Their Vietnam debut was in 1969.

The main production version of the Dragonfly was given the designation A-37B. This is powered by two 1 293-kg (2,850-lb)st General Electric J85-GE-17A turbojet engines installed in the wing roots. Maximum speed is 816 km/h (507 mph). A 7.62-mm Minigun is carried in the fuselage and eight underwing stations allow for a total weapon load of more than 2 270 kg (5,000 lb).

By the close of production in 1977, construction of the A-37B had totalled 538 aircraft. Today Air National Guard units of the U.S.A.F. fly Dragonflies for light attack and forward air control duties, and the air forces of Chile, Guatemala, Honduras, Peru and Viet-Nam continue operation of the type. Those used by the Vietnamese People's

Above: U.S. Marine
Corps Rockwell
International OV-10A
Bronco.

Left: Argentine FMA
IA 58 Pucará with the
weapons it can carry,
headed by two 20-mm
Hispano HA-2804
cannon and four 7.62-
mm FN-Browning
machine-guns.

Air Force were among the U.S. aircraft left after the fall of the South in the early 1970s.

An even lighter aircraft from Cessna has enjoyed considerable military success. In the 1960s the U.S.A.F. began deploying armed versions of the Cessna Model 337 Super Skymaster for forward air control (FAC) duties. The FAC version is designated O-2A and a considerable number remain in use with regular and Air National Guard squadrons. Of those acquired by other air forces, perhaps only those of Haiti remain in operational use.

Reims Aviation in France produces a number of Cessna aircraft under licence. A version of the FTB 337 (Model 337 Skymaster) was put into production for several military uses, including COIN, maritime patrol and training. The latest military derivative of the Model 337 series is, however, another U.S. type known as the Summit Sentry 02-337, which is based on the Model T337. Capable of a maximum speed of 302 km/h (188 mph) and of carrying a wide variety of bombs and rocket launchers on four underwing pylons, it is said to be suitable for the roles detailed above and a number of others including helicopter escort. A 210-hp Continental TSIO-360 piston engine is installed in the nose and rear of the pod-type fuselage in so-called 'pull and push' configuration. Customers are reported to have included Haiti, Honduras, Nicaragua, Senegal and Thailand (Navy).

When Fairchild started producing the Swiss Pilatus PC-6 Turbo Porter under licence in the U.S.A., it also developed an armed version for U.S.A.F. evaluation as the AU-23A Peacemaker. Powered by a 650-shp AiResearch TPE 331-1-101F turboprop engine, the Peacemaker could be armed with a 20-mm cannon firing from the door opening and with attack weapons carried on underfuselage and underwing pylons. Alter-

Cessna A-37B Dragonfly.

natively, camera or broadcasting equipment could be carried. Fourteen of the 15 Peacemakers evaluated by the U.S.A.F. were transferred to the Royal Thai Air Force, which subsequently received an even larger batch. Today two squadrons operate Peacemakers, totalling some 31 aircraft. The Thai Police aviation force also purchased five which remain in use.

North of the U.S. border, in Canada, light attack aircraft have been produced by Canadair and de Havilland Canada. As a derivative of its side-by-side two-seat CT-114 Tutor trainer, built for its home air force, Canadair produced the CL-41 light attack aircraft and armed trainer. Powered by a 1340-kg (2,950-lb)st General Electric J85-J4 turbojet engine installed in the rear fuselage, the aircraft is capable of a maximum speed of 774 km/h (480 mph), although lower speeds are attained with maximum fuel or while carrying weapons (including missiles) up to a maximum total weight of 1815 kg (4,000 lb). The Royal Malaysian Air Force was the only customer, which has 15 CL-41G Tebuans in service, although these are being replaced by Skyhawks.

De Havilland Canada's contribution is a COIN version of the DHC-6 Twin Otter Series 300M, first made available in 1982. It has provision for a machine-gun to be fired from the door opening and external light attack weapons can be carried at four stations under the wings. The crew is protected by armour and self-sealing fuel tanks reduce the risk from ground fire.

Above: Fairchild AU-23A Peacemaker with its weapon pylons showing clearly and a 20-mm cannon projecting from the door opening.

Left: Summit Sentry 02-337 on the attack.

A Royal Malaysian Air Force Canadair CL-41G Tebuan is a light attack and armed trainer version of the CT-114 Tutor.

The British influence

The United Kingdom has produced three important aircraft used currently for the demanding roles of attack, strike and close support, and has been co-producer of two more. One, the Tornado, has already been detailed. The smallest of these, and by far the lightest, has been the BAC 167 Strikemaster. Like the Canadair Tebuan, this too was developed as a light attack version of a side-by-side two-seat trainer (the Jet Provost, which itself has strike capability). The prototype Strikemaster flew for the first time in October 1967, 13 years after the prototype Jet Provost. The final Strikemasters built to order were delivered in 1978, bringing the total number completed then to over 140.

The Strikemaster is powered by a 1 547-kg (3,410-lb)st Rolls-Royce Bristol Viper Mk 535 turbojet engine installed in the rear fuselage. A maximum speed of 760 km/h (472 mph) can be attained and armament carried on four underwing stations can total 1 360 kg (3,000 lb). Current users include the air forces of Ecuador, Kenya, Kuwait, New Zealand, Oman, Saudi Arabia and Singapore.

The most versatile of British aircraft in this category must be the BAe Harrier. When this first entered R.A.F. service in 1969, with an operational conversion unit, No. 233 Squadron, it was the world's first fixed-wing V/STOL aircraft in use. Only with the appearance of the Soviet *Forger* some years later did the Harrier have a rival.

The Harrier is the production version of the experimental Hawker Siddeley P.1127 and Kestrel. The P.1127 was developed initially as a private venture, with the company taking the financial risks attached to such a revolutionary aircraft. On 21 October 1960 the first P.1127 performed its first hovering flight, albeit tethered, and its first untethered hover in the following month. By September 1961 the P.1127 had shown itself capable of transitions from vertical to horizontal flight and back again. In 1963 trials were conducted on board HMS *Ark Royal*.

As a result of earlier success, nine Kestrel evaluation aircraft were ordered for a combined test programme initiated by Britain, West Germany and the U.S.A. The first Kestrel flew in 1964. Development of a V/STOL aircraft of this type had not been without its problems but in August 1966 the first prototype of the Harrier proper made its maiden flight.

The Harrier entered R.A.F. service as the GR.Mk 1. Subsequent engine changes have brought all R.A.F. aircraft up to Harrier GR.Mk 3 standard, with one 9752-kg (21,500-lb)st Rolls-Royce Pegasus Mk 103 vectored-thrust turbofan engine exhausting through four rotatable nozzles. The position of these nozzles, which can move through 98° from a position pointing rearward, dictates vertical, horizontal or other flying modes. The R.A.F. has received 114 single-seat Harriers for close support and reconnaissance duties. A number were operated

The Royal Saudi Air Force fly Strikemaster Mk 80s and 80As.

during the Falkland Islands conflict, each having been modified hastily to carry AIM-9L Sidewinder air-to-air missiles in addition to its more usual weapons. Four of these managed the flight from the United Kingdom to the Falklands, landing on HMS *Hermes* (a feat in itself for non-naval pilots) in approximately 18 hours, with only a brief stop on Ascension Island. Each aircraft took on fuel for the second leg of the remarkable flight from R.A.F. Victor tanker aircraft. During the course of the action that followed the arrival of all the R.A.F. Harriers sent to the South Atlantic, only three were lost to ground fire. All pilots survived, Squadron Leader Bob Iverson being rescued by helicopter after two nights in a farmhouse.

Apart from two-seat training versions of the Harrier which retain fighting capability, delivered to the R.A.F. and Royal Navy (21 and four respectively), Harriers have been deployed by the U.S. Marine Corps and the Spanish Navy and Sea Harriers by the Royal Navy and the Indian Navy. Two-seaters have also been exported to Harrier/Sea Harrier-operating nations. Naval versions of the Harrier are detailed in Chapter Three.

R.A.F. Harrier GR.Mk 3s are capable of speeds higher than 1186 km/h (737 mph) EAS. For normal operations the weapon load can total 2270 kg (5,000 lb). However, the Harrier has been successfully tested with a 3630-kg (8,000-lb) load. Optional loads can include one or two 30-mm Aden gun pods plus a wide variety of conventional or laser-guided bombs, rocket pods and other weapons. A Ferranti laser ranger and marked target seeker is carried in the 'thimble' nose of each R.A.F. aircraft and a number of R.A.F. two-seaters.

Prior to its departure for the South Atlantic, this Harrier GR.Mk 3 at R.A.F. Wittering has been loaded with 2-in rocket pods and underfuselage 30-mm Aden guns for air defence and drop-tanks to extend range.

The Harrier has opened a new chapter in aerial warfare. For the first time it has enabled equipped air forces to operate from any area where there is a small flat piece of ground, from naval vessels or from conventional airstrips. It can move up with the land forces in a close support role, hide among natural landscape features, or can use its proven manoeuvring capability in an air-to-air combat role.

Two other aircraft of major importance to today's R.A.F. are the Hawker Siddeley Buccaneer and the SEPECAT Jaguar. The Buccaneer, as its name implies, was developed originally as a naval type, for low-level strike missions from aircraft carriers. Developed by the former Blackburn com-

pany, a prototype flew for the first time in April 1958. The Royal Navy received 20 development Buccaneers and 124 production aircraft, and the South African Air Force acquired 16 as S.Mk 50s for land-based use. Six S.A.A.F. S.Mk 50s remain operational today but, from October 1969, Royal Navy S.Mk 2Cs and Ds were transferred to the R.A.F.

In addition to the acquisition of Navy aircraft, the R.A.F. also received 43 newly built S.Mk 2Bs by 1977. R.A.F. designations for the Buccaneer are S.Mk 2A and S.Mk 2B, indicating minor differences between the aircraft themselves and the S.Mk 2B's ability to carry and launch up to four anti-radar and stand-off ground attack examples of the

The Harrier's unique ability to land and hide in woodland or in other natural camouflage gives the R.A.F. the ability to move up undetected with ground forces in a close-support role.

Martel missile, relating to the Navy's former S.Mk 2D.

The two-seat Buccaneer is powered by two 5035-kg (11,100-lb)st Rolls-Royce RB.168-1A Spey Mk 101 turbofan engines. Maximum speed at a height of just 61 metres (200 feet) is 1038 km/h (645 mph) and the typical range for a strike mission is 3701 km (2,300 miles). Four 1,000-lb high-explosive bombs or other stores can be carried on the rotating weapons-bay door (designed not to induce unnecessary drag during an attack run), and the weapons carried under the wings can bring the total load to 7257 kg (16,000 lb).

Buccaneers employed by the R.A.F. for strike against land targets are being replaced by early production Tornados. Those used for maritime strike missions will be the last to be replaced by Tornados and so will remain operational for some years. As a result, Buccaneers have been receiving Sea Eagle all-weather 'fire and forget' anti-shipping missiles to supersede the Martel.

The SEPECAT Jaguar is the result of a joint British and French venture to produce a supersonic tactical support aircraft for the R.A.F., French Air Force and for export as the Jaguar International. The company SEPECAT was formed during the 1960s by

A series of 68-mm SNEB rockets blast from their launchers.

the British Aircraft Corporation and Breguet Aviation, now British Aerospace and Avions Marcel Dassault/Breguet Aviation.

The first prototype to fly was configured as a French Air Force two-seat advanced training Jaguar E, flying initially in September 1968. Five production versions of the Jaguar have been built. The Jaguar A is the French Air Force's single-seat tactical support version, of which 160 had been delivered by the close of 1981. The first operational squadron was Escadrille 1/7 'Provence' in 1973. Nine squadrons are now similarly equipped, each aircraft able to carry various weapon loads including eight 1,000-lb bombs, AS.30, Martel AS.37 anti-radar or Magic missiles, rockets or the AN 52 tactical nuclear weapon. Fixed armament comprises two 30-mm DEFA cannon.

Forty two-seat Jaguar E trainers with combat capability were delivered to the French Air Force from 1972 and the R.A.F. received 38 similar operational training Jaguar Bs, the latter carrying the service designation Jaguar T.Mk 2. The R.A.F.'s single-seat version is the Jaguar S, military designated Jaguar GR.Mk 1; 165 have been delivered. Jaguar GR.Mk 1s currently equip six combat squadrons in England and West Germany, one reconnaissance squadron in each country and an operational conversion unit. Two 30-mm Aden cannon comprise the fixed armament of each Jaguar S and one on each Jaguar B.

The Jaguar International is the export version and is the most powerfully engined. It has either two 3650-kg (8,040-lb)st with afterburning Rolls-Royce Turboméca

R.A.F. Buccaneer S.Mk 2B, armed with two TV-guided AJ.168 Martel missiles and one anti-radar AS.37 Martel.

An R.A.F. Buccaneer, assigned anti-shipping duty and armed with four new Sea Eagle missiles.

Adour Mk 804 turbofans or two 4200-kg (9,270-lb)st with afterburning Mk 811s. Each Jaguar International can carry up to 4763 kg (10,500 lb) of external stores, which can include Magic or Sidewinder air-to-air missiles attached to overwing pylons. Operators are the air forces of Oman, Equador and India. The latter nation was allowed the use of a number of R.A.F. aircraft prior to the delivery of 40 Internationals. A further 45 Internationals are being assembled by Hindustan Aeronautics Limited in India from component parts. Eventually the International will be built under licence in India using home-produced components.

French Air Force Jaguars are powered by 3313-kg (7,305-lb)st with afterburning Adour Mk 102 turbofan engines. R.A.F. Jaguars have Adour Mk 104s, similarly rated to the Mk 804. Maximum speed is Mach 1.6 at high altitude and Mach 1.1 at sea level, making it most formidable.

Other nations contribute

A similar aircraft to the Jaguar is the product of collaboration between SOKO of Yugoslavia and CNIAR of Romania. Known to these countries as the Orao and IAR-93 respectively, it is a single-seat close support aircraft that can also perform interceptor duties if required. Two-seat

Facing page, top: Jaguar GR.Mk 1.

Facing page, bottom: French Air Force Jaguar As flown by the 11th Escadre.

Right: A Jaguar International of the Sultan of Oman's Air Force performs a low-level pass during a training exercise.

Below: Single- and two-seat prototypes of the Yugoslav Orao.

training versions are also built, which retain combat capability.

Design of the Orao/IAR-93 started in 1970 and prototypes built in each country made their maiden flights in October 1974. Fifteen pre-production aircraft were followed by initial production examples in 1981, each with two 1814-kg (4,000-lb)st Rolls-Royce Viper Mk 632-41R turbojet engines. The Romanian Air Force received 20 aircraft of this version as IAR-93As, in combat and training forms, and it is likely that a similar number were completed in Yugoslavia. Production thereafter switched to an improved version with 2268-kg (5,000-lb)st Viper Mk 633-47 turbojet engines. This has the designation IAR-93B in Romania, whose air force is to receive 165 in single- and two-seat forms. The number of Oraos to be built is not known. Maximum speed of the IAR-93B is 1160 km/h (721 mph). The fixed armament comprises two 23-mm twin-barrel cannon, and a wide variety of other weapons can be carried under the fuselage and wings.

Earlier, in 1967, SOKO had produced the prototype of a single-seat light attack version of its Galeb trainer, known as the J-1 Jastreb. Airframe and other changes were made to the Jastreb but the most important difference was the use of a single 1360-kg (3,000-lb)st Rolls-Royce Viper Mk 531 turbojet engine, increasing the maximum speed by 64 km/h (40 mph) to 820 km/h (510 mph). The Yugoslav Air Force received the standard J-1 Jastreb, which remains in major use, and the Zambia National Defence Forces operates six export J-1-Es. Three 0.50-in Colt-Browning machine-guns installed in the nose comprise the fixed armament and other weapons are carried on eight underwing stations.

A very light ground support and armed reconnaissance aircraft has come from Socata in France, based on the Gabier four-seat light aircraft. This is the R 235 Guerrier, powered by a 235-hp Avco Lycoming O-540 piston engine and carrying attack weapons or other stores on four underwing pylons. From Italy comes a similar aircraft built by SIAI-Marchetti (Aircraft Division of Agusta) as the SF.260W Warrior. This is just one of three 260-hp Avco Lycoming O-540 piston-engined military versions of the SF.260 light aircraft, carrying up to 300 kg (661 lb) of weapons or other stores. Warriors have been delivered to Burma, Dubai, Eire, the Philippines, the Somali Democratic

A Socata R 235 Guerrier carrying bombs and rocket packs.

Republic, Tunisia, Comoros and Zimbabwe.

Also of Italian origin are the light attack derivatives of the basic Aermacchi MB 326, and the MB 339K Veltro 2. The former aircraft first flew as a prototype tandem two-seat basic jet trainer in 1957 and production trainers were built subsequently for the Italian and other air forces. The MB 326GC represents a two-seat COIN derivative of the MB 326GB trainer. This was built under licence in Brazil as the EMBRAER AT-26 Xavante. The Brazilian Air Force received 166 and 16 were exported to Paraguay and Togo. Power is provided by a 1547-kg (3,410-lb)st Rolls-Royce Bristol Viper 20 Mk 540 turbojet engine. A typical weapon load is six 250-lb bombs, although heavier loads are permissible.

The MB 326K is another derivative of the MB 326 trainer but is a single-seater for operational training and light attack. Power is provided by a 1814-kg (4,000-lb)st Viper

Mk 632-43 turbojet engine and armament comprises two fixed 30-mm DEFA cannon plus 1814 kg (4,000 lb) of external stores. 'Ks' were exported to Dubai, Ghana, Tunisia and Zaïre, and South Africa received a small number before producing its own under licence as Atlas Impala Mk 2s. The Impala Mk 1 was a version of the MB 326M two-seat trainer and light attack aircraft.

The Aermacchi MB 339K Veltro 2 single-seat ground attack aircraft and operational trainer has the same relationship to the MB 339A two-seat trainer as the MB 326K has to the MB 326 two-seater. The prototype was first flown in May 1980 and limited production has begun. The single 1814-kg (4,000-lb)st Rolls-Royce Viper Mk 632-43 turbojet engine of the MB 339A is retained but two 30-mm DEFA cannon are fixed in the modified forward fuselage. Six under-wing stations carry attack weapons.

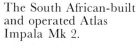

The South African-built and operated Atlas Impala Mk 2.

In August 1956 Fiat flew the prototype of a single-seat light strike fighter that was intended to be a standard aircraft for NATO air forces. In the event, only three nations ever acquired production G91s, namely West Germany, Italy and Portugal. Today G91s, known as Aeritalia G91s following the 1969 formation of this new company by Fiat and IRI-Finmeccanica, are operational only with the Italian and Portuguese Air Forces. Italian-used versions are the G91Y and G91R, R-1 and R-1A strike-reconnaissance aircraft, operated by five squadrons. G91Ts are tandem two-seat trainers. Each aircraft of the G91R series is powered by the 2270-kg (5,000-lb)st Fiat-built Bristol Siddeley Orpheus 803, but the improved G91Y changed to two 1850-kg (4,080-lb)st with afterburning General Electric J85-GE-13A turbojet engines. With these installed in the rear fuselage, maximum speed is 1110 km/h (690 mph) and the rate of climb is 5180 metres (17,000 feet) per minute. Armament comprises two

fixed 30-mm DEFA cannon plus 1816 kg (4,000 lb) of attack weapons carried under the wings. Portuguese G91R-3s and R-4s are similar to the Italian R-series aircraft, except that the R-3 has two DEFA cannon in place of the four 0.50-in Colt-Browning machine-guns of other Rs and trainers.

As described in earlier chapters, Swedish combat aircraft are produced in several versions to cover all major combat, reconnaissance and operational training roles. The AJ 37 attack version of the Viggen has been detailed alongside the interceptor version in Chapter One but an illustration of this is included here. Operational deployment of the follow-on aircraft to the Viggen, the Saab 2110 or JAS 39, by the Swedish Air Force is expected to begin in about 1992. It is for this reason that no further details of this aircraft are included here. The company has also produced a side-by-side two-seat basic trainer and light attack aircraft as the Saab 105, a mention of which can be found in Chapter Eight.

The newly developed prototype Aermacchi MB 339K Veltro 2 single-seat ground-attack derivative of the MB 339A two-seat trainer, armed with 30-mm cannon in forward fuselage fairings, rocket launchers and bombs.

Right: Italian Air Force Aeritalia G91Y strike-reconnaissance aircraft.

Below: Saab AJ 37 Viggen of the F7 Wing, Swedish Air Force, in snow outside a hardened shelter.

From Fitter to Frogfoot

Apart from the Sukhoi Su-7B, attack aircraft of Soviet origin are very modern and formidable. The prototype of the Sukhoi aircraft flew for the first time in 1955 and the Su-7B version (NATO *Fitter-A*) entered production three years later. It is a single-seater with the pilot accommodated under a 'blister' canopy. The mid-mounted wings are heavily swept, as is the tail unit. Several variants of the Su-7B were produced, the last as the Su-7BMK, including two-seat operational trainers. The Su-7BMK is powered by a 10000-kg (22,046-lb)st with afterburning Lyulka AL-7F-1 turbojet engine. This bestows a maximum speed of Mach 1.6 when no external weapons are carried or Mach 1.2 with weapons. Fixed armament is two 30-mm NR-30 cannon carried in the wings, and pylons under the fuselage and wings allow for 2500 kg (5,510 lb) of attack weapons. The Soviet tactical air forces and the air forces of 13 other countries received Su-7Bs. Today, Soviet Su-7B strength is down to approximately 150. Several of the other nations retain the Su-7B as a major component of their air forces.

The latest Sukhoi attack aircraft is that known to NATO as *Frogfoot*, an aircraft in the same class as the U.S.A.F's A-10A. It is powered by two engines installed in wing-root nacelles, which are likely to bestow a higher performance. However, in many other respects it is probably not such an advanced aircraft as the A-10A. Its wings are slightly swept and are of long span, allowing weapons to be carried on 10 stations. Further weapons can be attached under the fuselage, and a heavy calibre multi-barrel gun is carried. It is believed that a single squadron of *Frogfoots* has been used in Afghanistan since early 1982, with the role of developing operating techniques. *Frogfoots* and *Hind* attack helicopters could prove a formidable attack combination. Other *Frogfoot* units of the Soviet tactical air forces are now expected to be operational.

Of major importance to the Soviet tactical air forces is the single-seat ground attack derivative of the Mikoyan MiG-23 fighter, designated MiG-27. Although related, there are major differences between the MiG-23 and MiG-27, the most obvious of which is the revised configuration of the forward fuselage. The MiG-27 has no ogival nosecone covering the large radar dish of the fighter,

but instead has a sloping nose containing a laser rangefinder and marked target seeker. Power is provided by an 11500-kg (25,353-lb)st with afterburning Tumansky R-29B turbojet engine. Unlike the MiG-23, the MiG-27 has fixed air intakes and nozzle, suggesting transonic speed when carrying its weapon load of up to 3000 kg (6,615 lb) at low altitude. Maximum speed is thought to be Mach 1.5. A wide variety of weapon options are available to the MiG-27, including tactical nuclear weapons and missiles.

Two versions of the MiG-27 have been seen; both are single-seaters with variable-geometry wings. A 23-mm multi-barrel cannon comprises the fixed armament of each. *Flogger-D* (NATO name) was the original production version and many hundreds are operated by the Soviet and East German air forces. The later version (*Flogger-J*) has minor airframe changes,

Bottom: The Sukhoi Su-7UMK two-seat operational trainer version of the Su-7BMK single-seater is known to NATO as *Moujik*.

Below: Egyptian Sukhoi Su-7BM.

Below: The
Czechoslovak Air Force
Mikoyan MiG-23BN
Flogger-H single-seat
ground-attack aircraft.

including a slightly revised nose and extensions to the leading edges of the wing roots (not on all aircraft). Two underwing guns appear to be standard fittings. Both versions can carry *Atoll* missiles for self-defence.

Export versions of the MiG-27 fall under the MiG-23 designated series of aircraft, as each has variable air intakes and nozzle for its R-29 turbojet engine and the fighter's typical 23-mm GSh-23 cannon. In other respects, they are similar to the MiG-27, but with less sophisticated systems. Known to NATO under the reporting names *Flogger-F*

and *Flogger-H*, these attack aircraft have been exported to the air forces of Algeria, Bulgaria, Cuba, Czechoslovakia, Egypt, Ethiopia, Iraq, Libya, Poland, Syria, and Viet-Nam. India has also received 80 '*Hs*', and it has been reported that *Flogger-J* might be built under licence in that country.

Not a MiG

When China decided to develop its own tactical strike aircraft, probably in the early 1970s or late 1960s, it appeared prudent to base certain aspects of the aircraft on the nation's J-6 fighter. However, although the wings and engines of the J-6 appeared suitable with little change, the remainder of the aircraft had to be virtually entirely new. Known in China as the Qiangjiji-5 or Qiang-5, the attack aircraft is built at the Nanchang works and as such is known in the West as the Nanchang Q-5. NATO's own reporting name is *Fantan-A*.

The Q-5 has a modern appearance, with a pointed nose to the fuselage and side air-intakes for the engines. The adoption of a pointed nose was the result of a decision to fit an internal weapons bay in the centre fuselage, necessitating transfer of equipment forward. The canopy over the pilot's cockpit is faired into the fuselage aft, another breakaway from tradition. Fixed armament comprises two cannon carried in the wings. Other weapons carried in the bay and underwing can include conventional bombs or a tactical nuclear bomb. Maximum speed is thought to be Mach 1.35.

An attack force estimated at 500 aircraft is operated by the Air Force of the People's Liberation Army, thought to number *Fantans* as its most numerous type. The Aviation of the People's Navy also deploys the Q-5 but in a suggested fighter role. The Pakistan Air Force ordered 42 Q-5s, which have joined Chinese-built Shenyang F-6s.

In addition to purpose-built attack aircraft, most trainers are capable of light attack duties. Among the latest basic and advanced jet trainers are those with actual purpose-built attack derivatives. Some produced as single-seaters have already been mentioned, but typical of the most modern attack derivatives that have retained tandem seats is the Dassault-Breguet/Dornier Alpha Jet close support and NGEA versions, assigned to combat squadrons and capable of carrying 2 500 kg (5,510 lb) of weapons externally.

Bottom: The Chinese
Nanchang Q-5 *Fantan-A*
single-seat supersonic
tactical strike aircraft.

6 The Cobra's Bite

In the 1950s, France demonstrated in Algeria how armament on helicopters could be used offensively as well as defensively. What had begun as a method of defending transport helicopters from ground fire intensified quickly to encompass suppression of ground forces in preparation for landing and later actual attack on ground targets.

This new use for helicopters had not gone unnoticed by the military or aircraft manufacturers of other nations, but little was done immediately to advance the concept. The early 1960s were politically turbulent, with many 'hot spots' such as Southeast Asia and Cuba. Bell Helicopter, for one, recognized the shortcomings of ordinary transport helicopters armed for offensive missions and proposed the first-ever purpose-built attack helicopter as early as 1962. This was the Iroquois Warrior, a slim tandem two-seater capable of carrying a much heavier weapon load than normally practicable for helicopters.

The time was not right for such an advanced helicopter and it remained a proposal. Slowly the atmosphere changed and the U.S. Army began exploring the possibility of an attack helicopter. To save cost and time, the Army decided to issue a specification for an attack helicopter which would be based on an existing type, but would have a maximum speed of 287 km/h (178 mph). A short while later this specification was changed to include a speed of 370 km/h (230 mph). Such a speed was then very high indeed and Bell realized that its original idea for a tandem two-seat helicopter of completely new configuration was the only way of achieving the requirements in full.

As a means to an end, Bell built an experimental tandem-seat helicopter as a demonstrator, named the Sioux Scout. As its name suggests, it used components of the military Model 47. The Sioux Scout flew in 1963. For whatever reason, the U.S. Army suddenly warmed to the idea of a purpose-built attack helicopter, incorporating the very latest technologies. The AAFSS programme was initiated (Advanced Aerial Fire Support System). In the meantime, it was decided that armed versions of existing helicopters would have to be used until an AAFSS was ready.

In August 1964, however, U.S. Navy vessels came under attack off Vietnam, and U.S. Navy aircraft retaliated by attacking naval bases in the north. Rapidly the situation in Southeast Asia became worse. By early 1965 the war between the North and South had intensified and troop mobility was becoming a major problem as a result of heavy or unexpected ground fire. Bell was even more convinced that an attack helicopter would be required sooner rather than later and therefore put its Model 209 in hand. This helicopter, which became known as the HueyCobra, was based on the Sioux Scout but was more refined and incorporated Iroquois components.

In August 1965, the U.S. Army decided that it needed a 'stopgap' attack helicopter and this proposal attracted the consideration of several existing helicopters. Bell, meanwhile, had an ace up its sleeve. Because of the company's gamble to develop its Model 209 to prototype stage, it was able to demonstrate the only purpose-built attack helicopter in the following month. Army evaluation began in December. In 1966 Lockheed was awarded a contract covering engineering development of the AAFSS, which included prototypes, and Bell received an order for production Huey Cobras. In the event, the Lockheed AAFSS, which became known as the AH-56A Cheyenne, was ordered into production in 1968 and then cancelled. The HueyCobra, however, went from strength to strength.

In April 1966 Bell received a contract for 110 AH-1G HueyCobras. Delivery of these to the U.S. Army began in mid-1967 and by the autumn the first were operational in Vietnam. Their success was immediate. They proved capable of reaching their targets in half the time taken by an armed

Iroquois and could remain in the combat zone for much longer periods. They were also used to escort other troop-carrying helicopters. As the fuselage was only 0.97 metres (3 feet 2 inches) wide, the HueyCobra front-on was a very difficult target from the ground. For attack, the HueyCobra could fire its 7.62-mm six-barrel machine-gun carried in a turret faired into the front fuselage, under the nose. The gunner was positioned in the forward seat, giving him an excellent view of the target. Further weapons, which could be carried under the stub wings, included rocket packs or guns. These were normally fired by the pilot from the rear seat. However, the pilot could also fire the turreted gun and the gunner could fly the helicopter and fire the wing stores.

Such was the impact of this first-ever production attack helicopter that by the autumn of 1968 orders had reached 838, subsequently to reach 1,126. Later AH-IGs that came off production lines introduced improvements, including a new under-nose turret with guns and/or grenade launchers. On the power of a 1,100-shp Avco Lycoming T53-L-13 turboshaft engine, a level speed of 352 km/h (219 mph) was attained. Eight HueyCobras were also delivered to the Spanish Navy for anti-shipping duties and six initially to Israel. The U.S. Marine Corps received a twin-engined version as the AH-1J SeaCobra. The latter had several other changes, including differing avionics. Iran received 202 AH-1Js from 1974.

In 1981 the U.S. Army had a total of 987 HueyCobras in service. The total included AH-1Gs, AH-1Qs and AH-1Ss. The 'Q' was an anti-armour conversion of the AH-1G, modified to carry up to eight Hughes TOW anti-tank missiles. The AH-1S represents the latest version with TOW. Four sub-variants of the 'S' model have been produced. The U.S. Army currently has about 1,000 AH-1Ss and some 60 AH-1Gs.

The first variant of the 'S' is the Mod AH-1S. A total of 290 was produced by modifying AH-1Gs and all the AH-1Qs. Each has a 1,800-shp Avco Lycoming T53-L-703 turboshaft engine and provision for eight TOW missiles. Production proper of the 'S' began with an order for 100 new aircraft, known simply as Production AH-1Ss. Each has a T53-L-703 engine; a flat-plate cockpit canopy to lessen the sunglint problem which occurred with the original moulded canopy, avionics and other improvements. When carrying eight TOWs, maximum speed in level flight is 227 km/h (141 mph). Delivery of newly built HueyCobras of this version began in 1977.

The Up-gun AH-1S, of which 98 were delivered from 1978, is similar to the earlier version but has a new turret housing a

Spanish Naval Aviation Bell AH-1G HueyCobra anti-shipping helicopter, known to that service as Z.14.

20-mm or 30-mm multi-barrel cannon. It can carry 2.75-in rockets on the stub wings as well as TOWs.

The latest version of the 'S' is the Modernized AH-1S. This version incorporates all the improvements of the earlier versions plus new and very advanced avionics, added partly to improve weapon management and survivability. The last of 196 ordered will be delivered in early 1984. By the second half of this decade all earlier U.S. Army HueyCobras will have been modified up to the Modernized AH-1S standard.

In 1981 the U.S. Army National Guard received 27 Modernized AH-1S HueyCobras and the Japan Ground Self-Defence Force is to receive 54 assembled by Fuji. The U.S.M.C. continues to operate its AH-1Js, together with improved AH-1Ts. The speed of the AH-1J is 333 km/h (207 mph).

As a result of the HueyCobra's success, the cancellation of the Lockheed AAFSS and the end of the Vietnam conflict, the U.S. Army has not received a heavy attack helicopter of

the calibre originally specified. However, in the early 1970s a new programme was started called AAH or Advanced Attack Helicopter, which led eventually to the construction of prototypes by Bell and Hughes as YAH-63s and YAH-64s respectively. Bell had previously produced its own follow-on to its HueyCobra as the Model 309 KingCobra, under the same private-venture arrangements that had served the company so well before. KingCobra prototypes were built and flown, but, with the Army's announcement of the AAH programme, this helicopter was dropped.

In September 1975 Hughes flew the first of its YAH-64 AAH prototypes. The YAH-64 later became known as the Apache. At the end of the following year Hughes was named the winner of the AAH programme and thus development and evaluation of this helicopter continued. A further six Apaches were produced. For Hughes, getting authority to begin mass production has been long in coming, due partly to rising costs. However, against the reduced Army requirement for

U.S. Army AH-1S HueyCobra.

Hughes AH-64 Apache prototype carrying eight Hellfire anti-tank missiles on two of its four pylons.

446 Apaches, Hughes has received a contract covering manufacture of the first 11. Deliveries will start in February 1984.

The Apache is both larger and heavier than the HueyCobra/SeaCobra and can attain a speed of 309 km/h (192 mph) in level flight on the power of its two 1,536-shp General Electric T700-GE-700 turboshaft engines. Like the HueyCobra, it is a tandem two-seater. Armament comprises a 30-mm Chain Gun cannon in an underfuselage turret and 16 Hellfire anti-tank missiles or 76 2.75-in rockets carried under the stub wings, or a combination of missiles and rockets. These weapons, combined with the performance of the Apache and its very advanced avionics, makes it a very formidable attack helicopter, capable of day, night, and adverse weather operations.

Following the HueyCobra's lead

A similar layout to the Apache's has been selected by Agusta in Italy for its A 129. However, this is a light attack helicopter of smaller size and lighter weight than even the HueyCobra. On the power of two 815-shp Rolls-Royce Gem 2-2 turboshaft engines, it has an estimated maximum level speed of 270 km/h (168 mph). It is suitable also for advanced scout missions by day or night and in bad weather conditions. The A 129 carries no fixed or turreted weapons, but eight TOW anti-tank missiles, rockets, rocket or grenade launchers or machine-guns can be attached to the four stations under the stub wings.

Four prototype A 129s have been or are being built; the first flew in 1983. Production is expected to cover 60 attack A129s, for use by two Italian Army squadrons from 1986, and seven for training. A third squadron might also be so equipped at a later date. The helicopter will also be available for export.

Of all the world's other helicopters used in attack roles, there remains only one other that has been designed and built specifically for this role (rather than converted). This is the Soviet Mil Mi-24, known to NATO as *Hind*. Apart from the Soviet Union, which is believed to have well over 1,000 operational and where the manufacture of approximately 200 new aircraft a year is being undertaken, *Hinds* are used by five other Warsaw Pact nations and have been delivered to Afghanistan, Algeria, Cuba, Iraq, Libya and South Yemen.

The Mi-24 entered service with the Soviet forces in the early 1970s. Initial *Hind-A* and *Hind-B* versions have similar basic armament, comprising one 12.7-mm machine-gun in the nose and underwing pylons for 57-mm rocket pods. *Hind-A*, the most important of the initial versions, also has launchers for four *Swatter* anti-tank missiles. Each of these versions was developed to carry out heavy attacks on ground forces in the course of landing the eight troops accommodated in the main cabin, or to escort transport helicopters. As a result of this dual role, *Hind* has larger proportions and is much heavier than the U.S. Apache. Power is provided by two 2,200-shp Isotov TV3-117 turboshaft engines carried above the main cabin. Maximum level speed is unknown but it is likely to be high.

Hind-C appeared as a version without gun and missile armament, but was otherwise seen to be a similar helicopter to *Hind-A*. However, *Hind-D* proved very different. Whereas all previous versions had accommodation for a crew of four in the angular and heavily glazed cockpit, *Hind-D* introduced a completely redesigned nose with accommodation for a co-pilot/gunner and pilot in tandem in separate cockpits with individual canopies, the pilot's cockpit positioned behind and well above the nose cockpit. Directly under the forward cockpit is a turreted 12.7-mm four-barrel gun, which has sufficient movement to allow it to be used in an air-to-air role as well as in a ground attack role. Armament carried under the wings is the same as for *Hind-A*. This was the first real gunship version.

Bottom: The restyled nose of *Hind-D* with individual canopies for the weapon operator and pilot. Note the 12.7-mm gun in the undernose turret.

Below: Soviet Mil Mi-24 *Hind-A*, armed with a machine-gun in the nose and four UB-32 pods containing 128 57-mm rockets.

In the early 1980s *Hind-Es* joined other *Hinds* based in Europe to face NATO forces, and were stationed elsewhere. Similar to *Hind-D*, the '*E*' has the added capability of launching four *Spiral* anti-tank missiles. These missiles home on targets that have been illuminated by a laser designator and are believed to have a range approximately three times that of *Swatter*. A further version of *Hind* has since appeared with the nose gun replaced by a twin-barrel cannon mounted on the side of the nose.

Combining roles

The remaining attack helicopters to be covered in this chapter can be put in two main categories: anti-tank and naval. Of course, there are many helicopters not included in this chapter that are capable of carrying guns and launching rockets and missiles. For example, the French Aérospatiale Puma can be armed with a 20-mm cannon fired from the door plus 7.62-mm machine-guns, rockets and missiles as part of

its military equipment options. The U.S. Bell TexasRanger can count four TOW missiles among its possible armoury. It has been necessary, therefore, to include only those helicopters with specific attack versions.

From 1970 Aérospatiale began delivering examples of its SA 316B Alouette III, derived from the earlier but similar SE 3160 Alouette III. From the appearance of the Alouette III prototype in 1959 until the end of production in France in 1982, more than 1,400 of these helicopters had been built for service in 74 countries. SA 316Bs have been built under licence in India (as the Chetak), Romania and Switzerland. The French Army continues to operate SA 316Bs in an attack role, each carrying four AS.11 or two AS.12 missiles. Other weapons can also be carried by Alouette IIIs in service around the world. Indian Chetaks have been in production since the 1960s, but an armed version, specially prepared to launch four air-to-surface missiles, is under development for the Indian Army and Navy. The SA 316B

This Aérospatiale SA 316B Alouette III, operated by French Army Aviation, fires a Hot from one of its four launching rails.

Left: French Navy
SA 321G Super Frelon,
assigned to development
launches of the Exocet.

is powered by an 870-shp Turboméca Artouste IIIB turboshaft engine, bestowing a maximum cruising speed of 185 km/h (115 mph).

By far the largest French helicopter is the Aérospatiale SA 321 Super Frelon, which has been in production since the 1960s in military and commercial forms. The SA 321G was, however, the initial production version and 24 were built as anti-submarine helicopters for use by Flottille 32F of Aéronavale. This version entered service in 1970. The main task of these helicopters is to protect the five French nuclear-powered ballistic missile submarines around their base. They can also operate from the helicopter carrier *Jeanne d'Arc*, replacing the usual Lynx. Super Frelons patrol in groups of three or four, each carrying sophisticated detection and tracking equipment and four homing torpedoes. As an alternative, each helicopter (and the SA 321H utility helicopter) can be armed with two Exocet anti-shipping missiles for attacking surface vessels. Cruising speed is 248 km/h (154 mph) on the power of three 1,570-shp Turboméca Turmo IIIC$_6$ turboshaft engines.

The SA 342M is just one version of the Anglo-French Gazelle. It differs from previous versions by having a more powerful 859-shp Turboméca Astazou XIV M turbo-

shaft engine and by changes made to its avionics. Some 120 are required for French Army Aviation (Aviation Légère de l'Armée de Terre), each carrying four Hot anti-tank missiles. Deliveries of the initial batch ordered started in mid-1980 and to date approximately 42 are in use. Cruising speed is 264 km/h (164 mph). The SA 341 version of the Gazelle, with a 590-shp Astazou IIIA engine, is licence-built by SOKO in Yugoslavia. This version has been supplied to the Yugoslav Air Force and is of particular

A Yugoslav-built and operated Gazelle, without *Sagger* and *Grail* launchers.

A representation of the Aérospatiale SA 365F/AS.15TT Dauphin 2, with Agrion search radar under the nose on a pivoting mount.

interest as some examples carry Soviet *Sagger* anti-tank missiles and air-launched versions of the Soviet *Grail* anti-aircraft missile. *Grail* is normally used as an infantry shoulder-fired surface-to-air missile. This airborne adaptation gives the Yugoslav Gazelles real helicopter-fighter capabilities.

In 1980 Saudi Arabia placed large orders for French arms. Included was an order for 24 special military versions of the Aérospatiale SA 365N Dauphin 2, known as SA 365Fs. Each helicopter is powered by two 710-shp Turboméca Arriel 520M turbo-shaft engines and can cruise at 259 km/h (161 mph). Accommodating a crew of two, the first production SA 365F flew in July 1982. This and the next three helicopters are configured for search-and-rescue missions. The following 20 are being assigned anti-shipping duties, for operation from land and from the four Type F 2000 frigates under construction. Each frigate will carry one helicopter. Other roles could include

surveillance and the location of targets to be attacked with long-range anti-shipping missiles launched from naval vessels or coastal-defence bases.

In its anti-shipping (ASV) role, the helicopter produced for Saudi Arabia is designated SA 365F/AS.15TT. As this desig-nation indicates, armament comprises the AS.15TT lightweight all-weather anti-shipping missile, with a range of more than 15 km ($9\frac{1}{4}$ miles). Two missiles are carried each side of the fuselage on outriggers. The special detection and tracking radar associated with the helicopter's role is carried under and slightly forward of the nose. An anti-submarine version of the SA 365F, armed with torpedoes, is offered by Aérospatiale.

The SA 365N also forms the basis for the SA 365M Dauphin 2 military helicopter, which is being developed as an anti-tank helicopter (carrying eight Hot missiles), an attack helicopter (with two packs of 22

A Federal German Army MBB PAH-1 anti-tank helicopter, armed with six Hot missiles.

An Agusta A 109A in armed configuration.

68-mm **SNEB** rockets), and troop-carrying assault transport.

The Federal Republic of Germany's MBB BO 105 light helicopter has been a major success in civil and military forms since it first appeared as a prototype in the 1960s. Power is provided by two 420-shp Allison 250-C20B turboshaft engines. The Federal German Army deploys two main versions. The first of these is the BO 105 M liaison and observation helicopter, with accommodation for five persons including the pilot. The other is the BO 105P or PAH-1 anti-tank helicopter. The PAH-1, of which 212 have been delivered, carries three Hot missiles on outriggers each side of the fuselage. Maximum cruising speed is 220 km/h (137 mph). Seven Army squadrons operate these. Furthermore, 28 of the BO 105Cs, assembled in Spain by CASA for the Spanish Army, are assigned anti-tank duties.

The very different Italian Agusta A 109 twin-engined general-purpose helicopter first flew as a prototype in 1971. It had been designed with an emphasis on high performance and the result was a beautifully streamlined helicopter with a retractable undercarriage. Accommodation is provided for eight persons including the pilot. From the A 109A production version, Agusta has evolved several derivatives for military use and one for police work. Military versions of the latest and improved A 109A Mk II include an armed scouting helicopter, a command helicopter to direct attacking helicopters to their targets, electronic warfare and troop or stretcher-carrying utility helicopters, and those for attack and naval missions. The attack version can be used for anti-tank duties while carrying four or eight TOW missiles or it can be armed with guns and rockets for light attack missions. Anti-tank A 109A Mk IIs have been selected for service by Argentina, Libya and Yugoslavia. The naval variant can be equipped for most maritime roles in armed and unarmed forms. For anti-submarine work it carries one or two homing torpedoes and the necessary avionics. Air-to-surface missiles, including the well-proven AS.12, can be carried in an anti-shipping (ASV) role. A cruising speed of 272 km/h (169 mph) is quoted for the A 109A Mk II in anti-tank configuration, on the power of two Allison 250-C20B turboshaft engines.

Since 1952 Agusta has built U.S. Bell helicopters under licence, starting with the famous Model 47. Among the Bell helicopters manufactured in Italy at present is the Agusta-Bell 212ASW. This is an anti-submarine helicopter for shore- or ship-based operation and is equipped to detect submarines and attack them with two homing torpedoes or depth charges. It is based on the 14-passenger AB 212. It can also perform anti-shipping (ASV) missions armed with AS.12 air-to-surface missiles, or can perform search-and-rescue missions and other duties in unarmed form. The 1,875-shp Pratt & Whitney Aircraft of Canada PT6T-6 Turbo Twin Pac power plant allows a maximum speed of 196 km/h (122 mph). Operators include the navies of Greece, Iran, Italy, Peru and Turkey.

The AB 212ASW was developed to supersede the earlier Agusta-Bell 204AS, which itself had been based on the smaller and lighter single-engined AB 204B utility helicopter. The AB 204AS is still operated by Italian Naval Aviation (Aviazione per la Marina Militare) for anti-submarine and anti-shipping duties, although in smaller number than the AB 212ASW, which is now the main helicopter. The AB 212ASW serves on the Italian light carrier *Vittorio Veneto* and various cruisers, destroyers and frigates. The AB 204AS is powered by a 1,290-shp General Electric T58-GE-3 turboshaft engine and has a cruising speed of 167 km/h (104 mph).

A Spanish Navy Agusta-Bell 212ASW.

The mighty Sea King

Agusta also constructs, under licence, examples of the Sikorsky SH-3H (S-61) for anti-submarine and other duties, having previously built the SH-3D for the Italian Navy and for export. Customers for the Agusta-Sikorsky SH-3 have been Iran and Peru. Versions of the Sikorsky SH-3 have also been assembled in Canada as the CH-124 anti-submarine helicopter, in Japan by Mitsubishi for anti-submarine and other roles with the J.M.S.D.F., and in the U.K. by Westland as the modified Sea King (detailed later).

As mentioned above, H-3 is the U.S. military designation of the Sikorsky S-61, a very important helicopter originally designed for amphibious anti-submarine duties with the U.S. Navy and first flown as a prototype in March 1959. Subsequent versions of the S-61 have included military transports and 28-passenger commercial airliners. The first production version was the SH-3A Sea King, which entered U.S. Navy service in 1961 and remains in use. Power is provided by two 1,250-shp General Electric T58-GE-8B turboshaft engines. From the 'A' was developed the SH-3D, which is the U.S. Navy's standard ASW helicopter. Power is provided by two 1,400-shp T58-GE-10 engines, bestowing a maximum speed of 267 km/h (166 mph). Armament can weigh up to 381 kg (840 lb) and include homing torpedoes. The U.S. Navy received 72, and the Brazilian and Spanish navies received 22 and 4 respectively. The majority of ASW helicopters operated by 11 U.S. Navy squadrons and four of the Reserve are of this type.

Amongst the total number of U.S. Navy ASW helicopters is the SH-3H Sea King, which is a conversion of the SH-3D with improved ASW capability. This helicopter also undertakes a role in the important task of fleet-defence against missile attack, its electronic surveillance measurement equipment allowing it to detect on-coming missiles.

In Britain, Westland Helicopters began development of its own version of the Sea King ASW and search-and-rescue (SAR) helicopter after receiving a licence from Sikorsky in 1959 to produce a modified version. The Westland Sea King is based on the SH-3D but has two Rolls-Royce Gnome turboshaft engines, differing avionics and equipment, and a greater fuel capacity to increase endurance. Like the Sikorsky, the Westland Sea King has a watertight hull and its main undercarriage units retract into stabilizing floats which carry flotation bags which inflate in case of an emergency ditching.

The first Royal Navy version was the Sea King HAS. Mk 1, which first appeared in 1969. Mk 1s were later upgraded to Sea King HAS. Mk 2 standard, with more powerful

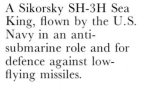

A Sikorsky SH-3H Sea King, flown by the U.S. Navy in an anti-submarine role and for defence against low-flying missiles.

A Royal Navy Westland Sea King releases a new lightweight Sting Ray torpedo.

1,660-shp Gnome H.1400-1 turboshaft engines, and then joined production examples in service. The first Sea King HAS. Mk 2 appeared in 1976. Mk 2s, in turn, are now being upgraded to Sea King HAS. Mk 5 standard, to supplement newly built examples.

The first Sea King HAS. Mk 5s joined the Royal Navy in 1980 and were among the helicopters operated during the conflict over the Falkland Islands. As a result of losses, production of new Mk 5s has been increased to 25. Like other Sea Kings, the HAS. Mk 5 has advanced search radar in a radome carried above the fuselage and dipping sonar. The crew of four includes an observer/navigator, whose job it is to coordinate data from the search and tracking radar and navigational equipment with sonar contacts. Each helicopter can both detect submarines and then attack them with four homing torpedoes or a similar number of depth-charges. A machine-gun can be carried in the door opening. Today the Royal Navy operates more than 40 Sea Kings in an ASW role, and uses others for SAR/training, utility, and a very small number as Sea King AEWs. The latter are of particular interest as they give *Invincible*-class carriers low-altitude airborne early warning of the type lacking when the Task Force fought in the South Atlantic. The Sea King AEW was developed in just 11 weeks, using two HAS. Mk 2s as prototypes. Each carries Searchwater radar in a large radome which is swung below the hull from the fuselage side when in use. Deployment began in August 1982. It is believed that five further AEWs are being completed by converting Royal Air Force HAR Mk 3 search-and-rescue Sea Kings.

Westland-built Sea Kings have been exported to Australia, Belgium, Egypt, West Germany, India, Norway and Pakistan, for ASW and SAR duties. Up to 22 persons can be carried in the main cabin in a SAR role.

A Swedish Naval
Aviation Kawasaki
KV-107/II, military
designated HKP 4.

The cruising speed at sea level is 208 km/h (129 mph).

Since 1962, when the first production helicopter flew, Kawasaki of Japan has enjoyed considerable commercial and military success with its KV107. This is a licence-built version of the Boeing Vertol Model 107 model II. Most military examples have been equipped for SAR, mine countermeasures or transport duties, but Swedish Naval Aviation (Svenska Marinen) uses the type for anti-submarine and mine countermeasures work under an HKP 4 designa-tion. Unlike other versions of the helicopter, which have two General Electric or Ishikawajima-Harima CT58 turboshaft engines, Swedish HKP 4s are powered by Rolls-Royce Gnome H.1200s installed side by side within the rear rotor pylon. The rotor drive system enables both forward and rear rotors to be powered by both or one engine. Swedish Naval examples also carry a British navigation system and the necessary avionics and equipment to perform their ASW/MCM roles. The Swedish Air Force also flies HKP 4s for SAR work.

Soviet helicopters – the most powerful

Soviet and other forces have long relied on helicopters built by Kamov and Mil. By far the most important to the Soviet Naval Air Fleet (Aviatsiya - Voenno - Morskovo Flota) is the Kamov Ka-25, known to NATO as *Hormone*. Distinctively configured, *Hormone* has two three-blade co-axial contra-rotating rotors and a tail unit comprising a central fin and outer fins and rudders. It was first seen in public in 1961. Today it is thought that some 250 are operational in an anti-submarine role from both ship and shore bases (*Hormone-A*), in unarmed SAR and utility roles (*Hormone-C*), and as an electronics helicopter (*Hormone-B*) to locate and give details of targets that can be attacked by *Sandbox* long-range anti-shipping cruise missiles carried in multiple launchers on board *Kiev*-class aircraft carriers and some submarines.

Hormone-As and *Bs* are carried on board *Kiev*-class aircraft carriers of the Soviet Navy (16 and three respectively), the nuclear-powered heavily missile- and gun-armed battle cruisers of the *Kirov* class, the helicopter cruisers *Moskva* and *Leningrad* (18 '*As*' each), on board the 10 *Kresta II* and seven *Kara* cruisers (*Hormone-As*), on the four *Kresta I* cruisers (*Hormone-Bs*), and on other vessels. The *Hormone-A* has an under-nose radome housing the search radar and carries dipping sonar and a towed magnetic anomaly detector as part of its operational equipment. Armament includes homing torpedoes, nuclear depth-charges or other weapons carried in the fuselage bay. Some helicopters have a deep rectangular container along the length of the underfuselage, aft of the radome, said to house wing-guided torpedoes, while others can carry air-to-surface missiles. The power from two 900-shp Glushenkov GTD-3 or 990-shp GTD-3BM turboshaft engines mounted side by side above the main cabin provides a maximum speed of 209 km/h (130 mph). Exported *Hormone-As* are in use in India, Syria and Yugoslavia.

Kamov Ka-25 *Hormone* Soviet Navy anti-submarine helicopters, photographed on board *Moskva*.

The new Kamov Ka-32 *Helix-A* on the helicopter pad of *Udaloy*, photographed during Soviet exercises in September 1981.

One of several new Soviet helicopters is the Kamov Ka-32. This has been named *Helix* by NATO and was first seen in 1981. It is said to have many civil applications but has also been seen on board the *Udaloy*, the first of about four new Soviet guided missile cruisers of this class. Indeed, the ship is as new as its two *Helix* helicopters. Other Ka-32s are probably deployed on the very new *Sovremenny* class of guided missile cruisers.

Two versions of the Ka-32 relate directly to *Hormone-A* and *B* and will supersede them. The new helicopter continues the Kamov predilection for co-axial contra-rotating rotors and multiple fins and rudders, the latter forming endplate surfaces as used previously on the light Ka-26. Although the overall dimensions are similar to those of the Ka-25, thereby enabling the Ka-32 to use Ka-25 facilities on board ship, it has a much larger main cabin. This will enable it to accommodate more than the 12 passengers or the cargo of the Ka-25.

In 1952 the first flight was made of a piston-engined Mil Mi-4. This was the Soviet equivalent of the U.S. Sikorsky S-55 and the two types were of basically similar configuration. The Mi-4 was put into mass production for many military and civil roles and was widely exported. A version known to NATO as *Hound-B* became a standard anti-submarine helicopter, but was superseded by the Ka-25 on board Soviet ships and by the Mi-14 for shore-based duty. However, the Mi-4 has been produced in China under the local name Zhishengji-5 or Zhi-5. Manufactured at the Harbin works, it is therefore best known in the West as the Harbin Z-5. It is powered by one 1,700-hp Huosai-5A or HS-5A piston engine, a Chinese-built Shvetsov ASh-82, and is likely to have a maximum speed of about 209 km/h (130 mph). Approximately 40 to 50 are operated by the Aviation of the People's Navy in an ASW role and for SAR.

To supersede land-based Mi-4 ASW helicopters, Mil produced its Mi-14. This is known to NATO as *Haze*. It is basically a Mil Mi-8 with modifications made to the airframe and equipment to make it suitable for its new role. These changes include the use of a new watertight boat-type hull to the lower fuselage and the addition of stabilizing sponsons in case of an emergency landing on water. The undercarriage is retractable. Operational equipment and armament are similar to those carried by the Ka-25 and power is provided by two Isotov TV3-117 turboshaft engines, rated at 2,200-shp each. Maximum speed is unknown but it is likely to be about 260 km/h (161 mph). The Soviet Naval Air Fleet is thought to deploy about 65 Mi-14s and 12 have been acquired by Bulgaria to equip one ASW squadron.

The Mi-8 itself is a large civil and military helicopter, which has been in production since the 1960s and is still being built. It is believed that the total number produced approaches 8,000, mostly con-figured and equipped for transport duties. Power is provided by two 1,700-shp Isotov TV2-117A turboshaft engines carried side by side above the main cabin. Maximum speed is 260 km/h (161 mph). Three of the military versions of the Mi-8 are heavily armed. The first, known to NATO as the *Hip-C* assault transport, is able to carry and launch 128 57-mm rockets or other weapons to suppress ground fire while landing perhaps 32 troops, freight or military vehicles. *Hip-E* is said to be the world's most heavily armed helicopter, able to carry up to 192 57-mm rockets and four *Swatter* anti-tank missiles at the same time. It also has a 12.7-mm machine-gun in the nose. The *Hip-C* and *E* are standard helicopters with the Soviet tactical air forces. An export version of the *Hip-E* is the *Hip-F*, which has six *Saggers* as its anti-tank missile armament.

This Soviet Navy Mil Mi-14 *Haze* shore-based ASW helicopter has its MAD bird carried against the rear fuselage, prior to being towed through the water to pick up magnetic signals from a submerged submarine.

Left: The Mil Mi-8 *Hip-E*, the world's most heavily armed helicopter, is seen here with a gun at the nose and 192 rockets carried in six launchers, but without the four *Swatter* anti-tank missiles it can carry above the rocket launcher racks.

135

An Army Lynx carrying 12 80-mm SURA rockets each side.

A helicopter for every role

Another British helicopter that made world news during the conflict over the Falkland Islands is the Westland Lynx. On 2 May 1982 two Royal Navy Lynx helicopters armed with Sea Skua missiles damaged the Argentine patrol vessel *Alferez Sobral* and sunk another named *Comodoro Somellera*. These helicopters had been called into action after a Royal Navy Sea King had been fired upon. Both vessels were of similar type, being two of three ex-U.S. *Sotoyomo*-class vessels of 800 tons, armed with one 40-mm and two 20-mm guns.

The Lynx is known as a Westland type but it is one of several helicopters developed under an Anglo-French agreement. It is a multi-purpose helicopter powered by two Rolls-Royce Gem turboshaft engines of 750-shp or 890-shp maximum continuous rating. Well over 300 Lynx helicopters have been ordered for the British Army, the navies of Britain and France, and for export. The British Army version is known as the Lynx AH.Mk 1. This is a general-purpose helicopter that can undertake armed and unarmed missions. The first flew in 1977. A very wide range of weapons can be carried by the Army version when required. During demonstrations even French Magic 550 air-to-air missiles have been fired successfully. Just over half the British Army Lynx AH.Mk 1s will be equipped to carry TOW anti-tank missiles. The first few became operational with Number 654 Squadron, Number 4 Regiment of Army Aviation in 1981.

Royal Navy versions are the Lynx HAS.Mk 2 and Mk 3, for anti-submarine, anti-shipping, and other duties including the transport of goods from shore to ship in the so-called vertical replenishment role. Eighty have been delivered, and many of these serve on board Type 42 destroyers, *Amazon*-class Type 21 frigates, *Broadsword*-class Type 22 frigates and *Leander*-class frigates. In an ASW role, these can each be armed with two homing torpedoes (including the new Sting Ray), or two depth-charges. The submarine to be attacked can be detected by dipping sonar or magnetic anomaly detector. For ASV missions, four Sea Skua or a similar number of other air-to-surface missiles can be carried, to be used against vessels detected by the search and tracking radar. The Lynx HAS.Mk 2 cruises at 211 km/h (131 mph).

The French Navy has received 40 Lynx helicopters for ASV duties, carrying AS.12 missiles, and others have been ordered by, or delivered to, the navies of Argentina, Brazil, Denmark, West Germany, the Netherlands and Nigeria. Norway has received a few ASW/ASV Lynx for its air force and the State of Qatar Police has received three general-purpose types.

The Lynx can be seen as a modern replacement for helicopters like the small Westland Wasp, which is still carried by some Royal Navy frigates as the Wasp HAS. Mk 1 anti-submarine helicopter. Lynx helicopters have replaced Wasps with the Royal Netherlands Naval Air Service (Marine Luchtvaartdienst) but others serve in very small number with the navies of Brazil (liaison and SAR only), New Zealand and South Africa.

The Wasp was developed as a naval version of the Scout and first appeared in 1962. It is powered by a 710-shp Rolls-Royce Bristol Nimbus 503 turboshaft engine, which

One of 12 Westland Lynx Mk 88 ASW helicopters flown from Federal German Navy frigates deploys its dipping sonar.

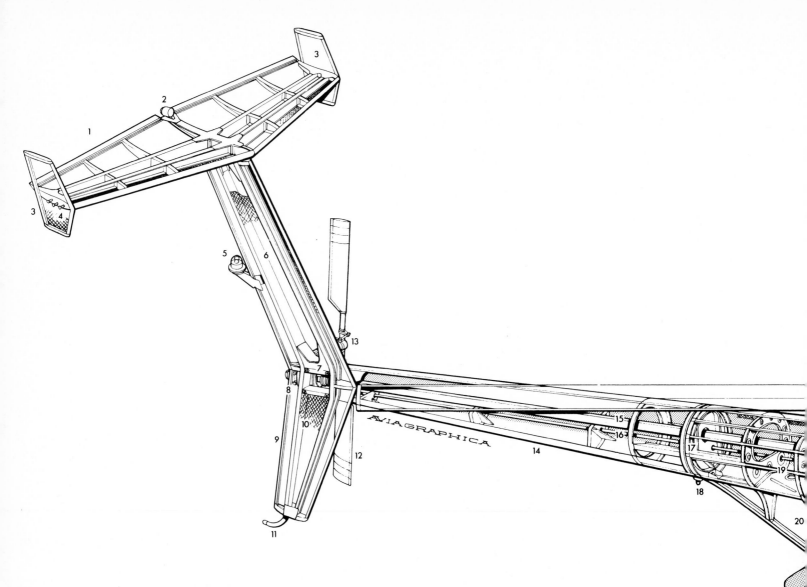

Plate V

Hughes 500 MD Defender

cutaway drawing key

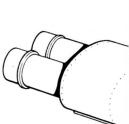

1 Horizontal stabiliser construction	24 Engine bay construction	48 Fuselage main frame
2 Tail navigation light	25 Sloping firewall	49 Control rod guard duct
3 Stabiliser end plates	26 Allison 250-C20B turboshaft engine	50 Rotor brake control
4 Honeycomb panels	27 Engine intake	51 Gunsight reticle image generator
5 Anti-collision beacon	28 Cooling air fan	52 Co-pilot's seat
6 Tailfin construction	29 Air intake plenum chamber	53 Crew seat armour plating
7 Fin attachment bolts	30 Intake filter by-pass door	54 Co-pilot's reflector gunsight, HGS-5 sub-system
8 Tail rotor gearbox	31 Communications aerial	55 Outside air temperature probe
9 Ventral fin	32 Rotor head fibre-glass tail fairing	56 Grab handle
10 Honycomb core panel	33 Intake filtered air particle separator	57 Ammunition magazine, 2,000 rounds
11 Tailskid	34 Engine air intake	58 HGS-5 gun system mounting
12 Two-bladed tail rotor	35 Rotor brake	59 General Electric, 7,62-mm M-134 Minigun
13 Tail rotor pitch control mechanism	36 Engine drive shaft	60 Electric gun drive
14 Tubular tail boom	37 Rotor gearbox	61 Cockpit canopy glazing
15 Tail rotor drive shaft	38 Rotor support mast	62 Co-pilot's weapon aiming viewfinder — XM65 (TOW) sight
16 Tail rotor control rod	39 Flexible strap, blade retaining rotor head	63 Co-pilot's control column
17 Tailboom joint ring	40 Rotor head fairing	64 Sight controller
18 Antenna	41 Blade attachments	65 Pilot's steering indicator
19 Fuselage tailboom extension frame construction	42 Lead lag dampers	66 Instrument panel shroud
20 Boat tail fairing construction	43 Aluminium spar rotor blades	67 Instrument panel pedestal/ avionics housing
21 Fuselage tailcone (only if BHO, item 23, is fitted)	44 Blade articulating links	
22 Engine compartment access doors	45 Pitch control rods	
23 Infra-red suppressor (Black Hole Ocarina) exhaust pipe	46 Rotor head swash plate linkage	
	47 Control rods	

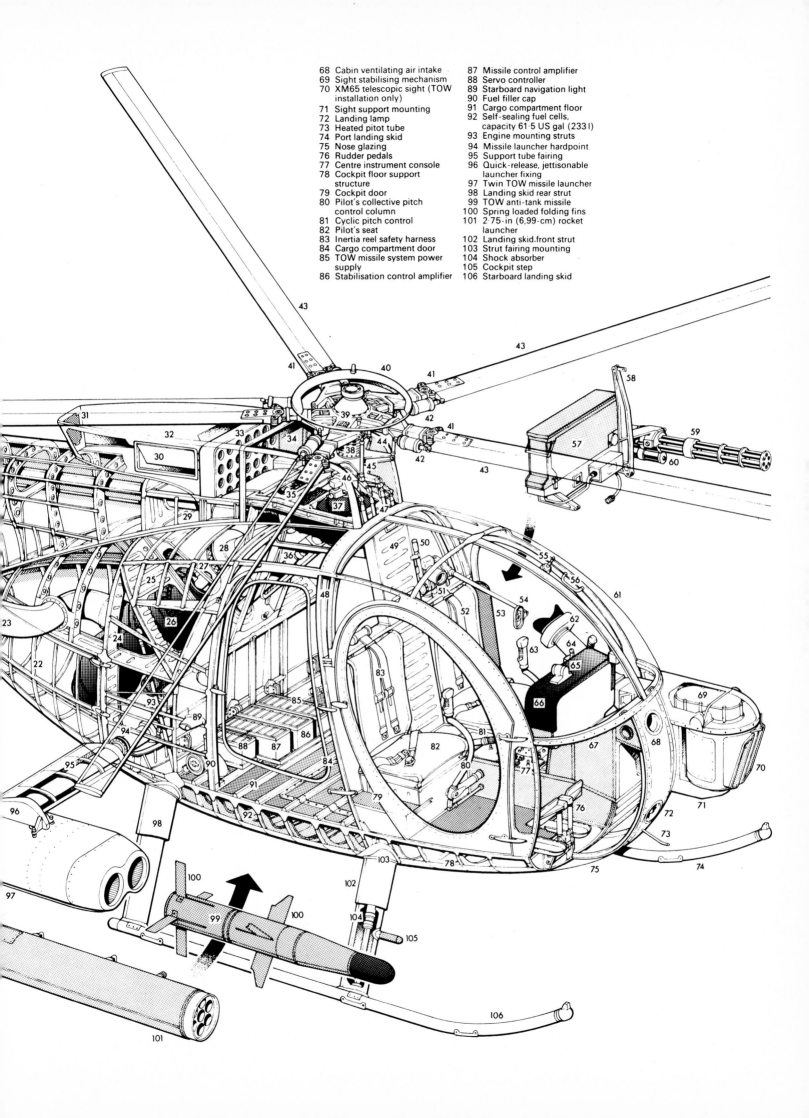

68 Cabin ventilating air intake
69 Sight stabilising mechanism
70 XM65 telescopic sight (TOW installation only)
71 Sight support mounting
72 Landing lamp
73 Heated pitot tube
74 Port landing skid
75 Nose glazing
76 Rudder pedals
77 Centre instrument console
78 Cockpit floor support structure
79 Cockpit door
80 Pilot's collective pitch control column
81 Cyclic pitch control
82 Pilot's seat
83 Inertia reel safety harness
84 Cargo compartment door
85 TOW missile system power supply
86 Stabilisation control amplifier

87 Missile control amplifier
88 Servo controller
89 Starboard navigation light
90 Fuel filler cap
91 Cargo compartment floor
92 Self-sealing fuel cells, capacity 61·5 US gal (233 l)
93 Engine mounting struts
94 Missile launcher hardpoint
95 Support tube fairing
96 Quick-release, jettisonable launcher fixing
97 Twin TOW missile launcher
98 Landing skid rear strut
99 TOW anti-tank missile
100 Spring loaded folding fins
101 2·75-in (6,99-cm) rocket launcher
102 Landing skid.front strut
103 Strut fairing mounting
104 Shock absorber
105 Cockpit step
106 Starboard landing skid

gives it a maximum speed of 193 km/h (120 mph). Armament normally comprises two homing torpedoes carried under the fuselage between the undercarriage legs.

An important attack helicopter based on an observation type is the Model 500MD Defender, which has been built for anti-tank, ASW, ASV and other roles. Military versions of the basic Hughes Model 500 began with the OH-6A Cayuse of 1963, which subsequently won a U.S. Army competition as a light observation helicopter. By 1970 the U.S. Army had received no fewer than 1,434. The export version of the Cayuse became the Model 500M, which has also been built under licence in Argentina (by RACA) and Japan (by Kawasaki). Power is provided by a 278-shp Allison 250-C18A turboshaft engine, allowing a maximum speed of 244 km/h (152 mph). The 11 operated by Spanish Naval Aviation (Arma Aérea de la Armada) are not typical of the Model 500Ms in use, being equipped and armed for anti-submarine and SAR duties. Submarine detection is by magnetic anomaly detector (MAD).

Five different versions comprise the actual Defender series. Defenders are also among the Model 500s built under licence by BredaNardi in Italy and Korean Air Lines in South Korea. The Model 500MD Scout Defender can be used to seek out enemy forces and, if required, attack them with guns, rockets and grenade launcher. Kenya, South Korea and Morocco operate this version.

A version of the Scout Defender with equipment designed to reduce its noise level is the Quiet Advanced Scout Defender. In operation, this 'quiet' helicopter can observe enemy forces and either attack them or call in the Model 500MD/TOW Defender armed with four TOW missiles to destroy armour. With the added armament of a 30-mm Chain Gun cannon, the latter helicopter is designated Model 500MD/MMS-TOW. Examples of the TOW Defender have been delivered to Israel and Kenya and built under licence in South Korea.

Naval duties are undertaken by the Model 500MD/ASW Defender, which is currently in service with the Taiwanese Navy. Using MAD and a nose-mounted search radar, the ASW Defender can locate submarines and surface vessels and attack with two homing torpedoes.

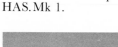

South African Wasp HAS.Mk 1.

The final version in the Model 500MD series is the Defender II. This is a multimission helicopter also capable of performing the land missions of previous versions (accordingly it has a wide range of optional equipment and armament). Interestingly, like the Yugoslav Gazelles mentioned earlier, the Defender II can be armed with Stinger anti-aircraft missiles in an air-to-air role. Normally, Stingers are employed as man-portable missiles for use by infantry. Other air-to-air missiles can be carried.

Not so well known to the public as the Sea King is the U.S. Navy's Kaman SH-2F Seasprite. The prototype made its maiden flight in July 1959 as a single-engined utility helicopter, and the first production examples entered U.S. Navy service in 1962.

Other missions followed, including search and rescue. Interestingly, the Kaman UH-2 was one of the five helicopters considered by the U.S. Army during the early 1960s as an interim armed attack helicopter, as detailed at the beginning of this chapter.

The first major modification of the Seasprite came in the latter 1960s, when early production UH-2s were uprated to UH-2C standard by having two General Electric T58 turboshaft engines fitted instead of the previous one. In the early 1970s two Seasprites were modified for evaluation in an anti-ship missile defence (ASMD) role, as part of the overall programme to consider a light airborne multi-purpose system (LAMPS) helicopter. As a result of successful tests, deployment of

A Hughes 500MD/TOW Defender in service with the Kenya Army.

Seasprites converted into SH-2D LAMPS helicopters, for roles including ASW and anti-ship surveillance and targeting, started at the end of 1971. Each SH-2D carried search radar in a 'chin' radome and MAD.

Modification of Seasprites into SH-2Ds was restricted to a small number as a more advanced version was being developed. This became known as the SH-2F and 88 utility Seasprites were converted accordingly. The SH-2Ds were converted later. The first SH–2Fs were deployed in the Pacific, by squadron HSL-33, in 1973. Production of additional SH-2Fs began recently. The U.S. Navy has eight squadrons equipped with the SH-2F. Power is provided by two 1,350-shp T58-GE-8F turboshaft engines, bestowing a maximum speed of 265 km/h (165 mph). A crew of three is usual, but an extra person can be carried while the helicopter remains LAMPS-equipped. With the sonobuoy launcher taken out, four passengers or two stretchers can be accommodated. Armament is one or two homing torpedoes.

The Sikorsky UH-60 Black Hawk is best known as an assault transport helicopter and is in large-scale service with the U.S. Army.

Other versions have been built, including an electronic countermeasures version (EH-60A) to intercept enemy communications and jam them and the EH-60B for stand-off target acquisition. However, a programme is now underway to evaluate the Black Hawk's ability to carry stores and fire weapons attached to a new external stores support system. The ESSS, as it is known, comprises the necessary modifications to the airframe to allow the attachment of four stores pylons under new stub wings. These pylons allow the attachment of up to 16 Hellfire 'fire and forget' anti-armour missiles or other weapons including anti-tank mines. The use of weapons or other external stores does not prevent troops from being accommodated in the main cabin and, indeed, allows the helicopter to suppress ground fire during landing or extend its range by attaching drop-tanks. The use of ESSS, which may become standard eventually, does not require changing the Black Hawk's standard two 1,560-shp General Electric T700-GE-700 turboshaft engines, which give the helicopter a maximum speed of 296 km/h (184 mph).

A U.S. Navy Kaman SH-2F Seasprite, photographed in 1980 during an inflight refuelling exercise, hovering over USS *Dewey*.

Left and below: This Sikorsky UH-60A Black Hawk is fitted with ESSS and carries 16 Hellfire anti-tank missiles.

A naval version of the Sikorsky Black Hawk is the SH-60B Seahawk. This has been developed for the U.S. Navy as a LAMPS Mk III helicopter to supplement (not replace) the Seasprite. Operational deployment begins in 1984. The U.S. Navy has a need for more than 200 Seahawks, each powered by two 1,690-shp T700-GE-401 turboshafts. The Seahawk is heavier than the Black Hawk and has an estimated maximum speed of 234 km/h (145 mph). Two homing torpedoes are included in its armament.

Another Sikorsky helicopter is the S-76, developed originally as a 12-passenger commercial helicopter. It is typical of many

modern types (such as the Italian A 109A and U.S. Bell Model 222) in having a very streamlined fuselage, twin engines and a retractable undercarriage for high performance. Sikorsky now offers an armed military version of the S-76 Utility known simply as the S-76 Military. This has engine type and retractable/non-retractable undercarriage options and can be armed. Inside the main cabin 12 troops or equivalent cargo can be accommodated. As a troop transport it has a cruising speed of about 269 km/h (167 mph), which is increased in anti-tank configuration or when the helicopter is used for other roles which allow a lighter take-off weight, such as search and rescue.

The Sikorsky S-76 Military, with a non-retractable undercarriage and armed with rocket pods.

Facing page: The SH-60B Seahawk, photographed in 1982 over the frigate USS *McInerney* during operational evaluation at sea.

7 Searching the Seas

In Chapters Three and Six, details have been given of aeroplanes and helicopters used to search out submarines and surface vessels and attack them. Those fixed-wing aircraft of Chapter Three are types flown from aircraft carriers and are, therefore, necessarily small. This chapter deals with the land-based fixed-wing aircraft used for maritime patrol and ASW.

It is accepted that the term maritime patrol includes the roles of over-water surveillance, anti-submarine and anti-surface vessel warfare, and search and rescue. It can also include other duties such as fishery protection. However, some aircraft in this chapter are purely anti-submarine types. This category of military aircraft is one of the few to incorporate amphibians and flying-boats.

The smallest of the flying-boats in use today is the Grumman HU-16 Albatross. Still flown by several navies and air forces, including those of Mexico, the Philippines and Thailand, only those belonging to the Hellenic Air Force are of the specially produced HU-16B anti-submarine version. Power is provided by two 1,425-hp Wright R-1820-76A engines and maximum speed is 380 km/h (236 mph).

Interestingly, because of Grumman's long-held tradition for producing many of the world's most important naval aircraft, a second Grumman type can be included in this chapter, known as the S-2 Tracker. First flown in 1952 and subsequently built in large number as a carrier-borne anti-submarine aircraft for the U.S. Navy, the Tracker is no longer in U.S.N. service. It remains in service, however, with several navies and air forces around the world. Untypical today are the S-2Es operated by both Argentine Naval Aviation and the Brazilian Naval Air Force, as these are carrier borne. The operators of the largest number of land-based aircraft are the Japan Maritime Self-Defence Force and the Republic of Korea Air Force. The S-2E version has two 1,525-hp Wright R-1820-82WA engines, can fly at 426 km/h (265 mph), and can be armed with depth-charges, other weapons in the bay and torpedoes or rockets carried under the wings.

Arguably the world's most important amphibious flying-boat, and one that is at the other end of the size range from the Albatross, is the Soviet Beriev M-12 Tchaika. Beriev flying-boats of various types have been standard equipment for Soviet

Grumman Tracker, operated by the 4th Air Group, J.M.S.D.F.

Left: Beriev M-12 (*Mail*), a standard maritime patrol amphibian with the Soviet Navy.

J.M.S.D.F. Shin Meiwa PS-1 anti-submarine flying-boat, photographed off Oshima Island.

forces since before the Second World War, and this current medium-range amphibian was first seen in public in 1961. Known to NATO as *Mail*, between 80 and 90 are believed to be in service with the Naval Air Fleet.

The *Mail* is of distinctive design, with high-mounted cranked wings and a tail-plane with marked dihedral supporting twin fins and rudders. The wing shape keeps the four-blade propellers well above the water. Power is provided by two 4,190-ehp Ivchenko AI-20D turboprop engines, bestowing a maximum speed of 608 km/h (378 mph). A heavily glazed nose compartment is occupied by the navigator/observer, and in front of him the radome housing search radar is carried. The long projection

from the rear fuselage is known as a 'sting' tail and contains a magnetic anomaly detector (MAD). Weapons are carried beneath the wings and in an under-hull bay. It should not be forgotten, also, that the Soviet Navy operates Tu-16 *Badgers*, Tu-22M *Backfires*, Myasishchev M-4 *Bisons*, Tu-142 *Bears* and Tu-22 *Blinders* in maritime roles.

Even larger than *Mail* is the Shin Meiwa PS-1, an anti-submarine flying-boat operated by the Japan Maritime Self-Defence Force. Unlike its search-and-rescue counterpart, the Shin Meiwa US-1, the PS-1 is not amphibious, although retractable beaching gear is fitted. The prototype flew for the first time in October 1967 and production aircraft went to the 31st Air Group.

Royal Thai Navy
Canadair CL-215
amphibian.

Nineteen are in use, most with Number 31 Squadron based at Iwakuni but a few are used as trainers. Each aircraft is powered by four 3,060-ehp Ishikawajima-built General Electric T64-IHI-10 turboprop engines. Maximum speed is 547 km/h (340 mph). Operational equipment includes search radar, MAD and dipping sonar, and armament can include four 150-kg anti-submarine bombs accommodated in the weapons bay plus four homing torpedoes and rockets carried under the wings.

The final flying-boat type to be detailed is the Canadair CL-215 amphibian. This is a multi-purpose aircraft that has found military and civil acceptance in maritime patrol, search-and-rescue, water bombing and utility roles. Firefighting as a water bomber is its primary role but the Hellenic Air Force operates seven for search-and-rescue, the Spanish Air Force has a number of its CL-215s assigned to SAR and coastal patrol duties, the Royal Thai Navy uses two for maritime reconnaissance and SAR, and the Yugoslav Air Force has four for SAR and transport work.

The prototype CL-215 made its maiden flight in October 1967. It is smaller than both the Beriev M-12 and Shin Meiwa PS-1 and is powered by two 2,100 hp Pratt & Whitney R-2800-CA3 engines. Cruising speed is 291 km/h (181 mph).

Patrolling from land

Typical of the large land-based maritime patrol aircraft is the British Aerospace Nimrod. This was developed as a modern replacement for the R.A.F.'s Hawker Siddeley Shackleton MR.Mk 3 force. The Shackleton itself dates from 1949 and has a configuration that reminds onlookers of the wartime Avro Lancaster bomber. Although a few Shackleton AEW Mk 2 airborne early-warning aircraft remained in service with the R.A.F. in the early 1980s, the MR.Mk 3 has long since disappeared. However, the South African Air Force continues to operate a handful of Shackleton MR.Mk 3s, each with two Rolls-Royce Bristol Viper 203 auxiliary turbojet engines housed in the same nacelles as the outer 2,455-hp Rolls-Royce Griffon 57A main engines, to boost take-off performance.

Returning to the Nimrod, this has been the R.A.F.'s standard maritime patrol aircraft for well over a decade and is expected to continue in service into the 1990s. Yet the Nimrod is based on the airframe of the de Havilland Comet 4C, an airliner no longer in commercial use. However, Nimrods are newly constructed, not conversions of airliners. Each has a slightly shortened Comet 4C fuselage, with the addition of an unpressurized pannier that runs below the original underfuselage from the nose to a point aft of the wings. This pannier houses the search radar in the nose section, and other operational equipment aft, plus nine torpedoes and bombs or auxiliary fuel tanks. Other weapons can be carried on two underwing pylons, which can include mines, bombs, air-to-surface missiles (including Harpoon) or Sidewinders for self-defence. Electronic support measures equipment is housed in a fairing on the tailfin and MAD is carried in the tailboom. The crew comprises 12 persons normally, and a small number of additional persons can be accommodated when required. With equipment removed from the rear fuselage, up to 45 troops can be carried. Power is provided by four 5507-kg (12,140-lb)st Rolls-Royce RB.168-20 Spey Mk 250 turbofan engines, but the pilot is free to decide to operate just two during cruising flight to extend the aircraft's endurance. Maximum speed is 926 km/h (575 mph) and endurance is normally 12 hours. Flight refuelling capability on some Nimrods can greatly extend endurance.

The prototype Nimrod made its maiden flight in May 1967 and initial production Nimrod MR.Mk 1s entered service in 1969, first going to No. 201 Squadron, R.A.F. Strike Command. Forty-three were built. Three aircraft were completed as Nimrod R.Mk 1s, serving with No. 51 Squadron in an electronic intelligence role, known as 'elint'. Currently, the entire fleet of Nimrod

An R.A.F. Nimrod MR.Mk 2, in new colour scheme, takes fuel from a Victor tanker.

147

One of three Kawasaki P-2Js recently modified to assume new roles, including electronic countermeasures.

MR.Mk 1s is scheduled to be converted, most to the more advanced MR.Mk 2 standard but 11 into Nimrod AEW.Mk 3 airborne early-warning aircraft (see next chapter). Delivery of MR.Mk 2 conversions began in 1979.

During the Second World War Lockheed designed an ASW/ASV patrol aircraft which eventually became the P2V Neptune. This was ordered into mass production for the U.S. Navy and subsequently for export, with more than 1,000 being completed by the close of production in 1962. A new designation system for U.S. military aircraft led to the Neptune being known thereafter as the P-2.

The final production version of the Neptune was the P2V-7 or, later, P-2H. Today, this is the only version in military service, serving with the navies of Argentina and France. The most significant changes made to this final version were to modernize its equipment and to use two 1 540-kg (3,400-lb)st Westinghouse J34 turbojet engines to supplement the standard two 3,500-hp Wright R-3350-32W piston engines. The maximum speed of the P-2H is 573 km/h (356 mph) without turbojets in use. Armament comprises up to 3 630 kg (8,000 lb) of bombs, torpedoes or depth-charges carried in the weapons bay, plus underwing rockets. Self-defence can be achieved by the optional use of a dorsal turret with two machine-guns.

During the period 1959 to 1965, Kawasaki in Japan completed 48 P-2Hs for the J.M.S.D.F. As production ended, the company began work on a developed version. This became the Kawasaki P-2J.

The prototype flew for the first time in 1966 and by the end of production in 1979 a total of 82 had rolled off production lines. The P-2J remains in service with the J.M.S.D.F. as its main maritime aircraft. Compared to the P-2H, the P-2J is longer, has a reduced wing span, is lighter, and is powered by two 3,060-ehp Ishikawajima-Harima-built General Electric T64-IHI-10E turboprop engines and two 1 400-kg (3,085-lb)st J3-IHI-7D turbojets. Its maximum cruising speed is 402 km/h (250 mph).

It was as a Neptune replacement that Breguet headed a consortium of European companies that produced the larger Br 1150 Atlantic, having previously been announced the winner of a NATO design competition that had attracted a great many different proposals. The first prototype made its maiden flight in October 1961 and the first production Atlantics were delivered to the French Aéronavale towards the end of 1965. Other recipients were the navies of West Germany and the Netherlands, and the Italian Air Force. Eventually, three ex-French aircraft were acquired by Pakistan. All of these nations continue to operate the Atlantic.

Power for the Atlantic is provided by two 6,106-ehp SNECMA-built Rolls-Royce Tyne RTy 20 Mk 21 turboprop engines, which bestow a maximum speed of 658 km/h (409 mph). The Atlantic's range is very long (9 000 km; 5,590 miles) and it can be armed with homing torpedoes, depth-charges, bombs, rockets and air-to-surface missiles (including Exocet) carried in the weapons bay and underwing.

Above: French Navy
Dassault-Breguet
Atlantic with its
retractable radome
lowered.

Left: The first P-3C
Orion to be built by
Lockheed for the
J.M.S.D.F.

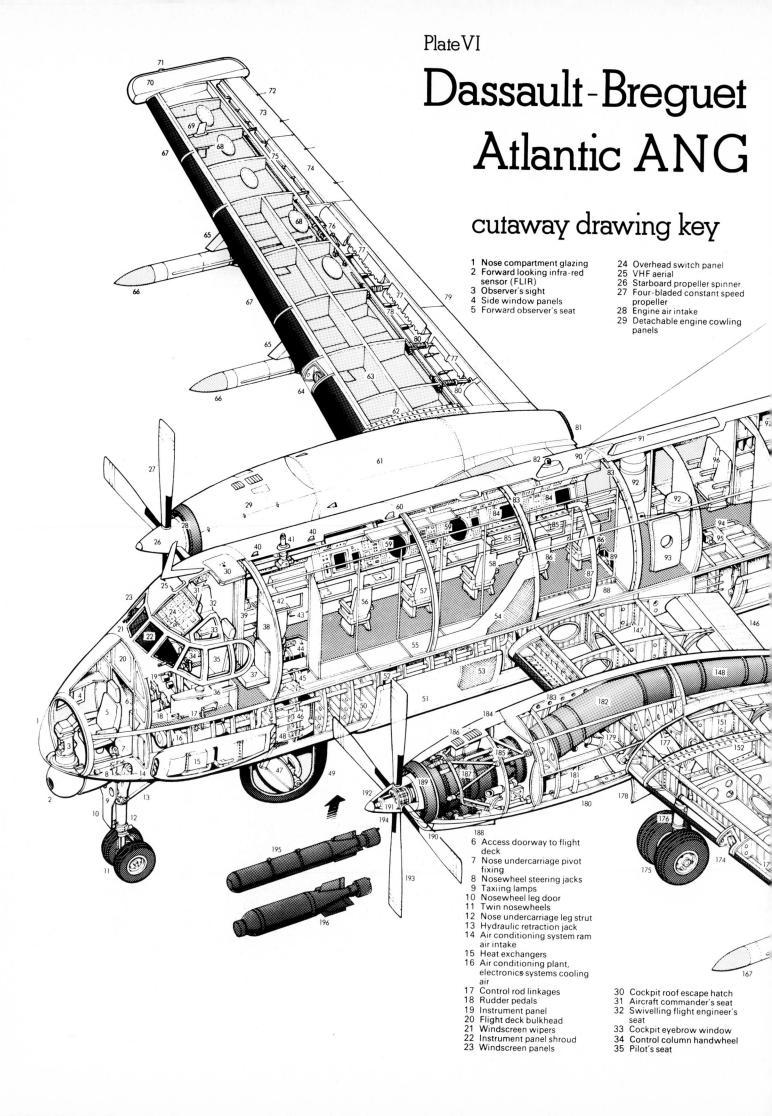

Plate VI

Dassault-Breguet Atlantic ANG

cutaway drawing key

1 Nose compartment glazing
2 Forward looking infra-red sensor (FLIR)
3 Observer's sight
4 Side window panels
5 Forward observer's seat

24 Overhead switch panel
25 VHF aerial
26 Starboard propeller spinner
27 Four-bladed constant speed propeller
28 Engine air intake
29 Detachable engine cowling panels

6 Access doorway to flight deck
7 Nose undercarriage pivot fixing
8 Nosewheel steering jacks
9 Taxiing lamps
10 Nosewheel leg door
11 Twin nosewheels
12 Nose undercarriage leg strut
13 Hydraulic retraction jack
14 Air conditioning system ram air intake
15 Heat exchangers
16 Air conditioning plant, electronic systems cooling air
17 Control rod linkages
18 Rudder pedals
19 Instrument panel
20 Flight deck bulkhead
21 Windscreen wipers
22 Instrument panel shroud
23 Windscreen panels

30 Cockpit roof escape hatch
31 Aircraft commander's seat
32 Swivelling flight engineer's seat
33 Cockpit eyebrow window
34 Control column handwheel
35 Pilot's seat

36 Side console panel
37 Folding observer's seat
38 Main cabin bulkhead
39 Curtained doorway
40 TACAN aerials
41 Periscope sextant mounting
42 Radio navigator's station
43 Moving map display
44 Starboard underfloor APU bay
45 Radome raising and lowering hydraulic motor
46 Fuselage lower lobe frame construction
47 Thomson-CSF Iguane search radar
48 Air conditioning system exhaust duct
49 Retractable radome
50 Weapons bay forward bulkhead
51 Externally sliding weapons bay doors
52 Door guide rails
53 Bomb door honeycomb construction
54 Fuselage pressurised section honeycomb skin panels
55 Port side radio and electronics racks
56 ESM, ECM and MAD systems operator's seat
57 Radar operator's seat
58 Tactical co-ordinator's seat
59 Display consoles
60 IFF aerial
61 Starboard engine nacelle fairing
62 Outer wing panel joint
63 Starboard wing integral fuel tank; total system capacity 5,086 Imp gal (23 120 l)
64 Landing/search light
65 Wing stores pylons
66 AM 39 Exocet air-to-surface missiles
67 Leading edge pneumatic de-icing boots
68 Wing access panels
69 UHF aerial
70 Wing tip ECM pod
71 Starboard navigation light
72 Static dischargers
73 Starboard outer aileron
74 Starboard inner aileron
75 Aileron mass balance weights
76 Aileron hydraulic jack
77 Spoiler/airbrake panels, open
78 Spoiler hydraulic jacks
79 Outboard, two-segment double-slotted flaps
80 Flap screw jacks
81 Starboard engine exhaust nozzle
82 Anti collision light
83 Wing/fuselage attachment main frames
84 Sonobuoy display consoles
85 Teleprinters
86 Sonobuoy operators' seats (two)
87 Electronics racks cooling air ducting
88 Wing centre-section carry through
89 Central flap hydraulic motor
90 Starboard escape hatch
91 DF aerial
92 Life raft stowage
93 Port escape hatch
94 Pressure floor beam construction
95 Bomb-bay door hydraulic motor

96 Crew rest area seating, port and starboard
97 Galley compartment
98 Dining table
99 Toilet compartment
100 Wardrobe
101 Curtained doorway
102 Rear observers' seats, port and starboard
103 Binocular mounting rail
104 Observation bubble window
105 Cabin doorway
106 Rear pressure bulkhead
107 Flare stowage rack
108 Sonobuoy stowage rack, maximum load 72 A or A3 sonobuoys
109 Rear fuselage frame and stringer construction
110 Tailplane mounting bulkhead
111 Fin root fillet
112 Tailplane leading edge de-icing boots
113 Starboard HF aerial cable
114 Starboard tailplane
115 Starboard elevator
116 Static dischargers
117 Fin leading edge de-icing boot
118 Fin construction
119 Fin honeycomb skin panels
120 Fin tip ECM aerial housing
121 Static dischargers
122 Rudder mass balance weights
123 Rudder construction
124 Rudder hydraulic jack
125 Tail navigation light
126 Tailboom extension
127 MAD boom
128 MAD detector head
129 Port elevator construction
130 Elevator hydraulic jack
131 Tailplane construction
132 Tailplane honeycomb skin panels
133 Leading edge de-icing boot
134 Port HF aerial cable
135 Rudder and elevator control rods
136 Rear entry hatch
137 Extending boarding ladder
138 Tail bumper
139 Tailplane trim feel units
140 Camera
141 Sonobuoy/flare launcher, in-flight loadable
142 Flare launcher door
143 AM 39 Exocet air-to-surface missile

144 Aft bomb bay door
145 Bomb door actuating mechanism
146 Inboard double slotted flap
147 Centre wing panel construction
148 Port engine tailpipe
149 Exhaust nozzle
150 Flap guide rails
151 Inner wing integral fuel tank bay
152 Outer wing panel bolted skin joint
153 Rear spar
154 Port airbrake/spoiler panels
155 Outboard two-segment double-slotted flaps
156 Flap rib construction
157 Aileron rib construction
158 Port inboard aileron
159 Port outboard aileron
160 Static dischargers
161 Wing tip ECM pod
162 Port navigation light
163 Wing rib construction
164 UHF aerial
165 Pitot tube
166 Port wing stores pylons
167 AM 39 Exocet air-to-surface missiles
168 Leading-edge de-icing boots
169 Aluminium honeycomb wing skin panels
170 Wing centre spar
171 Outer wing panel integral fuel tank bay
172 Leading edge honeycomb skin panels
173 Front spar
174 Port landing/search light
175 Twin mainwheels
176 Main undercarriage leg strut
177 Undercarriage leg pivot fixing
178 Mainwheel leg doors
179 Hydraulic retraction jack
180 Mainwheel bay doors, closed
181 Main undercarriage wheel bay
182 Heat shrouded exhaust pipe
183 Port engine nacelle construction
184 Engine cowling doors
185 Fireproof bulkhead
186 Engine bleed air and pre-cooler exhaust louvres
187 Rolls-Royce Tyne RTy.20 Mk 21 turboprop engine
188 Ventral oil cooler duct
189 De-iced engine air intake
190 Oil cooler ram air intake
191 Propeller hub pitch change mechanism
192 Spinner
193 Four-bladed constant speed propeller
194 Propeller blade root de-icing cuffs
195 Mk 46 lightweight torpedo
196 Depth charge

In May 1981 the first prototype of a revised version of the Atlantic took off for its initial flight. This is known as the Atlantic Génération 2 and has been developed to provide the French Navy with a replacement for the Atlantic and remaining Neptunes. Production deliveries will start in 1987 and 42 are required initially. These, too, are being constructed by the international consortium. The Atlantic Génération 2 will offer improved serviceability and maintenance. Secondary duties, as for the standard Atlantic, include fishery protection, minelaying, transport, AEW and SAR. The Atlantic's search radar is carried in a retractable radome under the forward fuselage.

In 1958 Lockheed was announced the winner of a U.S. Navy competition to provide a new anti-submarine aircraft, based on an existing aeroplane. Lockheed's proposal was based on the Electra airliner and became known as the Orion.

The initial production version was the P-3A, first going to VP-8 Squadron, U.S. Navy, in 1962. Today the P-3A is flown only by the U.S. Naval Reserve and in small number by the Spanish Air Force. The P-3B introduced more powerful 4,910-ehp Allison T56-A-14 turboprop engines. The U.S.N. received 124. All remaining P-3Bs can carry Bullpup air-to-surface tactical missiles as part of their armament but some were converted into EP-3B electronic countermeasures aircraft (followed by EP-3Es). P-3Bs are also flown in Australia, New Zealand and Norway, although the R.A.A.F.'s P-3Bs are being superseded by P-3Cs.

Lockheed CP-140 Aurora in the markings of the Canadian Armed Forces.

Soviet Ilyushin Il-38
May, photographed by
the Swedish Air Force.

The P-3C represents an advanced version of the Orion with important changes to the avionics. Power is provided by four engines similar to those of the P-3B, allowing a maximum speed of 761 km/h (473 mph). The large weapons bay can accommodate a 2,000-lb or three 1,000-lb mines, or eight torpedoes, up to eight depth bombs, or a joint weapon load of four torpedoes and two nuclear depth bombs. Torpedoes, mines, rockets or Harpoon anti-shipping missiles can be carried under the wings. More than 200 P-3Cs have been delivered to the U.S. Navy to date, and others have been exported to Australia and the Netherlands.

P-3C improvement updates have been incorporated into aircraft under production since the mid-1970s; the latest to improve anti-submarine avionics becomes standard from the spring of 1984. The second of these updates, which includes avionics changes and provision for the Harpoon missile, can be found on three U.S.-built P-3Cs delivered to the J.M.S.D.F. Further P-3Cs are being delivered to the J.M.S.D.F., all coming from the Kawasaki works. Also, under the designation CP-140 Aurora, the Canadian Armed Forces received 18 modified examples of the Orion between 1980 and 1981, each incorporating the data-processing ability of the Lockheed Viking and similar avionics.

The Soviet Navy operates several aircraft in maritime roles, some of which have been mentioned previously in this chapter. An aircraft used by the Soviet Naval Air Force about which little is known is the anti-submarine version of the Antonov

An-12 cargo transport (NATO *Cub*). It is reported to carry a nose radome and tailboom similar to those of the M-12 amphibian, and is probably still under evaluation. One of the force's main maritime patrol and ASW aeroplanes is the Ilyushin Il-38. This aircraft, known to NATO as *May*, is based on the Il-18 airliner and in most respects can be viewed as the Soviet equivalent of the U.S. Navy's Orion. However, it is believed that far fewer *Mays* are in operational service than Orions – probably between 50 and 60. This reflects the importance of the maritime versions of standard Soviet bombers and the M-12. A number of *Mays* are also used by the Indian Navy, with whom it is said to be regarded as an excellent aircraft.

Like the airliner, the Il-38 is powered by four 4,250-ehp Ivchenko AI-20M turboprop engines. It carries its search radar in an underfuselage radome aft of the nosewheel and houses MAD in a tailboom. An ECM or electronic intelligence (elint) aircraft, probably similar in role to the British Nimrod R.Mk 1, is also operational (as is an elint version of the An-12). This ECM aircraft is known to NATO under the revised airliner reporting name *Coot-A*. The usual range of weapons is carried and its maximum cruising speed is thought to be about 644 km/h (400 mph).

GAF Nomad Searchmaster L, the more sophisticated version of the Searchmaster with an undernose radome.

Small but effective

There are many smaller maritime aircraft produced around the world. All are based on existing aeroplanes and are suited ideally for coastal and medium-range duties with forces requiring cost-effective aircraft. From Australia comes the Government Aircraft Factories (GAF) Nomad Searchmaster B coastal patrol aircraft and the more sophisticated Searchmaster L. Both are powered by two 420-shp Allison 250-B17C turboprop engines and differ externally in having search radar in the fuselage nose and in an undernose radome respectively.

Operators include the Indonesian Navy. Up to 227 kg (500 lb) of weapons can be carried on four underwing stations.

EMBRAER of Brazil contributes the EMB-111, based on its successful EMB-110 Bandeirante. In service with the Brazilian and Gabonese air forces and the Chilean Navy, it is powered by two 750-shp Pratt & Whitney Aircraft of Canada PT6A-34 turboprop engines and can be armed on four underwing pylons. Search radar is housed in a nose radome.

The maritime version of the de Havilland Canada DHC-6 Twin Otter Series 300M, previously mentioned in Chapter Five, is

Brazilian Air Force EMBRAER EMB-111 maritime surveillance aircraft, fitted with a searchlight on the starboard wing and carrying 5-in HVAR rockets.

153

known simply as the Twin Otter 300 MR. It
has a search radar in an undernose radome
and can also be armed.

The French Dassault-Breguet Mystère-
Falcon 20 forms the basis of the U.S. Coast
Guard's HU-25A Guardian medium-range
surveillance aircraft and the French Navy's
Gardian maritime patrol aircraft. The
Guardian is powered by two 2 468-kg (5,440-
lb)st Garrett ATF3-6-2C turbofan engines
and the first of 41 was delivered in early 1982.
The French Gardian has two 2 359-kg
(5,200-lb)st ATF3-6A-4C turbofans. Both
can cruise at Mach 0.8.

A version of the German Dornier 128-2
has now joined the maritime patrol aircraft
market, powered by two 380-hp Avco
Lycoming IGSO-540-A1E piston engines
and with a search radar in an undernose
radome. The endurance of this aircraft is
nearly 17 hours.

The Israel Aircraft Industries Westwind I
business jet has a maritime derivative known
as the 1124N Sea Scan. Power is provided by
two 1 678-kg (3,700-lb)st Garrett TFE731-
3-1G turbofans. A search radar is housed in a
nose radome and for anti-submarine duties
ESM and MAD are employed. Armament,

Right: IAI Sea Scan, a military maritime version of the Westwind I business aircraft.

Below: Fokker F27 Maritime flown by the Royal Netherlands Naval Air Service.

carried on fuselage pylons, can include torpedoes or air-to-surface missiles for anti-shipping missions. The Israeli Navy operates a small number.

Two Italian aircraft fit into the maritime category. The first is the SIAI-Marchetti SF.260 Sea Warrior, a surveillance and SAR variant of the Warrior mentioned in a previous chapter. The second is the R.Piaggio P.166-DL3-MAR, a medium-range surveillance aircraft capable of carrying weapons under its wings. Power is provided by two 599-shp Avco Lycoming LTP 101-600 turboprop engines. A search radar is among the equipment and avionics options.

The Fokker F27 Maritime version of the Friendship is in service in the Netherlands, but the majority of the 14 so far delivered are operated in Angola, Peru, the Philippines, Spain and Thailand. Depending upon requirements, a search radar can be carried in an underfuselage radome. Power is provided by two 2,320-shp Rolls-Royce Dart Mk 536-7R turboprop engines. Like

some of the other aircraft detailed, roles can include surveillance, SAR, coastal patrol and fishery protection.

The Spanish CASA C-212 Series 200 Aviocar is offered in a maritime patrol and ASW version which, like the STOL utility transport, is powered by two 900-shp Garrett TPE331-10-501C turboprop engines. It can house a search radar in a modified nose and other equipment can include ESM and MAD. Weapons are carried on underwing pylons. So far 19 have been ordered, 12 for the Spanish Air Force and the government, four for the Uruguayan Air Force and three for the Venezuelan Navy.

The successful HS 748 airliner was chosen by British Aerospace when it, too, decided to produce a medium-range maritime patrol aircraft. Known as the Coastguarder, it can perform many missions, including anti-submarine and ASV, fishery protection, SAR and oil-rig patrol. Two 2,280-ehp Rolls-Royce Dart RDa.7 Mk 535-2 turbo-prop engines power the Coastguarder,

Uruguayan Air Force-operated CASA C-212 Series 200 maritime patrol aircraft.

157

which, in an ASW role, can carry homing torpedoes, depth-charges and missiles. Optional avionics and equipment includes ESM, MAD and ECM.

Military versions of the Pilatus Britten-Norman Islander are known as the Defender and Maritime Defender. The Defender can be used for many roles, both armed and unarmed, including light attack, SAR forward air control and troop transport. The Maritime Defender, as its name suggests, is basically similar but has a larger search radar in an enlarged nose. Fishery protection, SAR, coastal and oil rig patrol are some of its roles.

In the United States, Beechcraft has modelled its Maritime Patrol 200T on the Super King Air 200 passenger and executive light transport. Powered by two 850-shp Pratt & Whitney Aircraft of Canada PT6A-42 turboprop engines, it carries search radar in an underfuselage radome. The largest

Right: British Aerospace HS 748 Coastguarder demonstrator.

Below: The Pilatus Britten-Norman Maritime Defender can be identified by its larger nose which houses search radar.

number are currently operated by Japan's Maritime Safety Agency, which has 13, but other users include the Uruguayan Navy.

Indonesia operates three Boeing Model 737-200s as passenger transports and maritime surveillance aircraft, each carrying airborne multi-mission radar, and one Lockheed C-130H-MP maritime patrol/SAR version of the Hercules. Three other C-130H-MPs are used by the Royal Malaysian Air Force. A version of the Gates Learjet 35A executive jet, known as the Sea Patrol, is operated by the Finnish Air Force. The Sea Patrol was conceived for several maritime roles, including anti-submarine. Finnish aircraft are, however, used primarily as target tugs, although sea patrol and other duties are within their capability. Power is provided by two 1588-kg (3,500-lb)st Garrett TFE731-2-2B turbofan engines. Avionics and equipment for the Sea Patrol can include a sea surveillance radar in an underfuselage radome, with all-round sweep.

Finnish Air Force Special Missions Learjet, based on the Learjet 35A, prior to delivery.

8 The Back-up Force

An air force is only as good as its pilots. Given the most modern equipment, a force without well-trained pilots cannot hope to meet the challenge of combat with success. As important in different ways are the early-warning aircraft that give a defending force the time to prepare, the reconnaissance aircraft that can make possible the most advantageous disposition of forces, electronic countermeasures (ECM) aircraft to intercept and jam enemy communications and render anti-aircraft radars useless, transport aircraft, and flight-refuelling tankers. The latter, as demonstrated during the Falklands crisis, can provide an air force with its only means of getting to a trouble spot well outside its normal sphere of operations without delay.

As this chapter does not deal with combat aircraft in the strictest sense, albeit on the understanding that many of the jet trainers and others have important secondary combat capabilities, a brief mention only is made of each aircraft type included. Further, because of the very large number of different types of aircraft in each category that are in service around the world, only a representative few can be described in any detail and illustrated.

Beginning with trainers, there are three main categories. The primary trainer is the aircraft on which an instructor gives a pupil pilot his initial flight instruction. Typical of the piston-engined trainers with side-by-side seating are the Finnish Valmet L-70 Miltrainer (known to the Finnish Air Force

The latest U.S.A.F. tanker is the McDonnell Douglas KC-10A Extender, seen here refuelling a McDonnell Douglas F-15 Eagle.

ZA141

Above: One of the
R.A.F.'s new VC 10
K.Mk 2 flight refuelling
tankers, converted from
a commercial airliner.

Left: A U.S.A.F. Boeing
KC-135 Stratotanker
refuels a Boeing E-4
advanced airborne
command post.

Right: Finnish Air Force Valmet Vinka trainer.

Below: R.A.F.-operated British Aerospace SA-3-120 Bulldog Model 121.

Right: Yakovlev Yak-52, built in Romania by IAv Bacau.

Left: The Cessna T-41 Mescalero two- or four-seat trainer is used by the U.S. Army and Air Force and by services abroad.

as the Vinka) and the British Aerospace Bulldog. Both can be armed with weapons totalling more than 272 kg (600 lb) in weight. A piston-engined primary trainer with tandem seating is the Soviet Yakovlev Yak-52, now in production in Romania. A U.S. equivalent is the Beechcraft T-34, which began life in the 1950s as a piston-engined primary trainer but has been built over recent years in T-34C turboprop form. Weapon load is 544 kg (1,200 lb).

After a pupil pilot has completed flying on a primary trainer, he or she can progress onto a basic trainer. These normally have increased power and performance and tandem seating. Many of the newest trainers fit this category, including the turboprop-powered Brazilian EMBRAER EMB-312 Tucano, the Chilean/U.S. piston-engined IndAer (Piper) PA-28R-300 Pillan and the Swiss turboprop-powered Pilatus PC-7 Turbo-Trainer. All can be armed. The

Overleaf: EMBRAER EMB-312 Tucano prototype, known to the Brazilian Air Force as the YT-27. This Tucano carries rocket launchers under its wings.

163

Swedish Saab-91 Safir is a typical older-style basic trainer with a piston engine, and both the North American T-6 Texan and T-28 Trojan remain in use as basic trainers and light attack aircraft.

Two of the aircraft that can combine primary and basic training are the British NDN 1 Firecracker and the German RFB Fantrainer 400 and higher-powered 600. The Firecracker is powered by a piston engine and can carry armament of 16 81-mm rockets. The Fantrainer is also a tandem two-seater but has a turboshaft engine driving a five-blade ducted fan.

There are several turbojet-powered basic trainers in service, some advanced trainers, and others that combine basic and advanced training and actual combat roles. The term advanced trainer covers aircraft that can simulate actual combat duty. The Japanese Mitsubishi T-2 turbofan-powered advanced trainer and the turbojet-powered U.S. Northrop T-38A Talon basic trainer are supersonic. The oldest turbojet-powered advanced trainers are the U.S. Lockheed T-33 and the Soviet Mikoyan-Gurevich MiG-15UTI, both tandem two-seaters based on early single-seat fighters. Far more recent is the Chinese Shenyang JJ-5, similar in configuration to the MiG-15UTI but based on the MiG-17/J-5 single-seater.

Above: The civil registered NDN 1 Firecracker prototype, armed with 16 SURA 81-mm rockets.

Facing page: Swiss Air Force Pilatus PC-7/CH Turbo-Trainers photographed during a formation training flight.

Right: RFB Fantrainer 400 in camouflage.

166

Right: North American T-6 Texan in service with the Dominican Air Force.

Above: J.A.S.D.F. Mitsubishi T-2 supersonic trainer at the Hyakuri air base.

Right: Mikoyan-Gurevich MiG-15UTI (second from top) in the unlikely company of a fellow Egyptian MiG-21 and U.S.A.F. A-10A and F-16A during the exercise Bright Star 82.

Above: One of the
U.S.A.F.'s Northrop
T-38A Talon trainers
undergoes engine tests.

Left: Italian Air Force
Aermacchi MB 339A
trainer.

Plate VII

CASA C-101 Aviojet

cutaway drawing key

1 Pitot tube
2 Nose cone
3 ILS aerial
4 Nose compartment construction
5 Oxygen bottles
6 Nosewheel bay
7 Electrical access panel
8 Nosewheel doors
9 Radio and electrical equipment bay
10 Flush air intake
11 Nosewheel jack
12 Dowty Rotol nose undercarriage leg
13 Non-steerable nosewheel
14 Cockpit pressure bulkhead
15 Pressurisation valve
16 Frameless windshield
17 Sight unit (ground attack rôle)
18 Instrument panel shroud
19 Rudder pedals
20 Communications aerial
21 Control column
22 Cockpit floor level
23 Forward fuselage frame construction
24 Engine throttle control
25 Cockpit canopy external latches

26 Front cockpit rear bulkhead
27 Pilot's side console panel
28 Student pilot's Martin-Baker Mk E 10 zero-zero ejection seat
29 Ejection seat headrest
30 Side hinged cockpit canopy covers
31 Instructor's windshield

32 Rear cockpit instrument panel shroud
33 Inter-canopy bridge section
34 Rear cockpit floor level
35 Electrical equipment bay
36 Oxygen bottle
37 Air conditioning plant
38 Airbrake hydraulic jack
39 Port intake
40 Rear pressure bulkhead
41 Instructor's Martin-Baker ejection seat

42 Safety harness
43 Starboard integral wing fuel tank, capacity 76 Imp gal (345 l)
44 Starboard wing pylons
45 Cockpit canopy open position
46 AGM-65 Maverick television guided air-to-ground missile
47 Fuel tank filler cap
48 Starboard navigation light
49 Starboard aileron
50 Fixed aileron tab
51 Aileron hydraulic jack
52 Aileron control rods
53 Flap guide rail
54 Flap torque shaft
55 Starboard flap
56 Communications aerial
57 Control rod linkages

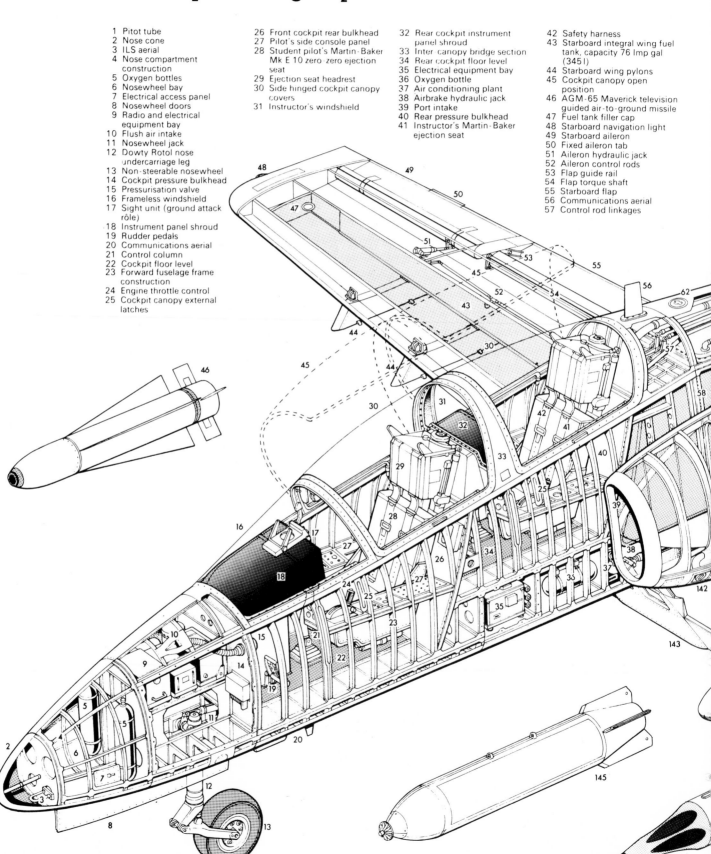

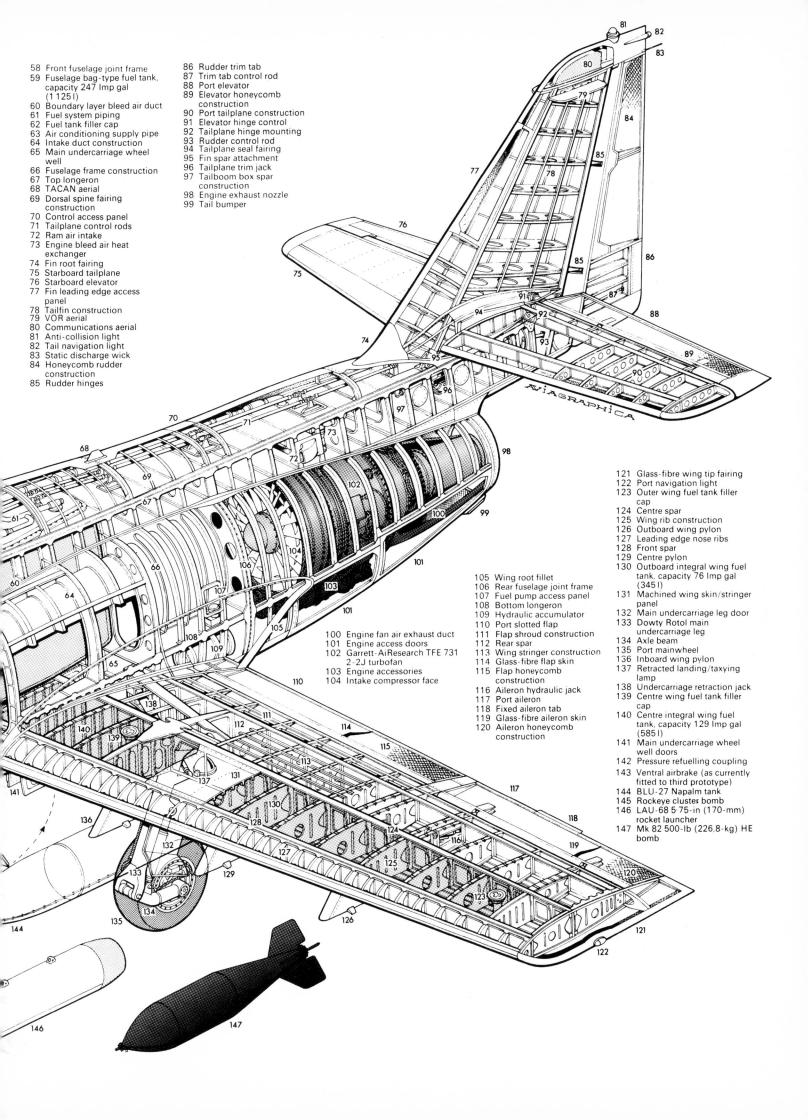

58 Front fuselage joint frame
59 Fuselage bag-type fuel tank, capacity 247 Imp gal (1 125 l)
60 Boundary layer bleed air duct
61 Fuel system piping
62 Fuel tank filler cap
63 Air conditioning supply pipe
64 Intake duct construction
65 Main undercarriage wheel well
66 Fuselage frame construction
67 Top longeron
68 TACAN aerial
69 Dorsal spine fairing construction
70 Control access panel
71 Tailplane control rods
72 Ram air intake
73 Engine bleed air heat exchanger
74 Fin root fairing
75 Starboard tailplane
76 Starboard elevator
77 Fin leading edge access panel
78 Tailfin construction
79 VOR aerial
80 Communications aerial
81 Anti-collision light
82 Tail navigation light
83 Static discharge wick
84 Honeycomb rudder construction
85 Rudder hinges

86 Rudder trim tab
87 Trim tab control rod
88 Port elevator
89 Elevator honeycomb construction
90 Port tailplane construction
91 Elevator hinge control
92 Tailplane hinge mounting
93 Rudder control rod
94 Tailplane seal fairing
95 Fin spar attachment
96 Tailplane trim jack
97 Tailboom box spar construction
98 Engine exhaust nozzle
99 Tail bumper

100 Engine fan air exhaust duct
101 Engine access doors
102 Garrett-AiResearch TFE 731 2-2J turbofan
103 Engine accessories
104 Intake compressor face

105 Wing root fillet
106 Rear fuselage joint frame
107 Fuel pump access panel
108 Bottom longeron
109 Hydraulic accumulator
110 Port slotted flap
111 Flap shroud construction
112 Rear spar
113 Wing stringer construction
114 Glass-fibre flap skin
115 Flap honeycomb construction
116 Aileron hydraulic jack
117 Port aileron
118 Fixed aileron tab
119 Glass-fibre aileron skin
120 Aileron honeycomb construction

121 Glass-fibre wing tip fairing
122 Port navigation light
123 Outer wing fuel tank filler cap
124 Centre spar
125 Wing rib construction
126 Outboard wing pylon
127 Leading edge nose ribs
128 Front spar
129 Centre pylon
130 Outboard integral wing fuel tank, capacity 76 Imp gal (345 l)
131 Machined wing skin/stringer panel
132 Main undercarriage leg door
133 Dowty Rotol main undercarriage leg
134 Axle beam
135 Port mainwheel
136 Inboard wing pylon
137 Retracted landing/taxying lamp
138 Undercarriage retraction jack
139 Centre wing fuel tank filler cap
140 Centre integral wing fuel tank, capacity 129 Imp gal (585 l)
141 Main undercarriage wheel well doors
142 Pressure refuelling coupling
143 Ventral airbrake (as currently fitted to third prototype)
144 BLU-27 Napalm tank
145 Rockeye cluster bomb
146 LAU-68 5·75-in (170-mm) rocket launcher
147 Mk 82 500-lb (226,8-kg) HE bomb

Right: First prototype SIAI-Marchetti S.211 lightweight and low-cost basic trainer and light attack aircraft.

Facing page, top: R.A.F. Hawk T.Mk 1, one of 90 modified to enable it to perform an emergency air-defence role carrying AIM-9L Sidewinder missiles.

Right: Iraqi Air Force Aero L-39Z Albatros, the armed version of the L-39 for weapon system training and light attack.

Facing page, bottom: Line-up of Yugoslav Air Force SOKO G2-A Galeb trainers.

Below: Alpha Jets in service with Groupement-Ecole 314, French Air Force, at Tours.

Some of the most modern basic and advanced trainers have the much-favoured tandem cockpit layout with the rear instructor's seat elevated for excellent forward vision. The new Argentine FMA IA 63 is so arranged and combines basic and advanced training. The Italian Aermacchi MB 339A, built to supersede the MB 326 (which has near level tandem seats), is similar in configuration and role, as is the fellow Italian SIAI-Marchetti S.211. Others are the Czech Aero L-39 Albatros, designed to follow the L-29 Delfin; the French/German Dassault-Breguet/Dornier Alpha Jet; the Spanish CASA C-101 Aviojet; the British Aerospace Hawk; and the Yugoslav SOKO Super Galeb (Galeb replacement). All of these are either capable of secondary attack duties or have versions assigned actual attack roles. In the case of the Hawk,

Right: The largest
operational Soviet
transport aircraft is the
turboprop-powered
Antonov An-22 Antheus
(NATO *Cock*), with a
wing span of 64.4 metres
(211 feet 4 inches).
Cargo is loaded via a
rear fuselage ramp. It is
reported that the An-22
will soon be joined by a
new transport similar to
the U.S. Galaxy.

Below right: Saab 1050e
light attack aircraft and
trainers, examples of the
export version of the
Saab 105. These are in
Austrian service.

Below: The Lockheed
C-130 Hercules is
operated in 55 countries.
Payload for the C-130H
is 19727 kg (43,399 lb),
or 92 troops/64
paratroops. This
U.S.A.F. C-130 airdrops
a Sheridan tank during a
NATO exercise, in a
technique known as
LAPES (Low Altitude
Parachute Extraction
System).

Above: The Soviet Antonov An-12 (NATO *Cub*) is a widely operated cargo transport, roughly equivalent to the U.S. Lockheed Hercules. Accommodation is provided for 20000 kg (44,000 lb) of cargo or 100 paratroops. Two 23-mm guns are carried in a tail turret. This An-12 belongs to the Egyptian Air Force.

Left: The huge lift-up nose of a U.S.A.F. Lockheed C-5A Galaxy makes loading even the largest of cargoes a straight-forward job.

173

Right: The Grumman
C-2A Greyhound is used
by the U.S. Navy to
carry cargo or personnel
from shore to aircraft
carriers in COD (Carrier
On-board Delivery)
duties. Maximum cargo
is 6818 kg (15,000 lb).

Below: The U.S.A.F.'s
McDonnell Douglas
C-9A Nightingale is
aptly named for its role
of aeromedical airlift. It
can accommodate 40
stretchers.

Above: The de
Havilland Canada
DHC-5 Buffalo is a twin-
turboprop transport
capable of STOL
operations. Accommo-
dation is for 8182 kg
(18,000 lb) of cargo or
41 troops. It is operated
by the Canadian Armed
Forces as the CC-115
transport and SAR
aircraft.

Left: The U.S.A.F.'s
Lockheed C-141B
StarLifter is between the
Hercules and Galaxy in
size and is capable of
carrying 41 310 kg
(90,880 lb) of cargo or
troops/paratroops.

90 in R.A.F. service are capable of carrying Sidewinder missiles in an emergency air defence role. Of course the side-by-side basic jet trainer is still very much in use and includes the Swedish Saab 105, the Indian HAL HJT-16 Kiran, the Canadian Canadair CL-41 Tutor, the U.S. Cessna T-37 and the British BAC Jet Provost. Interestingly, the jet trainer destined to replace the T-37 with the U.S.A.F., the Fairchild Republic NGT (military designated T-46A), is also a side-by-side two-seater.

Transports in military service can range from single-engined light aircraft to the massive Lockheed C-5 Galaxy operated by the U.S.A.F. The largest aircraft in the world, the Galaxy has a wing span of 67.88 metres (222 feet 8½ inches). It can accommodate troops, tanks and other vehicles, helicopters, missiles and other loads up to a total weight of about 100 228 kg (220,967 lb), yet still fly a distance of 6000 km (3,749 miles). Various military transports are illustrated, along with troop, cargo and flying-crane transport helicopters.

Right: The IAI Arava is a twin-turboprop light STOL transport. Its rear fuselage can swing open to provide access to the main cabin. Payload is 2351 kg (5,172 lb) of cargo or 24 troops/16 paratroops.

Facing page: This Italian Air Force Aeritalia G222 twin-turboprop transport accommodates 9000 kg (19,800 lb) of cargo or 53 troops/42 paratroops.

Right: The Transall C-160 is a French- and German-developed transport, operated by these and other air forces. These Luftwaffe C-160Ds can carry 17 000 kg (37,478 lb) of cargo or 93 troops/88 paratroops.

Right: The Kawasaki
C-1 is the standard
transport of the
J.A.S.D.F. Powered by
two turbofan engines, it
can carry 11 900 kg
(26,235 lb) of cargo or
60 troops/45 paratroops.
This C-1 is operated by
the 401st Squadron.

Above: Once the largest
helicopter in the world,
the Soviet Mil Mi-6
(NATO *Hook*) has a
rotor diameter of 35
metres (114 feet 10
inches) and can
accommodate 12 000 kg
(26,455 lb) of cargo or
90 troops internally.

Right: The Short
Skyvan STOL transport
is capable of carrying
2 722 kg (6,000 lb) of
cargo or 22 troops/16
paratroops.

178

Left: The Sikorsky S-64 Skycrane is known to the U.S. Army as the CH-54 Tarhe. It is a flying crane helicopter, which can carry a slung cargo (as shown) or can have a flat platform or enclosed pod fixed under the fuselage for vehicles, troops, and other loads.

Left: Aérospatiale SA 330 Puma HC.Mk 1, operated by the R.A.F. as a training helicopter. Pumas are also used by the R.A.F., the French services and others for assault and attack duties, with maximum accommodation for 20 troops.

Right: The Westland 30 is a new twin-engined and larger development of the successful Lynx, accommodating up to 17 troops. Here the demonstrator lands a mortar unit.

Right: The Sikorsky UH-60A Black Hawk is becoming the U.S. Army's standard combat assault transport helicopter, accommodating 11 troops. Here Black Hawks drop men of the 82nd Airborne Brigade.

Right: A Boeing Vertol Chinook HC.Mk 1 in R.A.F markings air-lifts a 9-ton armoured reconnaissance vehicle. As one of several operators of the Chinook, the R.A.F. uses its Chinooks for troop (44) and logistical support.

Left: The Westland Wessex, a derivative of the Sikorsky S-58, dates from 1958. This is one of two Wessex HCC.Mk 4s operated by the Queen's Flight, R.A.F.

Below left: Sikorsky CH-53E Super Stallion, operated by the U.S. Navy as a triple-engined multi-purpose helicopter. Internal and external payloads are 13607 kg (30,000 lb) and 14515 kg (32,000 lb) respectively, or 55 troops can be accommodated in the main cabin.

Electronic warfare

AWACS (airborne warning and control system) aircraft are assuming an ever more important role. These are used not only for the detection of hostile aircraft and missiles flying at low, medium and high altitude and at long range, but are employed for directing friendly interceptors onto them or directing tactical attack aircraft towards their targets. Some can also perform maritime surveillance and tasks like air traffic control.

All but the British Aerospace Nimrod AEW.Mk 3 are easily identifiable by their huge rotating surveillance rotodomes car-

ried above their fuselages. The smallest AWACS aircraft is the U.S. Grumman E-2 Hawkeye, designed as a carrier-based aircraft and in standard service with the U.S. Navy. Land-based examples are also operated by Israel and Japan.

The Boeing E-3 Sentry is the U.S.A.F.'s AWACS aircraft, based on a Boeing Model 707 airframe. It is also in service with NATO in Europe. The Soviet equivalent is the Tupolev Tu-126, based on the Tu-114 turboprop-powered airliner and known to NATO as *Moss*. An AWACS based on the Soviet Ilyushin Il-76 turbofan-powered freighter is in service (NATO *Mainstay*).

Bell UH-1 Iroquois general-purpose helicopters are in widespread use around the world, although Black Hawks are gradually taking over as the primary assault helicopters of the U.S. Army. Accommodation is for 1760 kg (3,880 lb) of cargo or up to 14 troops. These are UH-1s of the 52nd Aviation Battalion on exercise in 1980.

Right: The first Boeing E-3A Sentry AWACS aircraft for NATO operation.

Below: Soviet Tupolev Tu-126 AWACS aircraft.

Above: R.A.F. Nimrod AEW.Mk 3.

Left: A land-based example of the Grumman Hawkeye is this E-2C operated by the J.A.S.D.F.

183

Plate VIII

British Aerospace Nimrod AEW Mk 3

cutaway drawing key

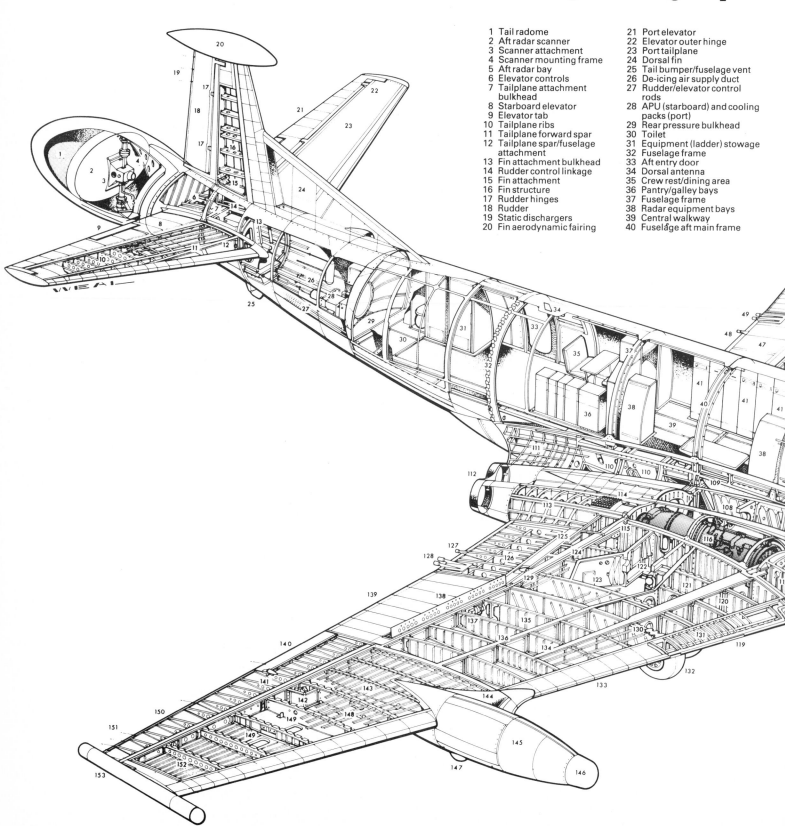

1 Tail radome
2 Aft radar scanner
3 Scanner attachment
4 Scanner mounting frame
5 Aft radar bay
6 Elevator controls
7 Tailplane attachment bulkhead
8 Starboard elevator
9 Elevator tab
10 Tailplane ribs
11 Tailplane forward spar
12 Tailplane spar/fuselage attachment
13 Fin attachment bulkhead
14 Rudder control linkage
15 Fin attachment
16 Fin structure
17 Rudder hinges
18 Rudder
19 Static dischargers
20 Fin aerodynamic fairing
21 Port elevator
22 Elevator outer hinge
23 Port tailplane
24 Dorsal fin
25 Tail bumper/fuselage vent
26 De-icing air supply duct
27 Rudder/elevator control rods
28 APU (starboard) and cooling packs (port)
29 Rear pressure bulkhead
30 Toilet
31 Equipment (ladder) stowage
32 Fuselage frame
33 Aft entry door
34 Dorsal antenna
35 Crew rest/dining area
36 Pantry/galley bays
37 Fuselage frame
38 Radar equipment bays
39 Central walkway
40 Fuselage aft main frame

41 ESM racks
42 Emergency escape window panels (port and starboard)
43 Undercarriage bay upper surface panel
44 Machined inboard wing skin
45 Rear spar
46 Flap jack fairing
47 Flap inboard section
48 Fuel vent
49 Fuel dump pipes
50 Flap outer section
51 Outer airbrake (upper and lower surfaces)
52 Port wing integral fuel tanks
53 Skin butt-joint rib
54 Wing outer fuel tanks
55 Aileron tab
56 Aileron tab hinge fairing
57 Port aileron
58 Static dischargers
59 EWSM port wingtip aerial
60 Wing leading-edge
61 Fixed slot
62 External fuel tank
63 Wing tank bumper

64 Leading-edge flow spoilers
65 Integral fuel tank
66 Fuselage forward main frame
67 Mission communications rack
68 Five tactical crew seats: from front (right) to rear, communications control officer, EWSM operator and three air direction officers
69 Seat rails
70 Window
71 Tactical situation display consoles
72 Tactical control officer
73 Dorsal antennae
74 Avionics modules
75 Crew entry door
76 Forward bulkhead
77 Emergency escape hatch
78 Navigator's station
79 Instrument consoles
80 Flight engineer's station
81 Co-pilot's seat
82 Eyebrow window
83 Cockpit roof structure
84 Pilot's seat
85 Windscreen panels

86 Windscreen wipers
87 Control console
88 Instrument panel
89 Support frames
90 Forward pressure bulkhead
91 Nose radar bay
92 Scanner mounting frame
93 Scanner attachment
94 Nose radar scanner
95 Nose radome
96 Fuselage/radome fairing
97 Twin nosewheels
98 Nosewheel leg strut
99 Nosewheel well
100 Underfloor equipment bay
101 Fuel cells (3) under cabin floor
102 Taxi light
103 Engine air intakes
104 Ram air to heat exchangers
105 Heat exchangers
106 Forward spar/fuselage attachment
107 Inboard engine bay (engine omitted)
108 Engine mounting frame
109 Rear spar/fuselage attachment
110 Life-raft stowage
111 Wingroot fillet structure
112 Exhaust pipes
113 Tailpipe frames
114 Thrust reverser (outboard engines only)
115 Rear spar frames
116 Rolls-Royce Spey 250 turbofan
117 Intake duct frames
118 Landing lamp

119 Leading-edge flow spoilers
120 Wing integral fuel tank
121 Forward spar
122 Main undercarriage pivot
123 Main undercarriage well
124 Rear spar
125 Auxiliary spar
126 Flap structure
127 Fuel vent
128 Fuel dump pipes
129 Flap jack fairing
130 Wing skin joint strap
131 Leading-edge de-icing ducts
132 Four-wheel main undercarriage bogie
133 Wing leading-edge
134 Abbreviated spar
135 Integral fuel tanks
136 Centre spar
137 Airbrake mechanism
138 Outer airbrake (upper and lower surfaces)
139 Flap outer section
140 Aileron tab
141 Aileron tab hinge fairing
142 Aileron hinge control linkage
143 Wing stringers
144 Fixed slot
145 External fuel tank
146 Weather radar
147 Wing tank bumper
148 Outboard fuel tank bays
149 Fuel tank access panels
150 Starboard aileron
151 Static dischargers
152 Outboard wing structure
153 EWSM starboard wingtip aerial

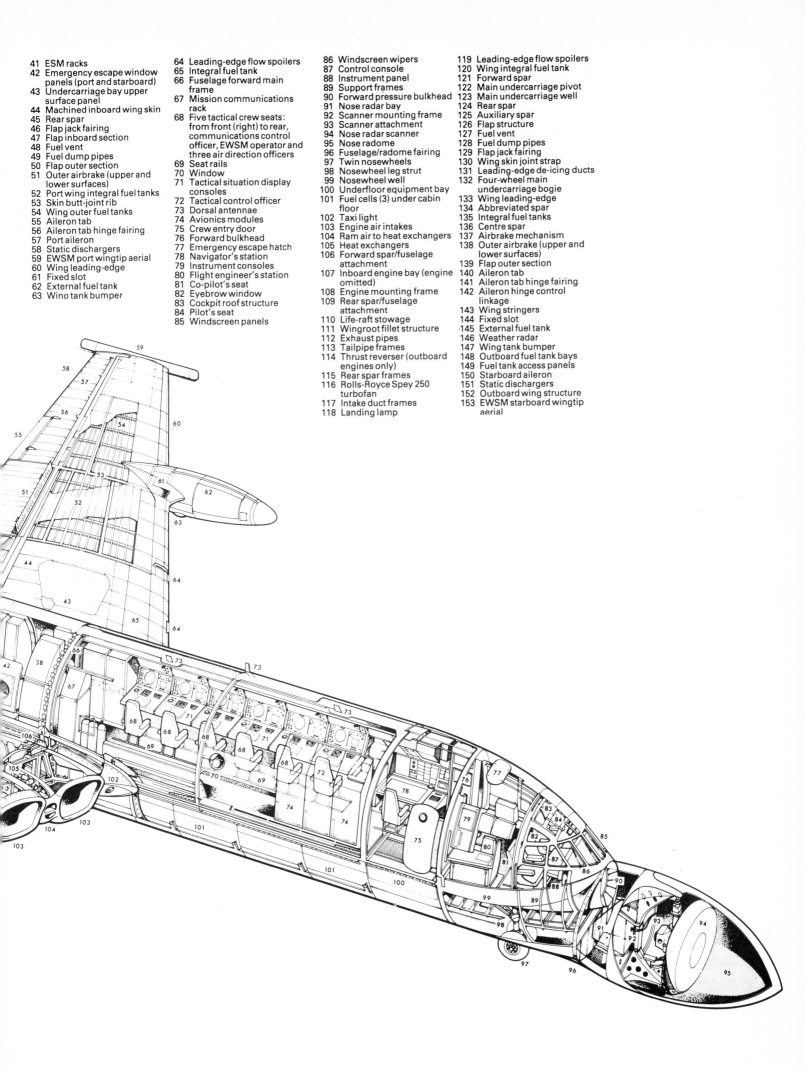

Above: Grumman-
converted General
Dynamics EF-111A
ECM aircraft.

Right: Grumman EA-6B
Prowler ECM aircraft,
operated by U.S. Navy
squadron VAQ-131 from
USS *Kitty Hawk*.

The British Aerospace Nimrod AEW. Mk 3 is an AWACS derivative of the maritime patrol Nimrod. It first entered service with the R.A.F. in 1983. Unlike the others, it has no rotodome but instead has radar scanners in bulbous radomes at the nose and tail. This configuration removes the obscuration effects the fuselage would otherwise cause.

The use of aircraft in an electronic warfare role is also becoming more widespread, in an attempt to jam enemy systems and prevent enemy anti-aircraft radars from picking up attacking aircraft. So important is this role that the U.S.A.F. has begun operating specially modified examples of the F-111A, known as EF-111As, to supplement other ECM types. The U.S. Navy and U.S. Marine Corps operate the Grumman EA-6B Prowler in a similar role from aircraft carriers and land bases, and other Navy ECM aircraft include a version of the Orion. The Soviet Union operates ECM versions of transport aircraft and bombers.

Spying from the sky

Four unique aircraft in service with the U.S.A.F. are the Boeing E-4 advanced airborne command post, the Lockheed SR-71A, U-2 and TR-1 reconnaissance aircraft. The E-4 is basically a modified Model 747 airliner, carrying the electronic systems necessary for it to provide a communications link with strategic forces in the event of an attack on the U.S. mainland and has the ability to launch intercontinental ballistic missiles if the normal control centres are no longer functioning.

The Lockheed U-2 and more recent TR-1 are U.S.A.F. single-seat high-altitude tactical reconnaissance aircraft, with huge wing spans to allow gliding flight with engine shut down to extend range. Operational ceiling of the TR-1A is 27 430 metres (90,000 feet). The strategic SR-71A is the world's fastest operational aircraft with a maximum speed (for short periods) of 3 717 km/h

This Soviet Antonov An-12 (*Cub-B*) conversion, which operates in an electronic intelligence role, is escorted by a Lockheed F-104G Starfighter of the Royal Norwegian Air Force.

(2,310 mph). It is a two-seater with a unique configuration, carrying the necessary photographic and electronic reconnaissance equipment to allow it to photograph 259000 sq km (100,000 sq miles) of territory in an hour. Specialized surveillance missions can also be undertaken.

Related to reconnaissance is the role of observation, a tactical mission to collect information on the enemy's movements and disposition. Aircraft used for this role are often army-operated and can include simple lightplanes of the Cessna O-1 Bird Dog type, helicopters, or can be as sophisticated as the Grumman OV-1 Mohawk, with its cameras, side-looking airborne radar, or infra-red or other sensors. The U.S. Army, the Philippines and Thailand use Mohawks.

Right: Lockheed TR-1A tactical reconnaissance aircraft.

Below: The Grumman OV-1D Mohawk sophisticated two-seat observation aircraft, in U.S. Army markings.

Epilogue

The myriad of other aircraft used in ambulance, communications, inspection, liaison, evacuation, survey, target tug, weather reconnaissance and other roles cannot be detailed – there are too many. These and previously mentioned non-combat types remain vital links in the military chain, training the crews to fly combat aircraft and transporting the supplies to keep them airborne. They provide detailed information to assist a strike or interception and can prevent anti-aircraft missile attack on weapon-carrying aircraft by ECM escort. True, they do not possess the glamour of fighter aircraft but who can doubt their worth.

Fighter aircraft have come a long way since the first air combats were fought in the skies of Europe during 1914–18. Today's advances in aviation technology are so rapid that what represented fiction yesterday becomes fact tomorrow. It is difficult to forecast what advances lie in store for the 1990s. Already in the U.S.A. a so-called voice interaction programme is underway, which involves the fighter aircraft warning the pilot of dangers by voice and allowing the pilot to perform certain functions by speaking a command. Only time will tell what else will follow!

The incredible Lockheed SR-71A, the world's fastest operational aircraft, is used for strategic reconnaissance by the U.S.A.F.

Abbreviations

AAFSS	Advanced Aerial Fire Support System
AAH	Advanced Attack Helicopter
ADV	Air Defence Variant
AEW	Airborne Early Warning
AGM	Air-to-Ground missile
AIDC	Aero Industry Development Center
AIM	Air Intercept Missile
AMRAAM	Advanced Medium-Range Air-to-Air Missile
ANG	Air National Guard
ARM	Anti-Radiation Missile
ASMD	Anti-Ship Missile Defence
ASMP	Air-Sol Moyenne Portée
ASV	Anti-Surface Vessel
ASW	Anti-Submarine Warfare
AWACS	Airborne Warning and Control System
BAC	British Aircraft Corporation
CAC	(Australia) Commonwealth Aircraft Corporation
CASA	(Spain) Construcciones Aeronáuticas S.A.
CNIAR	(Romania) Centrul National al Industriei Aeronautice Romåne
COD	Carrier On-board Delivery
COIN	Counter-Insurgency
D.A.	(Soviet Union) Dalnaya Aviatsiya
EAS	Equivalent Airspeed
ECM	Electronic Countermeasures
elint	electronic intelligence
EMBRAER	(Brazil) Empresa Brasileira de Aeronáutica S.A.
ESM	Electronic Surveillance Measurement
ESSS	External Stores Support System
EVS	Electro-optical Viewing System
FAC	Forward Air Control
FAST	Fuel And Sensor Tactical Packs
FMA	(Argentina) Fábrica Militar de Aviones
GAF	(Australia) Government Aircraft Factories
HAL	(India) Hindustan Aeronautics Limited
Hot	High-subsonic optically-guided tube-launched
IAI	Israel Aircraft Industries
IDS	Interdictor Strike
IFA	International Fighter Aircraft
J.A.S.D.F.	Japan Air Self-Defence Force
J.M.S.D.F.	Japan Maritime Self-Defence Force
LAMPS	Light Airborne Multi-Purpose System
LAPES	Low-Altitude Parachute Extraction System
LERX	Leading-Edge Root extensions
LWF	Lightweight Fighter
MAD	Magnetic Anomaly Detector
MAP	Military Assistance Program
MBB	(West Germany) Messerschmitt-Bölkow-Blohm
MCM	Mine Countermeasures
NATO	North Atlantic Treaty Organization
NORAD	North American Aerospace Defense Command
PVO	(Soviet Union) Protivio-Vozdushnaya Oboronastrany
R.A.A.F.	Royal Australian Air Force
RACA	(Argentina) Representaciones Aero Comerciales Argentinas S.A.
R.A.F.	Royal Air Force
RFB	(West Germany) Rhein-Flugzeugbau
S.A.A.F.	South African Air Force
SABCA	(Belgium) Société Anonyme Belge de Constructions Aéronautiques
SAGE	Semi-Automatic Ground Environment
SAR	Search and Rescue
SEPECAT	Société Européenne de Production de l'Avion E.C.A.T.
SNECMA	(France) Société Nationale d'Etude et de Construction de Moteurs d'Aviation
SRAM	Short-Range Attack Missile
st	static thrust
STOL	Short Take-Off and Landing
TFS	Tactical Fighter Squadron
TFW	Tactical Fighter Wing
TOW	Tube-launched Optically-tracked Wire-guided
TRAM	Target Recognition and Attack Multisensor
U.S.A.F.	United States Air Force
U.S.A.F.E.	United States Air Force Europe
U.S.A.N.G.	United States Air National Guard
U.S.M.C.	United States Marine Corps
V/STOL	Vertical/Short Take-Off and Landing

Index

Figures in italics refer to illustrations

A-4 Skyhawk 64–5, 94
  A-4G *65*
  A-4H *96*
  A-4M *63*
  A-4P *97*
  TA-4J *64*
A-6E Intruder 70–3
A-7 Corsair II 64–5, 94
  A-7D *95*
  A-7E *60–1*, *73*
  A-7H *94*
  A-7K *96*
  TA-7C *62*
A-10 Thunderbolt II *98–9*, *168*
A-37 Dragonfly 100
  A-37B *102*
A-109 helicopter *128*
A-129 helicopter 122–3
AB-204AS helicopter *129*
AB-212ASW helicopter *129*
AH-1G Huey Cobra 119–*120*
AH-1J Sea Cobra 120, 121
AH-1Q Huey Cobra 120
AH-1S Huey Cobra 120–*121*
AH-56A Cheyenne helicopter 119
AJ-37 Viggen 115–*116*
An-12 Cub 152, *173*
An-22 Antheus *172*
AN-22 missile 82
AN-52 missile 38
AS 11 missile *124*
AS 12 missile 124, 128, 129, 137
AS 30 missile 38, *42*
AT-26 Xavante 114
AT-33A Shooting Star 98
AU-23A Peacemaker 102–*103*
AAFSS programme 119
AAH programme 121
Acrid missile *20*, 21
Aden 30-mm cannon 14, 36, 37,
  57, 59, *106*, 109
Adour engine 52, 109–10
Aeritalia G91 115, *116*
  G222 *177*
Aermacchi MB 326 114, 171
  MB 339A trainer *170*, 171
  MB 339K Veltro 2 114, *115*
Aero L-29 Delfin trainer 171
  L-39Z albatross trainer *170*, 171
Aerospatiale SA 316B Alouette
  III *124–125*
  SA 365 Dauphin 2 helicopter
    126
  SA 330 Puma HC.Mk 1
    helicopter *179*
  SA 321G Super Frelon
    helicopter *125*
AGM-86B cruise missile *85*, 89
Agusta A109 helicopter *128*
  A 129 helicopter 122–3
Agusta Bell AB 204AS helicopter
  129
  AB 212ASW helicopter *129*
AiResearch TPE 331-1-101F
  engine 102
Ajeet 10, 36–37
Albatross – HU-16 144
Albatross trainer – L-39Z *170*,
  171
Alferez Sobral 136
Alizé 72
Alkali missile 8–9
Allison engines
  250-B-17C 153

250-C-18A 138
250-C-20B 128, 129
T56-A-14 150
TF41-A-1 94
TF41-A-2 64
TF41-A-400 94
Alouette III helicopter – SA 316B
  124–125
Alpha Jet trainer 171
AMRAAM missile 31
Anab missile 12, 15, 22
Antheus – An-22 *172*
Antonov An-12 Cub 152, *173*
  An-22 Antheus *172*
Apache helicopter – YAH-64
  121–122
Apex missile 21
Aphid missile 12, 20, 21
Arava *176*
HMS *Ark Royal* 54, 56, 105
ARM anti-radiation missile 44
Arriel 520M engine 126
Artouste IIIb engine 125
Ash missile 14–15
ASMP missile 18, 83
Astazou engines
  IIIA 125
  XIVM 125
  XVIG 100
Atar engines
  8B 62
  8K-50 62
  9C 22
  9K-50 17, 40, 83
Atlantic – BR1150 148, *149*, 150
Atlas Impala Mk 2 *114*
Atoll K13 missile 11, 12, *19*, 20,
  118
Avco Lycoming engines
  LTP101-600 157
  0-540 113
  T53-L-13 120
  T53-L-703 120
Avenger seven-barrel cannon 97,
  99
Aviojet trainer – C-101 171
Avon engines
  301 14
  207 35
AWACS aircraft *181–5*

B-1, B-1B *87–9*
B-52 Stratofortress *83–5*
BO-104 helicopter 128
Br 1150 Atlantic 148, *149*, 150
Backfire – Tu-22M *80*
Badger – Tu-16 *76–77*
Beagle – Il-28 *74–75*
Bear – Tu-95 *78–79*
Beechcraft T-34C trainer *163*
Beechcraft Maritime Patrol 200T
  158–9
Bell Helicopter
  Huey Cobra AH-1G 119–*120*
  AH-1Q 120
  AH-1S 120–*121*
  Iroquois Warrior UH-1 119,
    181
  King Cobra 121
  Sea Cobra AH-1J 120, 121
  Sioux Scout 119
Beriev M-12 Tchaika *144–145*
Blackjack 80
Boeing
  737-200 159
  E-4 *161*, 185
  Sentry – E-3A 181, *182*
  Stratofortress – B-52 *83–5*
  Stratotanker – KC-135 *84*, 161
Boeing Vertol Chinook HC.Mk 1
  helicopter *180*
Breguet

Alizé 72
  see also Dassault–Breguet
Bison – M-4 *77–78*
Brewer – Yak-28 15
Bristol Olympus Mk 301 engine
  80
Bristol Siddeley engines
  Orpheus 36–7
  803 115
BAC/British Aerospace
  Bulldog Model 121 trainer –
    SA-3-120 *162–163*
  Coastguarder – HS748 *157–158*
  Harrier 54–60 (*54–7*), 105–7
    (*107*)
  Hawk trainer *171*, 176
  Jet Provost trainer 176
  Nimrod 147–8
    AEW.Mk 3 *183*, 185
    MR.Mk 2 *147*
  Strikemaster – BAC167 *104*
Bronco – OV10 100
  OV10A *101*
Buccaneer 107–8, *110*
Buffalo – DHC-5 *175*

C-1 *178*
C-2A Greyhound 70, *174*
C-5A Galaxy transport *173*, 176
C-9A Nightingale *174*
C-101 Aviojet trainer 171
C-130H Hercules 159, *172*
C-141B Starlifter *175*
C-160D *176*
C-212 157
CAA-1 missile 9
CC-115 Buffalo *174*
CF-101F Voodoo 9–10
CH-53E Super Stallion helicopter
  181
CH-54 Tarhe helicopter *179*
CL-41 Tutor trainer 176
CL-41G Tebuan 103, *104*
CL-215 *146*
CP-140 Aurora 150, 151
Canadair CL-41 Tutor trainer
  176
  CL-41G Tebuan 104, *104*
  CL-215 *146*
Canberra 82
  B.Mk82 *81*
CASA C-101 Aviojet trainer 171
CASA C-212 Series 200 157
Cayuse – OH-6A helicopter 138
Cessna
  A-37 Dragonfly 100
    A-37B *102*
  Model 337 Skymaster 102
  O-2A Super Skymaster 102
  O2-337 Summit Sentry 102,
    103
  T-37 trainer 176
  T-41 Mescalero trainer *163*
Chain Gun 30-mm cannon 122,
  138
Cheyenne helicopter – AH56A
  119
Chinook HC.Mk1 helicopter *180*
Clemenceau aircraft carrier *58*, 61
CNIAR IAR-93 110, 113
Coastguarder – HS748 *157–158*
Cock – An-22 *172*
COIN aircraft *98–103*
Comodoro Somellera 136
USS *Constellation* 67
Continental TSIO-360 engine 102
Convair F-102 Delta Dagger 12
  F-106 Delta Dart 9, *12–13*
Coot-A – Il18 152
Corsair
  A-7 64–5, 94
  A-7D *95*

A-7E *60–1*, 73
A-7H *94*
A-7K *96*
TA-7C *62*
HMS *Coventry* 65
Cruise missiles
  AGM-86B *85*, 89
  ASMP 18, 83
  Sandbox 133
Crusader – F-8 10, 47, 61, 62, 64
  F-8E(FN) *59*, 64
Cub – An-12 152, *173*

DHC-5 Buffalo *175*
DHC-6 Twin Otter 103
  300MR *154*, 155
Dart RDa7 engine 72
Dassault-Breguet
  Atlantic – BR1150 148, *149*,
    150
  Guardian – HU-25A 155
  Mirage III – F1 13, *15–17*, 29,
    36, *38–39*
    IVA *82–83*
    5 *39–40*
    50 *39–41*
    2000 17–18
    4000 *40–42*
  Mystère B-2 *38*
    Super Mystère B-2 37
  Super Etendard *58*, 61–2
Dassault-Breguet/Dornier Alpha
  Jet trainer 118, 171
Dassault-Breguet *see also* Breguet
Dauphin 2 – SA 365 helicopter
  126
de Havilland
  Vampire 34
  Venom *35*
  Ghost engine 35
de Havilland Canada
  Buffalo – DHC-5 *175*
  Twin Otter – DHC-6 103
    300MR *154*, 155
Dédalo aircraft carrier 58
DEFA 30-mm cannon 41, 109,
  114, 115
  552 23
  553 17, 100
  554 18
Defender helicopter – 500M
  138–9
  500MD/TOW *139*
Delfin trainer – L-29 171
Delta Dagger – F-102 12
Delta Dart – F-106 9, *12–13*
Dornier 128-2 155
Dragonfly – A-37 100
  A-37B *102*
Draken – J35 *10–11*

E-2 Hawkeye 70, 181, *183*
E-4 *161*, 185
E-266M 27
E-3A Sentry 181, *182*
EA-6B Prowler 70, *184*, 185
EF-111A *184*, 185
EMB-111 153
EMB-312 Tucano trainer 163,
  164–5
Eagle – F-15 *25–8*
  Enhanced Eagle – F-15E 94, *95*
EMBRAER AT-26 Xavante 114
EMBRAER EMB-111 153
EMBRAER EMB-312 Tucano
  trainer 163, *164–5*
English Electric Canberra 82
  B.Mk82 *81*
English Electric Lightning F
  13–14
Enhanced Eagle – F-15E 94, *95*

USS *Enterprise* 67
ESSS *141*
Exocet missile 18, *58*, 61–2, 125

F-1 Mirage III 13, *15–17*, 29, *36*, 38–*39*
F-1 Mitsubishi 52–*53*
F-2 32
F-4 Phantom II 13, *44–6*, 66, 79
F-5 A & B 47–*48*
F-5E & F Tiger *36*, 48–*50*
F-5G Tigershark *50*
F-6 9
F-8 Crusader 10, *47*, 61, 62, 64
    F-8E(FN) *59*, 64
F-14 Tomcat 27, 66–8
    F-14A 67
F-15 Eagle *25–8*, *160*
    F-15E Enhanced Eagle 94, *95*
F-16 Fighting Falcon *28–31*, 42, 94, *168*
F-27 Maritime *156*, 157
F-35 Draken 11
F-51D Mustang 8, *32*
F-86 Sabre *33–34*
F-100 Super Sabre *34*
F-101 Voodoo 9
F-102 Delta Dagger 12
F-104 Starfighter *41–43*
F-105 Thunderchief *44*
F-106 Delta Dart 9, *12–13*
F-111 90–*91*
    EF-111A *184*, 185
F/A-18 Hornet 9, 42, *68–70*
F/A 18L *50–51*
FB-111A *86–7*
Fairchild AU-23A Peacemaker *102–103*
Fairchild Republic
    A-10 Thunderbolt II *98–9*, *168*
    NGT T-46A trainer *176*
Falcon missile *10*, 11, 13, 19
Falkland Islands conflict *54–57*, 61–2, 65, 80, 82, 94, 100, 106, 131, 136
Fantan A *118*
Fantrainer 400 trainer *166*
Farmer-C – MiG-19/SF 8
FAST pack 27, 94, *95*
Fencer – Su-24 90, *92*
Fiddler – Tu-28P *14–15*
Fighting Falcon – F-16 *28–31*, 42, 94
Finback – J-8 24
Firebar – Yak-28P *15*
Firecracker trainer *166*
Firestreak missile 14
Fishbed – MiG-21 *11–12*
Fishpot – Su-11 12
Fitter – SU7B; Su-17 *51–53*, 117
Flagon – Su-15 *21–22*
Flogger – MiG-23 *19*, 20, *118*
    MiG-27 20, *117–8*
FMA IA 58, IA 66, Pucará *101*
FMAIA 63 trainer *171*
FN-Browning 7.62-mm machinegun 100, *101*
Foch aircraft carrier 61
Fokker F 27 Maritime *156*, 157
Forger – Yak-36MP *57–8*, 60–1
Foxbat – MiG-25 19, *20–21*
Foxhound – MiG-25M 21
Foxhunter radar 25
Fresco – MiG-17 8, *32–33*
Frogfoot 117
Fulcrum – MiG-29 21

G2-A Galeb trainer *171*
G91 115, *116*
G222 117
GB-15 glide-bomb *91*

G Sh-23 23-mm cannon 20, 118
GAF Nomad Searchmaster *152*, 153
Galaxy transport – C-5A *173*, 176
Galeb trainer – G2-A *171*
Garrett engines
    ATF3-6-2C, ATF3-6A-4C 155
    T76-G-416/417 100
    TFE-731-2-2B *159*
    TFE 731-3-1G 155
    TPE 331-10-501C 157
    TPE 331-11-601W 100
Gates Learjet 35A Sea Patrol *159*
Gazelle helicopter – SA 342 *125*, 126
General Dynamics
    F-16 Fighting Falcon *28–31*, 42, 94, *168*
    F-111 90–*91*
        EF-111A *184*, 185
        FB-111A *86–7*
    YF-16 50
General Electric
    five-barrel 25-mm cannon 59
    GAU-8/A Avenger seven-barrel cannon 97, *99*
    M61 20-mm multi-barrel cannon 27, 31, 42, 44, 46, 70
General Electric engines
    F101-GE-102 89
    F404-GE-100 50
    F404-GE-400 50, 70
    J3-IHI-7D 148
    J47-GE-27 34
    J79 23
    J79-GE-2 45
    J79-GE-11A 41
    J79-GE-15 45
    J79-GE-17A 46
    J79-GE-19 42
    J85-GE-13 48, 115
    J85-GE-17A 100
    J85-GE-21B 48
    J85-J-4 103
    T58-GE-3 129
    T58-GE-8B 130
    T58-GE-8F 140
    T58-GE-10 130
    T64-IHI-10 146
    T64-IHI-10E 148
    T700-GE-401 143
    T700-GE-700 122, 140
    TF34-GE2 72
    TF34-GE100 97
Genie missile 10, 13
Ghost engine 35
Glushenkov engines GTD-3, GTD-3BM 133
Gnat 10, *35–7*
Grail missile 126
Greyhound C-2A 70, *174*
Grumman
    HU-16 Albatross 144
    C-2A Greyhound 70, *174*
    E-2 Hawkeye 70, 181, *183*
    A-6E Intruder *70–3*
    OV-1D Mohawk *186*
    EA-6B Prowler 70, *184*, 185
    F-14 Tomcat 27, 66–8
        F-14A 67
    S-2 Tracker *144*
Guardian – HU-25A *155*
Guerrier – R 235 113

H-5 74
H-6 *75–76*
HF-24 Marut 37
HJT-16 Kiran trainer *176*
HS748 Coastguarder *157–158*
HU-16 Albatross 144
HU-25A Guardian *155*
Harbin H-5 74

Harbin Z-5 helicopter 134
Harpoon missile 72, 73, 147, 151
Harrier *54–7*, *58–60*, 107
    AV-8A *56*, 58
    AV-8B *57*, 58, 59
    RAF Harrier GR.Mk3 *55*, 57, *106*
    GR.Mk5 58, 59
    Sea Harrier FRS.Mk1 *54–5*, 56
    Harrier II 59
Hawk T.Mk1 trainer *171*, 176
Hawker Siddeley
    P.1127 105
    Ajeet 10, *36–37*
    Buccaneer *107–8*, 110
    Gnat 10, *35–7*
    Hunter *34–6*
    Kestrel 105
Hawkeye E-2 70, 181, *183*
Haze helicopter – Mi-14 *134–135*
Helix A helicopter – Ka32 134
Hellfire anti-tank missile 122, 140, *141*
Hercules – C-130H 159, *172*
HMS *Hermes* 54, *55*, 56
Hind helicopter 117, *123–4*
    Hind-A *123*
    Hind-D *124*
HAL (Hindustan Aeronautics Ltd)
    Invincible *36–7*
    HJT-16 Kiran trainer 176
    HF-24 Marut 37
Hip helicopter – Mi8 *135*
Hispano HA-2804 20-mm cannon 100, *101*
Hook helicopter *178*
Hormone helicopter – Ka25 60, *133*
Hornet CF-18, F/A-18 9, 42, *68–9*, 70
HOT anti-tank missile 125, 126, *127*, 128
Hound-B helicopter – Mi-4 134
Huey Cobra helicopter
    AH-1G *119–120*
    AH-1Q 120
    AH-1S *120–121*
Hughes helicopters
    YAH-64 Apache *121–122*
    OH-6A Cayuse 138
    500M Defender *138–9*
    500MD/TOW 139
Hughes MA-1 guidance & control system 12
Hughes TOW anti-tank missile *120–1*, 122, 128
Hunter *34–6*
Huosai HS-5A engine 134
HVAR 5-in rocket *153*

IA-58, IA-66 Pucará *101*
Il-18 Coot-A 152
Il-28 *74–75*
Il-38 May *151*, 152
Il-76 181
HMS *Illustrious* 56
Iluyshin
    Il-18 Coot-A 152
    Il-28 *74–75*
    Il-38 May *151*, 152
    Il-76 181
Impala Mk2 *114*
In-flight refuelling 57
IndAer/Piper PA-28R-300 Pillan trainer *163*, *166*
Intruder A-6E *70–3*
Invincible *36–7*
HMS *Invincible* 54
Iroquois Warrior helicopter – UH-1 119, *181*
Islander 158

Isotov engines
    TV2-117A 135
    TV3-117 *123*, 135
IAI (Israeli Aircraft Industries)
    Arava *176*
    Kfir *22–4*
    Lavi *23–4*
    Nesher *22–23*
    1124N Sea Scan *155–156*
Ivchenko engines
    AI-20D 145
    AI-20M 152
IWKA-Mauser 27-mm cannon 25, 92

J-1 Jastreb 113
J-5 *32–3*
J-6 *8–9*
J-7 11
J-8 Finback 24
J-35 Draken *10–11*
JA-37 Viggen 11, *18–19*, 29
JJ-5 trainer 166
JM-61 multi-barrel cannon 52
Jaguar *108–10*, *110–12*
Jastreb – J-1 113
Jet Provost trainer 176
Jianjiji J-6, JJ-6, JZ-6 *8–9*
J-8 Finback 24
USS *John F. Kennedy* 61

Ka-25 helicopter 60, *133*
Ka-32 helicopter *134*
KC-10A Extender *160*
KC-135 Stratotanker *84*, 161
KV-107/II helicopter *132*
Kaman helicopters
    SH-2 Seasprite *139–40*
        SH-2F *140*
    UH-2 139
Kamov helicopters
    Ka-25 60, *133*
    Ka-32 *134*
Kangaroo missile 79
Kawasaki
    C-1 *178*
    KV107/II helicopter *132*
    P-2J *148*
Kelt missile 76, 77
Kestrel 105
Kfir *22–4*
Kiev aircraft carrier *57*, 60–1
Kingfish missile 76, 77
Kipper missile 77
Kiran trainer – HJT-16 176
Kitchen missile 79, *80*
Klimov VK-1A engine 33, 74
Kormoran missile *43*
Kuznetsov NK-12MV engine *78–9*

L-29 Delfin trainer *171*
L-39Z Albatross trainer *170*, *171*
L-70 Miltrainer (Vinka) *162–163*
LAPES *172*
Lavi *23–4*
Learjet 35A Sea Patrol *159*
LERX *57*
Lightning F *13–14*, 77
Lockheed
    SR-71A *185–6*, *187*
    T-33 trainer 166
    TR-1A 185, *186*
    U-2 185
    CP-140 Aurora *150*, 151
    AH-56A Cheyenne helicopter 119
    C-5A Galaxy transport *173*, 176
    C-130H Hercules 159, *172*
    P-2 Neptune 148

190

P-3 Orion 150–1
P-3C *149*
F-104 Starfighter 41–43
C-141B Starlifter *175*
S-3 Viking 72–3
S-3A *72*
Luz missile 23
Lycoming 0.540 piston engine 113
Lynx helicopters
AH.Mk1 *136*
HAS 136–*137*
Lyulka engines
Al-7F-1 12, 117
AL-21F-3 51

M-4 77–78
M-12 Tchaika 144–*145*
M 39 20-mm cannon 50
MB 326 114, 171
MB 339A trainer *170*, 171
MB 339K Veltro 2 114, *115*
Mi-4 helicopter 134
Mi-6 Hook helicopter *178*
Mi-8 helicopter 135
Mi-14 helicopter 134–*135*
Mi-24 helicopter 123–4
Hind-A *123*
Hind-D *124*
MiG-15 8, 32
MiG-15 UTI trainer 166, *168*
MiG-17 Fresco 8, 32–*33*
MiG-19 8
MiG-21 Fishbed 8, 11–*12*, 13, *168*
MiG-23 Flogger 8, 12, *19*, 20, 118
MiG-25 Foxbat 19, *20–21*
MiG-25M Foxhound 21
MiG-27 Flogger 20, 117–8
MiG-29 Fulcrum 21
McDonnell Douglas
F-15 Eagle 25–8, *160*
F-15E Enhanced Eagle 94, *95*
KC-10A Extender *160*
Harrier 54–7, 58–60
F/A-18 Hornet 9, 42, 68–70
CF-18 *68*
TF/A-18A *68*
C-9A Nightingale *174*
F-4 Phantom II 13, 44–6, 66, 79
A-4 Skyhawk 65, 94
A-4G *65*
A-4H *96*
A-4M *63*
A-4P *97*
TA-4J *64*
F-101 Voodoo 9
CF-101F *9–10*
MAD 135, 138, 145, 146, 147, 152, 155, 158
Magic missile 17, 18, 42, 109, 110, 136
Mail – M12 144–*145*
Maritime – F27 *156*, 157
Martel missile 107–8, *109–10*
Marut – HF-24 37
Matador – TAV-8S 58
Matra 530, 550 missiles 17, 18, 38
May – Il-38 *151*, 152
MBB BO *128*
MBB PAH-1 helicopter *127*, 128
Melbourne aircraft carrier 65
Mescalero trainer – T-41 *163*
Mikoyan E-266M 27
Mikoyan-Gurevich
MiG-15 8, 32
MiG-15 UTI trainer 166, *168*
MiG-17 Fresco 8, 32–*33*
MiG-19 8
MiG-21 Fishbed 8, 11–*12*, 13, *168*
MiG-23 Flogger 8, 12, *19*, 20, *118*

MiG-25 Foxbat 19, *20–21*
MiG-25M Foxhound 21
MiG-27 Flogger 20, 117–8
MiG-29 Fulcrum 21
Mikulin engines
AM-3 76
AM-3D 77
RD-3M 77
Mil helicopters
Mi-4 134
Mi-6 Hook *178*
Mi-8 135
Mi-14 Haze 134–*135*
Mi-24 123–4
Hind-A *123*
Hind-D *124*
Military helicopter – S76 *143*
Miltrainer – L-70 *162–163*
Minsk aircraft carrier 60
Mirage
III – F 1 13, *15–17*, 29, *36*, *38–39*
IVA *82–83*
5 39
50 39–40
2000 17–18
Super Mirage 4000 40–*42*
Mitsubishi F-1 52–*53*
Mitsubishi T-2 supersonic trainer 166, *168*
Mitsubishi ASM-1 missile 52
Mohawk – OV-1D *186*
Mongol – Mig-21 12
Moskva aircraft carrier *133*
Moss – Tu-126 181, *182*
Moujik 117
Mustang
F-51D *32*
P-51 8
Myasishchev – M-4 77–78
Mystère B-2 37, *38*

NR-30 cannon 8, 11, 51, 117
Nanchang Q-5 *8–9*, *118*
NDN 1 Firecracker trainer *166*
Nene RD-45 engine 74
Neptune – P-2 148
Nesher 22–*23*
Nightingale – C-9A *174*
USS *Nimitz* 67
Nimrod 147–8
AEW.Mk3 *183*,*185*
MR.Mk2 *147*
Nomad Searchmaster *152*, 153
North American
Mustang
F-51D 8, *32*
P-51 8
F-86 Sabre 33–4
F-100 Super Sabre *34*
T-6 Texan trainer 166, *168*
T-28 Trojan trainer 166
XB-70 Valkyrie 20, 87
North American *see also* Rockwell International
Northrop
F-5A & B 47–*48*
F-5E & F Tiger *36*, 48–50
F-5G Tigershark 50
F/A 18L 50–*51*
T-38A Talon supersonic trainer 166, *169*
YF-17 50

O-2A Super Skymaster 102
O2-337 Summit Sentry 102, *103*
OH-6A Cayuse helicopter 138
OV-1D Mohawk *186*
Orao/IAR-93 110, *112*, 113
Orpheus engine 36–*7*

P-2 Neptune 148
P-2J (Kawasaki) *148*
P-3 Orion 150–1
P-3C *149*
P-51 Mustang 8
P.166-DL3-MAR 157
PA-28R-300 Pillan trainer 163, 166
PAH-1 helicopter *127*, 128
PC-7/CH Turbo-Trainer 163, *167*
PS-1 145–146
Panavia GR.Mk1 Tornado 24–25, 42, *92–3*
Peacemaker – AU-23A 102–*103*
Pegasus engines
11–21 59
Mk104 56–7
Phantom II – F-4 13, 44–6, 79
Phoenix missile 67, 68
R.Piaggio P.166-DL3-MAR 157
Pilatus PC-7/CH Turbo-Trainer 163, *167*
Pilatus Britten-Norman Defender 158
Maritime Defender *158*
Pillan trainer – PA-28R-300 163, *166*
Piper/Indair PA-28R-300 Pillan trainer 163, *166*
Pratt & Whitney engines
F100-PW-100 26
F100-PW-200 29
J52-P-8A 37
J52-P-8B 72
J52-P408A 65
J57-P20 62
J57-P21A 34
J57-P43WB 85
PW2037 85
TF30-P-1 90
TF30-P-3 86, 90
TF30-P-7 86
TF30-P-8 64
TF30-P-9 90
TF30-P-100 90
TF30-P-408 64
TF30-P-412A 68
TF30-P-414A 68
TF33-P-3 85
Pratt & Whitney Aircraft of Canada engines
PT6A-34 153
PT6A-42 158
PT6T-6 129
Prowler EA-6B 70, *184*, 185
Pucará – IA 58, IA 66 100, *101*
Puma helicopter – SA 330 *179*

Q 5 *8–9*, *118*

R 235 Guerrier *113*
R.530 missile 64
RF-35 Draken 11
Reconnaissance aircraft *185–6*
Red Top missile 14
Republic F-105 Thunderchief 44
RFB Fantrainer 400 *166*
Rockwell International B-1, B-1B *87–9*
OV-10 Bronco 100
OV-10A *101*
Rockwell International *see also* North American
Rolls Royce engines
Avon 109 82
Avon 203 35
Avon 207 35
Avon 301 14
Bristol Nimbus 503 137–8
Bristol Olympus Mk301 80
Bristol Viper

203 147
Mk531 113
Mk535 104
Mk540 114
Mk632–43 114
Mk633–47 113
Dart RDa7 72
Mk535-2 157
Dart Mk536-7R 157
Gem-2-2 122
Gnome H1200 132
H1400-1 131
Griffon 57A 147
Nene RD-45 74
Pegasus 11-21 59
Mk103 105
Mk104 56–7
RB.168-1A Spey Mk101 108
RB.168-20 Spey Mk250 147
Tyne R Ty 20 Mk21 148
Rolls-Royce/Turbomeca Adour engine 52, 109–10

S-2 Tracker *144*
S-3 Viking 72–73
S-64 Skycrane helicopter *179*
S-76 Military helicopter *143*
S.211 trainer *170*, 171
SA-3-120 Bulldog Model 121 trainer *162–163*
SA 316B Alouette III 124–125
SA 321G Super Frelon helicopter 125
SA 330 Puma HC.Mk 1 helicopter *179*
SA 342 Gazelle helicopter *125–126*
SA 365 Dauphin 2 helicopter *126*
SF.260 Sea Warrior 157
SH-2 Seasprite helicopter 139–40
SH-2F *140*
SH-3 Sea King helicopter *130*
SF.260W Warrior 113–14
SR-71A *185–6*,*187*
Su-7 Fitter-A 51, 117
Su-9, Su-11 12
Su-15 Flagon *21–22*
Su-17 Fitter 51, *52*
Su-20 Fitter *52*
Su-22 52
Su-24 90, *92*
Saab-91 Safir trainer 166
Saab 105 trainer *172*, 176
Saab Draken
F35 11
J35 *10–11*
RF-35 11
Saab Viggen
AJ37 115–*116*
JA37 11, 18–19, 29
Saab-Scania RB04E, RB05A missiles 19
Sabre – F-86 *33*-34
Super Sabre – F-100 *34*
Safir trainer 166
SAGE system *12–13*
Sagger anti-tank missile 126, 135
Sandbox cruise missile 133
SAR 94
Sea Cobra helicopter – AH-1J 120, *121*
Sea Eagle missile 57 108, *110*
Sea Harrier 54–7, 58–60
Seahawk helicopter – UH 600 *142–143*
Sea King helicopter – Sikorsky SH-3, Westland HAS *130–131*
Sea King AEW helicopter 131
Sea Patrol *159*
Sea Skua missile 136

191

Seasprite helicopter – SH-2
  139–40
  – SH-2F *140*
Sea Warrior – SF.260 157
Sentry – E-3a 181, *182*
SEPECAT Jaguar 108–10, *110–12*
Shackleton MR.Mk3 147
Shafrir missile 23
HMS *Sheffield* 62
Shenyang
  F-2 32
  F-6, FT-6 9
  J5 32–3
  J-6 8–9, *118*
  J-8 Finback 24
  JJ-5 trainer 166
Shenyang Wopen-6 engine 9
Shin Meiwa PS-1 *145–146*
Shooting Star – AT-33A 98
Short Skyvan *178*
Shrike missile 44
SIAI-Marchetti
  S.211 trainer *170, 171*
  SF.260 Sea Warrior 157
  SF.260W Warrior 113–14
Sidewinder AIM-9L missile 11,
  18, 19, *25*, *26*, 31, 34, 38, 42,
  44, 46, 48, 50, 52, 54, 57, 64,
  67, 68, 70, 92, 100, 106, 110,
  147
Sikorsky helicopters
  UH-60A Black Hawk 140–*141*,
  180
  S-76 Military *143*
  UH-60B Seahawk *142*–143
  SH-3 Sea King *130*
  S-64 Skycrane *179*
  CH-53E Super Stallion *181*
Sioux Scout helicopter 119
Ski-jumps 54–6
Skycrane helicopter – S-64 *179*
Sky Flash missile *18*, *25*, 31, 50
Skyhawk – A-4 65, 94
  A-4G *65*
  A-4H *96*
  A-4M *63*, 65
  A-4P *97*
  TA-4J *64*
Skymaster Model 337 102
  Super Skymaster – 0-2A 102
Skyvan *178*
SNEB rocket 128
SNECMA engines
  8B 62
  8K-50 62
  Atar 9B 38
  Atar 9C 22, 38
  Atar 9K-50 17, 40, 83
  M53 18, 41
Socata R235 Guerrier *113*
SOKO
  G2-A Galeb trainer *171*
  J-1 Jastreb 113

Orao 110, 113
Sparrow missile *26*, 31, 42, *46*, *67*,
  68, 70, 94
Spiral anti-tank missile 124
SRAM *86*, 89
Standard anti-radiation missile 70
Starfighter – F-104 41–*43*
Starlifter – C-141B *175*
Sting Ray torpedo *131*
Stinger missile 139
Stratofortress – B-52 *83*–5
Stratotanker – KC-135 *84*
Strikemaster – BAC167 *104*
Sukhoi
  Su-7 51, *117*
  Su-9, Su-11 12
  Su-15 Flagon *21–22*
  Su-17 Fitter 51, *52*
  Su-20 Fitter *52*
  Su-22 52
  Su-24 90, *92*
Summit Sentry – 02-337 102, *103*
Super Frelon helicopter – SA321
  125
Super Mystère B-2 37
Super Skymaster – 0-2A 102
Super Stallion helicopter – CH-
  53E *181*
SURA 80-mm rocket *136*, *166*

T-2 supersonic trainer 166, *168*
T-6 Texan trainer 166, *168*
T-28 Trojan trainer 166
T-33 trainer 166
T34C trainer *163*
T-37 trainer 176
T-38A Talon supersonic trainer
  166, *169*
T-41 Mescalero trainer *163*
T-46A trainer 176
TAV-8S Matador 58
TR-1A 185, *186*
Tu-16 76–77
Tu-22M *80*
Tu-22 79–80
Tu-95 78–79
Tu-126 Moss 181, *182*
Talon supersonic trainer 166, *169*
Tanker aircraft 160
Tarhe helicopter – CH-54 *179*
Tchaika – M12 144–*145*
Tebuan – CL-419 103, *104*
Texan trainer – T-6 166, *168*
Thunderbolt II – A-10 97–9
Thunderchief – F-105 44
Tiger – F-5E & F *36*, 48–*50*
Tigershark – F-5G 50
Tomcat – F-14 27, 66–8
  – F-14A *67*
Tornado – GR.MkI 24–25, 42,
  92–3

TOW anti-tank missile 120–1,
  122, 128, 136, 138
Tracker – S-2 *144*
Trainer aircraft *160–76*
Transall C-160D *176*
Transport aircraft *172–8*
Transport helicopters *178–81*
Trojan trainer – T-28 166
Tucano – EMB-312/YT-27
  trainer 163, *164–5*
Tumansky engines
  R-9BF-811 9
  R-11 11, 24
  R-13 22
  R-13-300 11–12
  R-25 12
  R-27 20
  R-29 20
  R-29B 52, 117, 118
  R-31 21
Tupolev
  Tu-16 76–77
  Tu-22 79–80
  Tu-22M *80*
  Tu-28P 14–*15*
  Tu-95 78–79
  Tu-126 Moss 181, *182*
Turboméca engines
  Adour 52, 109–10
  Arriel 520M 126–7
  Artouste IIIB 125
  Astazou IIIA 125
  Astazou XIVM 125
  Astazou XVIG 100
  Turmo IIIC 125
Turbo-Trainer – PC-7/CH 163,
  167
Turbo-Union RB.199-34R engine
  25, 92
Turmo IIIC engine 125
Tutor trainer – CL-41 176
Twin Otter
  DHC-6 103
  DHC-6 300MR *154*, 155

U-2 185
UH-1 Iroquois Warrior helicopter
  119, *181*
UH-2 helicopter 139
UH-60A Black Hawk helicopter
  140–*141*, 180
UH-60B Seahawk helicopter
  142–143
Udaloy *134*

Valkyrie – B-70 20
Valmet L-70 Miltrainer (Vinka)
  162–163
Vampire 34
VC10K.Mk2 refuelling tanker *161*

Veinticinco de Mayo aircraft carrier
  65
Veltro 2 – MB339K 114, *115*
Venom *35*
Viggen 37 11, 18–19, 29
  115–*116*
Viking – S-3 *72*–73
Vikrant aircraft carrier 57–8
Vinka trainer – L-70 *162*–163
Volvo Flygmotor RM 8A, 8B
  engine 19
Voodoo – F101 *9*–10, *68*
Vought
  A-7 Corsair II 64–5, 94
  A-7D *95*
  A-7E *60*–1, *73*
  A-7H *94*
  A-7K *96*
  TA-7C *62*
  F-8 Crusader 10, *47*, 61, 62, 64
  F-8E(FN) *59*, 64
Vulcan 80–2
  B.Mk2 *81*
Vulcan 20-mm multi-barrel
  cannon 13, 65, 68, 84, 94

Warrior – SF 260W 113–14
Wasp helicopter 137–*138*
Westinghouse J 34 engine 148
Westland helicopters
  30 *180*
  Lynx *136*–7
  Sea King 55
  Wasp 137–*138*
  Wessex 181
Wild Weasel – F-4 46
Wopen-6 engine 9
Wright engines
  R-1820-76A 144
  R-1820-82WA 144
  R-3350-32W 148

XB70 Valkyrie 20, 87
Xavante – AT-26 114
Xian
  H-6 75–76
  J-7 11

YAH-64 Apache helicopter
  121–*122*
Yak-28P *15*
Yak-36MP *57–8*, *60*–1
Yak-52 trainer *162*, 163
YF 16 50
YF 17 50
YT-27 Tucano trainer 163, *164–5*
Yakovlev
  Yak-28P *15*
  Yak-36MP *57–8*, *60*–1
  Yak-52 trainer *162*, 163